THE
house
ALWAYS WINS

THE
house
ALWAYS WINS

Creating the Home You Love—
Without Bursting Your Budget

Marni Jameson

Da Capo
LIFE
LONG

A Member of the Perseus Books Group

Designed by Lisa Kreinbrink
Set in 12-point Goudy by the Perseus Books Group

Cataloging-in-Publication data for this book is available from the Library of Congress.

First Da Capo Press paperback edition 2009
HC: 978-1-60094-067-5
PB: 978-0-7382-1312-5

Published by Da Capo Press
A Member of the Perseus Books Group
www.dacapopress.com

Da Capo Press books are available at special discounts for bulk purchases in the United States by corporations, institutions, and other organizations. For more information, please contact the Special Markets Department at the Perseus Books Group, 2300 Chestnut Street, Suite 200, Philadelphia, PA 19103, or call (800) 255-1514, or e-mail special.markets@perseusbooks.com.

1 2 3 4 5 6 7 8 9

For Paige and Marissa,
and for Dan, who makes so much possible

Contents

PART I—LET'S GET REAL
Design basics: Finding your dream house and discovering your style

PART II—DECISIONS, DECISIONS
Selecting wall treatments, flooring, counters, tile, and cabinetry

PART III—THE GOODS ON THE GOODS
Furnishing your home: Copying good looks,
using what you have, finding what you need,
getting deals, buying quality

PART VI—TAKING IT OUTSIDE
Tackling the yard: From design to maintenance, decks to patio furnishings

PART VII: HOMES FOR THE HOLIDAYS
Create festive tables, deck the halls, and get ready to party

PART VIII: HOME ECONOMICS
Make your household dollars go farther without feeling the pinch

Foreword

by Dominique Browning

UNTIL JUST RECENTLY I had no idea anyone could love mud-rooms as much as I do. And not just mudrooms, but laundry rooms, garages, and basements as well—all those black holes of interior design, waiting for someone to coax forth their real potential. That someone turns out to be Marni Jameson, a supercollider force in the design world. This is no surprise for readers lucky enough to have been following her journey through three house renovations in the syndicated newspaper columns she has been writing. For the rest of us—well, welcome to a world of messy and hilarious reality.

Marni is like a lot of my friends. They know what they want, but they get paralyzed with indecision on the way to getting it. What color should the bathroom be? What fabric goes with that carpet? What should I do with all these knickknacks? Then again, Marni is unlike my friends, because she actually figures out the answers—and then tells the rest of us how to avoid disasters. And she seems to have an infinite patience for the whole process of designing a home, which, as anyone knows who has done this even once, is simply the management of one problem after another, on the way to realizing an impossible dream.

In fact, Marni seems to have made every mistake in the book, which is why she is such a valuable friend to have. Whether she is organizing the stuff on her coffee table, or clearing up the tangle of cords that drive her crazy (everyone has her own poison, after all), or dealing with furniture mistakes—and we all know how big those can be—Marni is open-hearted and generous about sharing her hard-won knowledge. Somehow, she hasn't been ruined by her experiences; she manages to be funny about it all. She gets knocked down, and she picks herself up, brushes herself off, and gets right back to fighting with those tricky design devils. This is a book for those of us who love our homes, and want them to look beautiful—without having to get rid of pets, children, husbands, and other pesky, messy trouble makers. She's even got advice for those of us with children who want to paint their walls black.

Marni says she isn't interested in visions of design ideals, something home magazine editors know a great deal about, but I know a dreamer when I hear one. Take her fantasy of the perfect mudroom, for instance. Not only was she meditating for months on exactly which elements would organize her family's comings and goings from the house every day—just the right arrangement of bins and hooks and benches—but she was also scheming and plotting to get her husband to build it out for her—as a Mother's Day present, on top of it all. That, as far as I'm concerned, is about as close to an ideal vision of design as anyone needs to get.

If you ever felt that the renovation gods had singled you out for torture, if you ever felt forsaken in a cruel world of plumbers and painters, if you ever felt like simply handing the keys over to your contractor and slamming the door shut on your house, forever, then you need to be led from the wilderness. I would suggest forming a single line behind Marni. This woman is fearless. And when you are done with this book, you will be too.

Dominique Browning was editor in chief of *House & Garden* magazine for twelve years. She is the author of *Around the House and in the Garden: A Memoir of Heartbreak, Healing, and Home Improvement* and *Paths of Desire: The Passions of a Suburban Gardener.*

Preface
Come On In

LIKE MOST PEOPLE, I have a dream of how I want my home to look. My vision is of a tasteful, timeless home, neither too cluttered nor too sterile. Pretty but not pretentious. Distinctive yet humble. A homey—but not homely—picture reflecting those who live inside, taken, of course, in the most flattering light. I want a haven that welcomes me when I come in from the war-torn world, a refuge that says come in, relax, recharge. And okay, as long as I'm being honest, I want a house that's nicer than the neighbors' house. Finally, my fantasy home is one that, because of the improvements I've made, is worth more than the sum of what I paid for it plus what I've sunken into it, including therapy bills.

In today's economy, that dream is harder to realize. But if you're determined—and I am—you can have a beautiful home on a budget.

In the year since the hardcover version of *The House Always Wins* came out, the housing market dropped like a plumb line. When I originally wrote this book, people were still "moving up." They were building or buying that next dream house. A fortunate few still are, but most homeowners are coming to terms with the fallen housing market and the tough economy. If they're not moving down or out, they're staying put and making do. They are dancing to an updated version of an old tune: If you can't live in the house you love, honey, love the house you're in.

That means getting creative on a shoestring. This book is still about how to do that. It's for anyone who wants to turn his home—new, old, or otherwise—into a dream home without over-spending.

For me it's a passion. As a habitual home improver, I've de-signed, built, and decorated three homes from the ground up. I've made mistakes, learned a lot, and tried to find humor in the worst of it. Several years ago, my experiences triggered a weekly syndi-cated home design column. Readers apparently identified with my quest because the column, "At Home with Marni Jameson," soon began appearing in major metropolitan newspapers across the country and in Canada. As I shared my perilous but educational journey through home design and improvement, many readers wrote to thank me for letting them know they weren't alone in their difficult and sometimes disastrous attempts at home improve-ment. The columns made them smile when they felt like suing, and, I believe, spared an instance or two of domestic homicide. The gut-spilling, gossipy, advice-ridden columns grew into this book.

Here I chronicle the journey of buying, finishing, decorating, and landscaping my most recent home. Although my current home lies in the Colorado foothills, just outside Denver, the prob-lems I encountered and dealt with are universal ones that afflict homeowners everywhere, whether they're building, moving, re-modeling, or redecorating.

When my husband and I bought this house, it was under con-struction. We moved into a large vanilla box on a bulldozed one-acre lot that had as much ambience as strip mall in Barstow. Since then, it has become a place we love to call home, and has appreci-ated nicely. Even after adjusting for the dismally low market, it's worth more than what we paid plus what we spent on improve-ments. What's more, our home has graced the cover of our metropolitan newspaper's real estate guide as an example of fine living in the region (if they only knew).

Apparently, I've fooled a few people, and here I share everything I've learned—and wished I'd known sooner—about transforming a plain or even ugly or out-of-date home, into a place others envy, and, more important, into your dream home, all while staying married to a thrifty husband and not breaking the bank.

Unlike other home design books and shelter magazines, I share the dirt. My home projects don't go swimmingly. They are fraught with a chronic shortage of time and money, gender differences (My husband thinks Astroturf makes perfectly fine carpeting and can double as a putting green.), contractors flaky as pie crust, migraine-inducing choices, escalating costs, taste wars (my two daughters want to paint their walls black and lime green), dogs who consider the house their agility course, unwelcome surprises (ground failure, rattlesnakes, squirrels in the attic), and routine disaster. Still, knowing I work against the odds, I stubbornly continue to try to create a beautiful living space.

Reading this book will both hearten and teach you. You'll find comfort knowing you're not the only one who struggles with home improvements, and you'll discover useful, hard-won lessons from the trenches. You'll witness home improvement as it really is—not as depicted in a TV makeover special. You'll learn when, from a cost standpoint, to do a job yourself and when to hire a pro. You'll learn my favorite cheapskate ways to cut costs without compromising style. And you'll explore the question that drives me: What are the guiding lights in home design for the average busy family on a budget who really lives in their home?

We start by discussing how to choose a home, moving in, and setting up a new-to-you house. After we explore my home design philosophy, we'll discuss how to find inspiration and create a home design plan, including a color scheme and a budget. Then we'll roll up our sleeves and take on designing your home from the walls in. We'll tackle backgrounds: walls, floors, and windows. We'll shop for furniture and accessories, like rugs and art. And from there we'll decorate specific rooms, such as kids' rooms, laundry rooms, and the home office. Then we'll tackle the yard. When every square inch of your home is your dream home, we'll give it some holiday glam and throw a party. Finally, in a new-to-this-edition section on Home Economics, at the end of the book, we'll look at ways to save energy and cut costs throughout the house.

I hope that the humor and humanity in each chapter will spur you on to stay with the cause of beautifying your home and make your journey more fun, more affordable and less frustrating. I also hope it helps you not take it all so seriously, which you won't if you remember this: Just as in Las Vegas, the house always wins.

PART I

Let's Get Real
Design basics:
Finding your dream house
and discovering your style

Pick the Right House in the Right Place

What to look for when buying an old or new home

I LOOK AT IT THIS WAY. It was either this, a blonde, or a red Corvette. My husband, Dan, woke up one day, metaphorically speaking, and said he wanted a change. I figured something like this was coming, since he'd recently rounded the treacherous bend of his fortieth birthday. "I'm sick of the corporate rat race," he ranted. "Sick of working for others."

"Don't be such a cliché," I said. "It's just your midlife crisis talking."

"I want to live somewhere else, experience more of the world."

"Everybody goes through times like this," I said, hoping to dispatch the mood. See, I was hoping Dan's midlife crisis would be minor and fleeting, like, over in an afternoon, so I could get on with mine.

"I want to buy my own business and move out of state."

"Honey," I said, being the incredibly supportive wife that I am, "you know I'd move with you to the end of the earth, as long as I got a great house and didn't take a knock in my standard of living."

That would sweep his daydream into the dustbin. "Beyond that, darling, feel free to self-actualize all you want." Looking back, I now see I should have thrown in big white diamonds while I had some leverage. This is what started our upheaval, and our quest for a new house, one that we hoped would eventually be our dream house.

Obvious as this sounds, we knew that to create our dream house, we had to start with a house that had a few things going for it, like, for one, it had to be in the right place for us. Depending on one's lifestyle and priorities, that might mean a place close to work and good schools, or near family, friends, excellent restaurants, and great skiing. Although both Dan and I were born and raised in Southern California—and still lived there—we had not chosen it. Our parents had. As we grew older and had children of our own, certain aspects of the local lifestyle had caused us to question whether we wanted to raise our kids there. The cost of living and the traffic worsened every year. While Southern California has a lot going for it, the thought of somewhere else proved tempting. Where would we choose if we were doing the choosing? That started us looking.

If you are already living in the house you plan to commit to, one you can make your dream house, at least for a while, skip to the next chapter. But if you're planning to move, or debating whether to fix up the house you live in or move to another one that has more of what you want, read on for what to consider when choosing new digs. DISCLAIMER: Keep in mind that the views expressed in this chapter come from a slightly obsessive, semideranged woman living with a man who at the time of these events was going through a midlife crisis, and who was primed to jettison his good job and sell his home. In other words, we could be nuts.

Where Would You Choose if You Were Choosing?

"Pick a city, any city," Dan said, handing me a book: *The Places Rated Almanac: Your Guide to Finding the Best Places to Live in the United States and Canada.* "And I'll make it work."

"What if that city is right here, where we live now?" I asked, flipping through the phone-book-like tome, which each year examines and ranks more than 350 metropolitan areas.

"Then we'll stay. But do you really want to be sitting here twenty years from now talking about the time we almost lived somewhere else but didn't have the guts?"

Ooh. Now I can fend off almost any brand of criticism but the kind that implies I lack nerve. When Dan wasn't looking, I cracked the book. I looked at top cities and what made them so great, which made me think hard about what I want out of the place I live. When I heard Dan coming, I shoved the book under the sofa like a box of bonbons.

When Dan explained to me all the tax advantages of selling (see box) I grew more interested but was still unconvinced. To show him I was game, I agreed to put our house on the market, with a private pocket listing, at a price I thought high, given the slow market. We had two offers in eight days and agreed to sell. Our agent said our house sold quickly (and for 250 percent more than we paid for it seven years earlier) because of the way we had decorated and landscaped it. So the good news for you is maybe I really do know what I'm talking about. The bad news: If you follow my advice, you, too, could sell your house in a nanosecond and become homeless.

Meanwhile, alongside Dan's midlife reincarnation and the fact that we'd sold our home, another factor conspired to fuel our relocation. The same week our house sold, Dan left his corporate job.

While most people out of a job and a home in the same week would consider lying down in heavy traffic, Dan acted as if he were on jailbreak. "I'm not sure we should be so happy about this," I said, trying to ground him, which was like trying to tether a tornado with a kite string.

"You don't get it," he said.

"No. I really do," I said, noting how the gray in his hair was overtaking the dark. "Time is passing and that's a problem beyond Grecian Formula."

"We can go anywhere!"

Anywhere?

If you get an itch to move away, but don't know how to start, try this:

- **Ask** why you live where you live, and whether somewhere else might suit you better? Or put it this way: Do you spend a lot of time complaining about situations—bad schools, high crime rate, heavy traffic—that would go away if you lived somewhere else?
- **Consider** whether you could find satisfying employment elsewhere, or whether your job is the kind that would let you work from anywhere.
- **Evaluate** cities based on objective (not anecdotal) evidence. Because everyone's definition of quality of life is different, focus on what matters to you. *The Places Rated Guide* looks at nine categories: cost of living, arts, health care, jobs, recreation, transportation, education, climate, and crime. Fold in the subjective stuff: family, friends, and familiarity with your local turf, to create your own balance sheet.
- **Visit** a place if it strikes you. Visit again in a different season. If you have children, visit the schools.
- **Use the Internet** to compare real estate prices in different cities. www.realtor.com is a great place to start.

I pulled the book from its hiding place, and we started reading to-gether. We narrowed the list of cities to five, then researched our finalists for real estate values, schools, and business opportunities. We settled on the Denver area, which ranked fifth in our guide. It had the right combination of what mattered to us: outdoor recre-ation, arts, education, a promising business for sale, and it wasn't here. A little online research proved we could make the proverbial California real estate trade—buy twice as much house and more land for less than we were selling our house for—and still have a decorat-ing budget, which is why I'm now kicking myself for not throwing in those diamonds. So we started house hunting three states away.

Here's the gist of the tax law that fueled Dan's enthusiasm:*

- **In 1997,** the U.S. Congress revised the federal tax code to say, es-sentially, that if you have owned and lived in your primary resi-dence for two of the past five years, you qualify for up to $250,000 of tax-free profits if you're single, and $500,000 if you're married when you sell your house.
- **Before,** the law required sellers to either buy a more expensive home or pay taxes on the gains (if they purchased a less expensive home or rented). The old law made an exception for individuals over age fifty-five. Now age doesn't matter. In our case, because we were in our forties, we could buy a better house for less money and not pay tax on the gains. Check with your tax advisor about your situation.
- **Expert advice:** Before you cash out, know (unlike us) whether you are going to rent, buy down, buy up, or move out of state. Then consider the long-term tax implications of that decision, including the possi-ble loss of a mortgage interest deduction if you don't buy again.

*Note: You'll see the symbol throughout the book before points that can help save you money, add value, or protect you from financial loss.

House Buying: Old vs. New—
So Much for Character

Next thing I know, Dan's online, in this brave new world of real estate, house hunting in another state. "We're NOT buying a house over the Internet," I say.

"*Everyone* does it like this," Dan says. Everyone is his shorthand for: the rest of the world except for troglodytes like me. Last time we bought a house, back in 1997, this sort of virtual house hunting wasn't too common. Now it's de rigueur to market homes through the ether.

"Check out this view!" he says, clicking to a virtual tour of a home that looks built but isn't yet.

"Hooey," I say, to an admittedly seductive mountain panorama. "Besides, I don't want a new house."

"*Everyone* wants a new house," he says.

Not me. I've paid my new house dues. Our last house was new. We bought a lot and a plan and built it our way, as they say in the hamburger ads. The house before that was ancient, built in 1936; we bought it, tore most of it down, and rebuilt it, so it was like new. Both times, the process involved blood, sweat, tears, lots of money, threats of domestic homicide, and heavy drinking. Now I want something in between, old but not ancient. I want character, patina, and charm. I want a house that can tell stories on a street with grown-up trees.

Besides, I can't face the mind-boggling new house choices: light fixtures, faucets, granites, ceramics, flooring, cabinets. I want to benefit from someone else's thoughtful decisions, aggravation, and good taste. I want turnkey.

"Let's go look at this place," he says, "then we can see all the already-built homes you want." We add this home under construction to the list of homes on the outskirts of Denver that we plan to view. Then we head off to Colorado to look at actual houses.

When we visit this virtual house in person, it's actually in the framing phase—meaning it doesn't yet have walls—and I'm already creeped out. If you look at it online the place is built, furnished, and landscaped. I feel as if someone is selling me something with smoke and mirrors. We push open the door with no handles. I see Dan's face and know I'm sunk. He's not looking at the house; he's looking through it, the way he looks through me when I'm standing in front of the TV and the Lakers are playing. His eyes lock on the snow-capped mountain view. Just my luck, this clear day seems ordered to feature it.

As he stands gawking as if he's stumbled onto a photo shoot for the *Sports Illustrated* swimsuit edition, I walk the house looking for reasons to rule it out. Darn if it doesn't have everything we want: enough bedrooms and baths, an office, a loft (my library!), a bigger yard, and the right price tag. Dan keeps making funny noises like he needs more air.

Over the next three days our broker, Tom, takes us to see thirty-three other houses. Soon the virtual home becomes the house against which we measure all others. Between showings, Tom tactfully fields "feedback calls" from brokers representing houses we've toured:

"She likes it . . . but wants a bigger kitchen."

". . . but wants higher ceilings."

". . . but needs more storage."

". . . but the flow seemed awkward." (Like you need to drop breadcrumbs to find your way out.)

He doesn't mention anything that calls attention to the sellers' hygiene, taste, or odd lifestyle: locker-room smells, mirrored ceilings, living room hot tubs. As I eavesdrop, I realize that the problem with these older houses is that they're dated. The cramped kitchens, baths, and storage spaces were designed long before eating, primping, and chronic consumption became leading national pastimes.

Patios are cracked. Windows stick. Finishes are tired. Suddenly, I remember why I bought and built my last two homes. I wanted an old home then, too, but couldn't find old done my way.

"Maybe," says Tom, as if he's mind reading, "We should look at some newer construction." It's a pride-swallowing moment. We

---

When home shopping, here's what to look for, and what to overlook:

- **Be sure** you like everything about the home that is impossible or hard to change:
  - Great location and lot
  - Homes in the neighborhood of equal or greater value
  - Good light
  - Good bones and flow
  - No code violations or environmental issues. If you're buying an older home, inquire about the presence of lead and asbestos, the levels of each, and any abatement programs.
- **Be encouraged** if the house has hard finishes you like, as these are costly to change:
  - Cabinetry
  - Stone and tile
  - Hard flooring
  - Outdoor hardscape, such as patios, decks, pools, and built-in barbecues
- **Don't worry** if it doesn't have the following finishes, because they're easy to change:
  - Nice carpet
  - Fresh paint in a color that fits your palate
  - Light fixtures or window treatments that suit your décor
  - Up-to-date appliances
  - Pleasing outdoor softscape, such as lawns and planter beds

When making your final decision, remember: It's better to have too much nerve than too little.

look but again don't find the right combination of finishes and flair. This is how we come full circle to the virtual house with the view. As I re-walk the just-framed house, I see not what's in and wrong, as in all the other homes I've been through, but what's not in and could be. For the first time in these exhausting days of house hunting, the bluebird in my little heart wakes up to sing. I'm dialing in my vision, and it doesn't include tearing anything out or living with someone else's vision. I know the work that lies ahead. I've done it before. But I also know the satisfaction.

"You really like this place, don't you?" I say to Dan.

"You'd get to do it all your way."

So it took seeing nearly forty homes to realize there's no shortcut to getting what you want. The Perfect House—the one with character, charm, patina, finishes you love, a finished yard and mature foliage, for just the right price—doesn't exist. But, for me, in five or six years it will. And it will be right here. And it can for you, too. So here we go again.

Background Check

The importance of homework

"HAVE FUN!" DAN HOLLERED as he dropped me off at the design center near our soon-to-be home. I should have felt excited; after all, I was finally getting to pick out the finishes for my dream house. But, in fact, I was verging on a home-design breakdown. For the builder to have the home done in five months, as promised, I needed to make a heap of decisions, and I was only in town for one day. I had eight hours to select flooring for the whole house, and tile and stone treatments for the kitchen, laundry room, and four baths, before I had to catch a plane.

"Plenty of time," I said to the design center rep, who, when setting the appointment, warned that most people needed a few days to select finishes for a home like this. "I've done two homes before," I assured her. "I'll be quick," I lied.

Truth is, any one of these decisions would normally take me two weeks: five days of searching for inspiration in magazines and researching materials; five days of gathering samples, resources, and opinions; and four days of hand-wringing coupled with an increased ingestion of headache tablets.

Because I was also busy working, selling our current home, researching and applying to area schools in our new city, and shoring up my husband's career change (read midlife crisis), I wasn't exactly spending my evenings by the fire poring over issues of *House Beautiful*.

I entered the design center determined to be like Chainsaw Al: efficient, decisive, on a budget. That mindset lasted until I hit the showroom, which was packed with tantalizing samples: decorative tile, marble, limestone, wood. I began to swoon. My resolve to make swift decisions unraveled like a cheap sweater. I lost my design compass and needed a chair. Having seen this reaction before, the design center rep quickly ordered a cup of caffeine. Once I revived, we got to work. Every so often she looked at her watch and suggested we quicken the pace. As I tried to divine my way through the bewildering options, my creative courage turned to cowardice. I made timid and reluctant choices, driven more by the clock than by conviction.

"How did it go?" Dan asked when he picked me up.

"I need professional help."

"I know that, but how did it go?"

"Awful."

"Why? You were supposed to pick exactly what you've always wanted."

"Just because I know what I want doesn't mean I know how to get it," I said. Then I set out all the choices I'd made.

"Hmm," he said cautiously, knowing that if he said the wrong thing I might crack a piece of tumbled marble over his head. "Looks like a nice hotel."

"Exactly! A hotel, not a home. Not *our* home. I was going so hard for understatement, I didn't make any statement."

"You need professional help," he agreed.

The next day I called the design rep and, in a fit of panic and uncertainty, canceled everything. I pulled the plug on every design choice I'd made. I called the builder and said I didn't care if I delayed the project. During the next two weeks, I did what I should have done—my homework.

The point of this false start is to let you know that these background decisions take time, planning, and thought. Don't rush through them, but do educate yourself. Take the time to define your style and explore your options, because they are overwhelming. Frankly, the whole experience gave me a new respect for bachelors who can't commit.

A few weeks later, I returned to the showroom armed with photos from home décor magazines—or shelter magazines, as they are called in the trade—as well as a clearer head and a godsend—an interior designer. When I first spoke with Karlie Adams, of Denver, on the phone, she gave me the tough-love advice I needed.

Before we could choose backgrounds, she said, I needed to define my style. Lesser designers will forge ahead and give you a look they think is right, but not Karlie. She told me to pore over design books and magazines, tour some model homes in the area, and gather photos of interiors I liked, and of my current home furnished. Then we could meet in person. You'll read how it all turned out in Part II, where we tackle background decisions, but first we need to slow down and ask some tough questions: Can your house ever look like a model home? What is good design, anyway? How do you find your personal decorating style and express it? Let's find out.

Reality Check

Why your home will never look like a model home, and how it can still look great

DON'T THESE PEOPLE HAVE DOGS, or kids? Don't they get newspapers or mail? I ask myself this every time I open a shelter magazine. I want to scream: How do you get to live like this? The magazine homes always look so unattainably perfect. I used to feel the same way years ago when I looked at—before I banned— fashion magazines. All those models with their perfect skin and no body fat. Now instead I look at gorgeous homes and compare, not skin tone and thighs, but kitchens and kids' rooms.

Is it just my house that has carpet stains and torn screens, thanks to pets who can't find pet doors? Am I the only home with an urgent pile of paperwork so high the pieces on top get nosebleeds? Is my kitchen table the only one chronically cluttered with half-finished children's crafts—usually involving some combination of glue, paint, dried pasta, and glitter? Does anyone else avoid decorating because just the thought of picking a paint color is paralyzing? Have other couples started a three-month redecorating project and twelve months later found that the cost has tripled, their favorite fabric has been discontinued, their marriage is in a shambles, and the contractors have all gone to the bar?

Sometimes, in an optimistic moment, I look around my home and try to visualize any part of it being magazine worthy. Perhaps with the right lighting, camera angle, and stylist, it could be. What would it take? And why can't my home look like a model home?

An interior design friend of mine who is often hired to decorate model homes made me feel better one day when she told me the secret of why real homes will never look like models.

"Designing a model home interior is entirely different from doing residential design," she said.

"How so?" I asked.

"Because people don't live there. We create a possibility that can never exist. Our job is to sell a dream."

I admit I've been duped by such dreams. I've swooned in model homes that suck me in because they're perfect. I want perfect! I study the backgrounds, the furniture, the fixtures, the accessories, and think: This doesn't look so complicated. Surely my home can look like this.

But hard as I try, my home never does. And it never will.

Next time you're in a model home, before you go all weak in the knees and soft in the head, think about what you see: The boy's room has only three toys: a bat, a ball, and a glove. On the wall are a ball cap, two baseball pennants, and a signed Cal Ripken poster. The girl's room has three princess books, one doll, a tutu, and a tiara. The parents' closet has four perfectly pressed outfits all in the same tasteful color, three pairs of never worn shoes, and a hat one would wear to the Kentucky Derby. The table is set with unstained placemats and pristine, pressed cloth napkins; it looks as if the wave of a wand would put dinner on the table without a mess in the kitchen and with everyone in the family getting along.

Like that's real life. In reality, kids' interests change like the weather. One week they're aspiring soccer or tennis pros, the next week dancers or race car drivers, then they hit their Ninja rock star

Okay, so if it's all a façade, what exactly stands between real home design and model home design? In other words, what does a model home have that our homes probably never will?

- **A fresh start.** When designing a model, designers begin with a clean slate. They come in at the ground level and specify every single finish and detail in the home—tile, grout, wall colors, flooring, cabinetry—to make sure the whole house coheres. Most of us make do with what's there.
- **No baggage.** Model designers don't come to the project with favorite pieces of art they've collected or furnishings they're attached to. Instead, they custom order and select art, mats and frames, and every stick of furniture to coordinate with the interior scheme.
- **No arguments.** Model home designers don't have to argue with spouses or kids over how to do a room. They just get their way.
- **Real money.** Because builders know that the more decked out the model is, the more homes and upgrades they will sell, and the faster they will sell them, they give designers the budget and okay to do the whole house. I can only dream.
- **Smoke and mirrors.** Model designers order furniture that allows foot traffic to flow and that makes rooms look larger when necessary.
- **Less stuff.** Because their goal is to let people see the home and its architecture, not the stuff, they allow zero clutter.
- **False fronts.** When staging bookshelves, they select books for their covers, not their contents. Sometimes they cover all books on a shelf in the same leather. Who buys books for their covers?
- **Theme rooms.** Designers typically peg one child's room for, say, a boy golfer, and another for a girl horseback rider. In the boy's room, they'll have four golf shirts, a bag of clubs, three golf hats, and golf ball handles on the faucet. The girl's room will have tall riding boots, a crop, and some jodhpurs. No kid is that one dimensional.
- **Storage style.** Model master closets feature a monochromatic wardrobe that ties into the master décor, meaning all the outfits go with the bedspread, and who buys clothes that way?

phase. Plus, they have stuff: school papers, singing hamsters, gum wad collections, Russian nesting dolls, ant farms, and boxes of dead butterflies. Parents' closets are a mayhem that reflect career changes, expanding and shrinking waistlines, outfits in style three presidents ago, and nothing suitable for the winner's circle at the Derby. Most kitchens are just a blizzard of mail and manic meal making. In short, model homes are to lived-in homes what movie sets are to real life.

"Most people know models are just for show," my friend said. "They don't really think their homes will look like that."

"No, of course not," I said. "Who would think a thing like that?"

So let's all get right over this fantasy that we can make our homes look like models, and instead ponder the real question: *What is good design anyway?*

I start there, and call my brother, Craig Jameson, an architect in private practice. Craig used to teach architectural design at the University of North Carolina and has a master's in architecture from Cornell University. Design, he said professorially, is measured by how eloquently an object performs its duties. "The well-designed object, whether a teaspoon, a dress, or a house, achieves a high level of function and poetic success through an economy of means."

He told me about a shack in Montana, a shelter about six feet square. The builder/occupant apparently lacked access to standard roofing materials. So, when this guy (though I'm not convinced it wasn't a woman) was ready to put on the roof, he went to a nearby junkyard full of old cars, gathered a bunch of old license plates, and shingled the roof with them. "It was a work of art: direct, poetic, resourceful, inspired, highly functional, and even beautiful," Craig said.

License plates as roofing? Must be a Warhol thing. But it did give me hope. Good design is not about money and grandeur, but about thoughtfulness and simplicity.

The notion jived with something Michael Graves, the eminent architect and designer from Princeton, had told me during an interview. He said that the best object ever designed was the egg. Although he credits God, not humans, Graves deemed the egg perfect: smooth to easily come out of the hen, comfortable for her to sit on, self-contained in an aesthetically pleasing package, good to eat, nice to hold. Next best, he thought, was the paper clip. Both are functional without excess.

But what does all this have to do with our homes? Simply this: Well-designed homes, too, should be comfortable, self-contained, aesthetically pleasing, and superbly functional.

How do you get there? To answer that, I interviewed top design experts from every corner of the home improvement industry. I combined their responses with my own been-there experiences to create a logical, affordable, step-by-step approach to making your home yours—but better. I think that in doing so, I have divined an honest place between the surreal homes depicted in models, magazines, and TV shows and the real world, where people actually live in their homes. Here are my well-honed criteria for good home design:

- Your home needs to function and absorb your lifestyle.
- Your home needs to reflect you—but beautifully.
- Your home needs to be your haven, a calm port where you come to relax and recharge.

You need to achieve all this while balancing your family life, career, calendar, and budget. So before you buy a stick of furniture or paint a single wall, think about who you are, what you do, and what your household really needs.

4

Find Your Style and Create Your Plan

Think like Plato: Who are you and what are you doing here?

THE IRONY OF WHAT I DO is that everyone assumes I know what I'm doing. Here I am a home design columnist stumped when building and designing my own home. With Karlie's assignment—to do my homework before we selected my new home's colors and backgrounds—weighing on my mind, I went to a party. I met a woman there who got right down to the core of my crisis.

After the usual first-meeting patter—Where do you live? Who does your hair?—came the inevitable: What do you do? When I told her I was a home design columnist, she got a horror-stricken look that I'm used to. Translated, it means, "I'm never having this woman to my place." Then she just came out with it: "Okay, so tell me, is your home all tricked out?"

"Get me another drink," I cried.

"You're kidding?"

"Heck no! That's the point. First of all, I don't even have a home at the moment. I'm building one. And second, when it comes to decorating, I'm just like most people dealing with the same three-pronged trap—no money, no time, no courage."

"But it's your business."

"My business is making myself feel better by letting readers know they're not alone as we try to make our homes look like something better than the dog's breakfast."

Her relief was visible. Then she nailed one of the biggest problems do-it-yourself, or DIY, home decorators face, and that I was facing. "My problem," she said, "is that I like so many looks I don't have a look."

"Ahh," I said. "I know. One minute a sleek modern look sweeps me away. Next I'm in love with rooms filled with cozy English florals, when suddenly a Tuscan-styled home with terracotta paved floors turns my head. They're all great looks, but not in the same house."

"So how do you *commit* to just one?"

"I suppose it's like marriage," I say. "Success requires love, discipline, and not yielding to temptation."

As usual, I found myself spouting the same advice I needed to follow. Fortunately, Karlie helped me stay faithful to myself before I took off on a series of ill-fated affairs with styles that just weren't me.

When I first started looking at homes in Colorado, I was taken with all the Rocky Mountain–inspired interiors. I walked through model homes decorated with heavy wood furniture, rough hewn timbers, and color schemes in muted shades of olive, rust, and brown. I loved it all. The homes made me feel as if I were in a mountain lodge, which meant vacation. If my home looked like this, I thought, I would always have that vacation feeling. That, of course, is pure tripe. I mean, wherever you live, you always drag yourself with you.

Nevertheless, because I needed a design scheme fast for the house to be done in time, and we needed to pick those backgrounds, I decided this look was it! When I met to show Karlie, who was born and raised in Denver, I was sure that she would have this style down and that she would be happy to help me achieve it. I showed her the local interiors I loved, and then some pictures of my former home in California. She said we needed to talk.

"This look is great, but it's not you," she said bluntly. "This is too Beaver Creek. Your style is much more European. Everything I can see about you leans toward French Country, and an Old World look. Look at the furniture you've already bought. The lines in these model homes are too beefy for you, the furniture too heavy, the granite counters too thick, the colors too somber. It would be a mistake."

I felt as if I were talking to a psychic, not a designer. How did this woman, who barely knew me, know that inside I'm really a French woman born in the wrong country? I envisioned the typical Colorado lodge–style armchair sitting by the typical Colorado fireplace, and it did seem like something Paul Bunyan would sit in, not five-foot-three me. I would feel like Goldilocks in Papa's chair, not like the dignified matriarch I aspire to become. In that Oprah moment, I stopped trying to reinvent myself and my new interior into something I wasn't. Rather, I was going to be myself but in a new place.

So, short of finding a psychic interior designer, how do you figure out your style? I floated the question by Stephen Drucker, editor in chief of *House Beautiful*. When I told him how Karlie helped me stumble onto my style, he said, "You were very lucky. Most people have a blind spot about what their style is."

However, a good place to start, said Drucker, is by going through stacks of home design magazines. "Tear out pictures of any rooms you like. When you have fifty interiors, then go back and look through them. A look will emerge."

Only you can define your style, but here are questions you should ask yourself, or at least temporarily consider, when honing a look. To start, you have to answer some big philosophy questions, the kind Plato and Socrates contemplated and pontificated about at length. Only you need to do it faster. . . .

What Am I Doing Here?

Many people wrongly approach decorating by first focusing on a color scheme. But the first question to ask is more basic. What are you planning to do in your home? By defining your purpose here, you will define your lifestyle. In great design, function comes first, form second. We've all seen beautiful, gratuitous designs in fashion and interiors that look terrific, but that finally are useless. The home of an executive bachelor who is a gourmet cook should be very different from that of a family with four kids and two dogs. Drucker agrees. He said, "Be brutally honest when analyzing how you live. If you never entertain, turn your dining room into a library."

Your home's purpose changes with your life stages. Whether you're single, raising a family, or are an empty nester, everything that is most important to you—your relationships, interests, activities, and goals—will determine the answer to just about every home-design question you will need to ask yourself. Will you need fabrics that are durable, or can they be finer? Do you need lots of shelves for books, a place for a computer, a home office? Do you need to make your home safe for small children? Do you need a place where teenagers can hang out and eat pizza? All this will dictate what comes next.

Where Did I Come From?

Don't try to be someone you're not. Consider your heritage and express that in your home, even if, like me, you're a melting pot mongrel. I'm a fifth-generation Californian from English/Scottish roots, but I lived in France during the early years of my life and carry its indelible influence. I married a man from German-Irish extraction. All of this pretty much means that no one in my family tans. But how that shows up in my home is through a design style I would call Old World European with French Country leanings and a few nods to the west. I like a lot of other looks, but this one suits me.

And while you don't have to be a slave to one style, if you do pick one—modern, traditional, country, ethnic—try to be consistent. Mexican, Scandinavian, and Early American are all distinctive looks. But blend them and you'll wind up with a camel wearing plaid and stilettos.

Where Are You?

Before you commit to a design direction, look at the architecture of your home and notice the styles around you, in your neighborhood and region. Architecture and geography should have a bearing on your décor. When we lived in San Juan Capistrano, California, the look was largely Mediterranean (a lot of orange stucco). Mexican, Italian, and rustic interiors played well. In the Colorado Rockies, lodge-style homes with stone exteriors and

---

TIP: Here's a quick way to determine your style that *House Beautiful* editor Stephen Drucker suggested. Look around your house and pick out three items that you could not give up because it would break your heart to part with them. If you picked a cream canvas sofa, a pine table, and a woven throw, you're a country girl.

brown tones prevail. If you have a colonial home in New England, going with a Moroccan decorating scheme would be a mistake. Your home décor needs to go with your home's architectural style and should integrate with your environment.

Okay, so with those big questions in mind—your lifestyle, your heritage, and your location—you can dial in your plan. Below you'll begin to see how. . . .

Plan Before You Spend

Before I started writing journalism full time, I had a public relations agency in Los Angeles, where I blended my love of writing and graphic design with my fundamental inability to have a boss. I ran it for twelve years before selling. For nine of those years, I taught public relations at the University of California at Los Angeles. All those years, the most important point I would drive home to my students, clients, and staff was this: *Don't make a move without a plan.* The same holds true in home design. Not having a plan, whether in public relations or in home design, is like flying an airplane without a destination; you set out for Orlando and wind up in Des Moines.

Similarly, in home design you need to define your goals, including the look you want. You need to figure out who can help you achieve those goals (vendors, psychotherapists, suppliers, bartenders, contractors) and then find the pieces and finishes to get the job done—within your budget. And yes, you should know in advance what it will all cost. Very few people can afford to decorate without a budget. Building a realistic one before you start can mean the difference between finishing a room with money left for the mortgage, and living in a shoe.

Why plan? Besides giving you a design direction, having a plan offers many other advantages:

- **You can go at your own pace.** If you're like me, you can't afford to do every home improvement you want at once. But if you have your plan, you can chip away at your decorating scheme one step at a time, knowing you're on course.
- **You'll make fewer—or maybe no—design blunders.** The people who don't have a plan are the ones who impulsively buy a leopard-print chair then can't make it work. (In Chapter 20, you'll read of my mother-in-law's red sofa saga, which she could have avoided with a plan.)
- **You'll save money.** If you know your design goals, you'll know when to say no. A seaside getaway isn't a Manhattan loft, so it shouldn't look like one inside. Good design is about limits, and about editing out—or not bringing home in the first place—what doesn't belong. I love a lot of things that would look wrong in my home. Cool as they may be, I can pass on that antler light fixture, or a chrome-and-glass bar cabinet, because they don't fit my look or my plan.
- **You'll give your house a sure hand.** The nicest home interiors aren't the ones with the finest furnishings. They're the ones that cohere. Every room, while different, feels as if it's furnished with the same sensibility.
- **You'll create an ad buffer.** President's Day, Labor Day, Mother's Day, even tax time (like I ever get a refund) are all opportunities those clever PR and advertising types seize upon to declare open season on your wallet. They try to convince you that this is the weekend you have to buy that new sofa, washer, or mattress. Their motto: *Let your children pay off your Visa card! Buy those new copper rain gutters today!* But you can resist because you have a plan. The plan protects you from making stupid, reckless home improvements just because an ad attacked you when you had a day off to shop. So before you're tempted to blow the grocery money on an impulsive home design mistake, make and stick to a plan. (For more ways to find inspiration, see Chapter 18.)

Here's what your home improvement plan needs:

- **A vision bag.** This will hold all the ideas, samples, and cost estimates that you will compile to make your home fabulous. I use a large leather satchel, but a banker's box would also work. The container should be large enough to hold bulky files, and sturdy enough so that it won't decompose. This is key, since visions—at least mine—can take many years to realize. If you're one of those irritating people who can afford to decorate your whole house at once, fine. Use a large paper shopping bag.
- **The big picture.** Every plan should include a floor plan of your home; furniture layouts (do these in pencil on graph paper); a color scheme with swatches of your main fabrics and paint colors; other background finishes, including a piece of stone or tile, carpet, or flooring; and inspirational photos. These are the dominant tones and themes that will guide your whole house. This is your design compass. Some people like to tack these items to a portable design board, which is great.
- **Lighting plan.** Don't forget to consider the lighting as you go, particularly if you can work this into a construction phase. Lighting is often overlooked, but it adds the crowning glow. Work to create layered lighting. Use overhead lighting to pinpoint what you want to highlight—the fireplace, the art, the coffee table—then add ambient light at eye level from wall sconces and from table, floor, and task lamps. Finally, add candles to make magic.
- **One file for each room in the house and the yard.** Include files for transitional spaces, such as the entryway, mudroom, hallway, and patio areas. On the inside cover of each file, write a to-do list of the projects and pieces you will need to finish the room. Next to each entry, pencil in a budget number. (Pencil is key.) Or staple the room's itemized budget (see next tip) inside the folder's cover. I also like to put a star next to priority items. In the folder, stash a floor plan of the room, including the furniture layout, swatches and samples, inspirational pages torn from magazines, pictures of window treatments, photos of fixtures and furnishings, and names of contractors and suppliers. Include possible ideas. Weed out

("Here's what your home..." continues)

rejects later. Also include measurements and vendor estimates for specific projects you'd like done in that room, such as built-in shelves or faux finish paint.

- 🐷 **A budget.** Creating a decorating budget is much easier than creating a remodeling budget—which always involves those infamously skyrocketing construction costs. With a decorating budget you also have a much better shot at actually spending what you expect to, if, that is, you plan well.

🐷 Here's my AFFORD plan for creating a decorating budget:

- *Ask* what your dream is for each space, and make a wish list. Include everything you will need to purchase or do to finish the room. Be thorough and idealistic. (You can cut back later.) Factor in wall treatments, built-ins, furniture, lighting, window treatments, flooring, art, and accessories. List items you have and items you need to buy. Add in repairs you'll need to make.
- *Figure* out what you can realistically afford. If you think you'll be short, keep saving until you can afford to see the project through, or opt for the pay-as-you-go plan and move slowly, which is how I operate. The idea is to have a realistic sense of how much you can spend on the house as a whole before you shoot your wad on one custom wall unit. (See prioritizing section below.)
- *Fudge* a little. That is, leave an extra 10 to 15 percent in your budget for surprises, which are inevitable no matter how well you plan.
- *Organize* bids and gather prices for each item. For services you plan to contract out—painting, wallpaper hanging, carpentry, electrical work—get a few estimates so you're working with good numbers. Be sure contractors include costs for materials. For window

Now that you know your style, you need a plan, including a budget, for every room in your house. See boxes for more on how and why (which mostly boils down to saving yourself from spending lots of money you would later regret), and for some basic guidelines that you should know before you begin.

Every six months, sit down with your partner (ideally when the stock market is up) and decide which home improvements are next on the list. Dan and I almost never agree: He wants new yard mulch, while I want bathroom wallpaper. But it doesn't matter. I keep the list, and he forgets.

("Here's my AFFORD plan..." continued)

treatments, know the fabric you want, price per yard, and how much you'll need. Include drapery lining, trim, hardware, and installation costs. In other words: Think of everything. For furniture pricing, go shopping and do research online, figure in delivery charges and tax. The goal is to avoid surprises.

- *Revise.* With pricing in hand, list every task you need to do and every purchase you need to make, and arrange these in the order you will need to follow to achieve your goal. (We'll discuss the ideal decorating sequence later.) Some people like to use an Excel spreadsheet for this task, which helps you track estimates and actual costs as you go to keep you honest. Or you can use a paper spreadsheet and a pencil. Once you tally what everything will cost, grab the smelling salts. If you factored in everything, you're probably in for a shock. Now, bargain with yourself—ask what you must have and where you can cut. If you won't be happy without hardwood floors, then maybe you can forego wallpaper for paint. Keep refining your dream list until it matches what you can afford.
- *Decorate.* Well, almost. Before you begin, you have a little more preparation to do. See box on ordering your priorities.

Finally, create a permanent record. Save your photos and samples even after you've purchased or installed the décor. They not only prove you are making progress but also create a helpful home portfolio. If you're ever shopping for art or an area rug for that room, you have the room's colors and design elements in hand.

Setting priorities is easy when you use the logic of a Vulcan. As mere humans, however, we can use these four criteria to determine what to do next in each space:

- **First,** do necessary home repairs to ensure the soundness of the home: Repair a leaking roof, or treat mold or termite damage, for example.
- **Second,** do any improvement that adds to the base value of the home, such as built-in desks or bookcases, or upgraded appliances.
- **Third,** acquire decorative items, starting with furnishings for the most public rooms and ending with the most private (which explains why my master bedroom may never be done).
- **Finally,** ditch all of the above criteria if you find exactly what you want at a fire-sale price, meaning you'll have more room in your budget to splurge on something else. (Though I have other priorities, if I stumble across the perfect area rug to finish off my dining room, and it's a steal, I'm buying it, even if the roof leaks.)

PART II

Decisions, Decisions

Selecting wall treatments, flooring, counters, tile, and cabinetry

Eat your vegetables before dessert, my mother used to say. The same principle applies to home decorating. You have to tackle the tough part—selecting the backgrounds—before splurging on the fun stuff like that new artwork or a silk floral centerpiece. It takes a little discipline, but backgrounds, which some people call "the shell" of your home, should be selected, or in place, before the chatchkes. The shell includes the finished surfaces: walls, floors, ceilings, cabinets, window coverings, and counters.

You have to start with the backgrounds, says designer Gary Gibson, then move in: "Don't start with a blue sofa then get stuck." He advises clients to keep backgrounds low in contrast by using similar, harmonious tones. Soften glaring white walls by painting them wheat or another light neutral color, then cover your floors in materials slightly darker than the walls. That doesn't mean to avoid saturated color, but if you paint the walls pale sage, and add a eucalyptus carpet, you will have a neutral, harmonious background to build on.

5

The Big Picture

Start with something certain

I HADN'T HAD THIS MUCH RIDING on a decision since choosing my college major. In fact, choosing a major is a lot like the daunting task of choosing backgrounds, or surface materials: The ripple effect impacts all future choices. The wrong background, either in your home or on your resume, can send you in a misguided direction for life.

How will the carpet and paint you pick today work with the furnishings you have or plan to purchase? Are they versatile enough for the long haul? For example, would you be able to change the furnishings without having to redo the backgrounds in, say, ten years? Does this mean you can't change the bedspread? Will the colors become dated or limit your other choices too much? Are any of your selections too juvenile, too old-fashioned, too feminine or masculine, too formal or rustic, or too busy or boring? Would they negatively affect resale? And the queen of all worries: What will your choices say about you?

This is why so many rooms are beige, and why my first round of timid background choices would have given the impression of a generic hotel.

The good news is, once you've pinned down the backgrounds, future decisions become easier. But the pressure is on, because these decisions will, or should, impact every other decorating decision you make. These early choices are tough in part simply because you have so many options. I welcomed news of a study confirming that one reason people in our society are so stressed is because we have too much choice. Scientists didn't need to do a study, however; all they had to do was look at the shampoo aisle. This too-much-choice phenomenon is particularly true in the home design arena. With home improvement now a national pas-

---

Back at the design center, with a clear design direction and Karlie, whom I had hired for eight hours to help me navigate the sea of samples, we got much of the job done. Here's what I learned:

- **Start with something certain.** When picking backgrounds for your home, use swatches of furnishings you know will be in the home, or colors from an area rug or piece of artwork you know you plan to use. Keep an eye on color forecasts (See Chapter 18), so that you can select colors that are trending up, not down. Or shoot for non-trendy neutrals that are always in style. Build on that. I used a large oil painting, which my husband and I both love, and which hangs in our living room. I had the artist paint the colors in the painting on a small canvas, which I carried around when shopping for backgrounds.
- **Think flow.** The whole house doesn't have to match, but it should flow. That is, the tile or stone you choose in the guest bath should look at home in the kitchen. Color consistency and compatibility give a home a sure hand.
- **Look carefully at the undertones.** The biggest color mistake DIY decorators make is choosing two background colors that don't share the same undertone, or the cast that underlies a color. For instance, put two reds together and you might see that one has a blue undertone, and the other pulls orange. If you go with the bluer red, you'll want to pair it with pinks that also have a cooler,

time more popular than football (seriously, just drop by Lowe's or Ikea on Sunday), those in the industry are capitalizing on consumers' passions. They're not only rolling out the red carpet but also the celadon, buckwheat, and songbird blue carpets, which come in berber, frieze, loop, and cut pile. And the choices just keep growing.

The trick to managing this array of choices is to have a master plan, then break every decision down into small, methodical steps.

("Back at the design center, ..." continued)

bluer undertone. Whites can pull many colors, including taupe, tan, yellow, or cream. A beige carpet with a yellow undertone will look wrong against a beige wall with a taupe undertone.

- **Stay true to your style.** Decide if you're going modern, traditional, country, Old World, or eclectic, then don't switch gears. Successful houses cohere. While this seems limiting, it helps narrow the overwhelming field of choice. (See the next chapter.)

- **Get help.** If you really feel overwhelmed, find an interior designer who's a good fit for your project. I found Karlie by asking who designed a model home nearby that I loved. She visited my new home site. During the second round of finish selections, she quickly dialed in choices that she knew I would like and that would work both with the furnishings I had and with the new house's architecture. Her $800 consulting fee was worth it, considering that I was investing many thousands in finishes.

- **Make a deal.** Be sure you have a payment agreement up front with your designer. Not all will work on a consulting-only basis, but many will. Because I bought the finishes directly, not through her, I didn't pay a consulting fee plus a mark-up on purchased materials. Plus, her better choices cost less overall than the choices I initially made. And the real bonus? She pulled together a look that was way more me—or the me I wanted to be—than any look I could have cobbled together on my own.

Despite the mind-blinding frustration, at every step I worked a little harder, dug a little deeper, and relied on experts, so I—and now you—could get it right.

As we worked on the backgrounds, I learned to break the process down into smaller steps. Starting with wall color, we then moved to flooring, then tile, cabinets, counters, and window coverings. As we made each decision, we made sure each built on the prior choice, so we built a cohesive look. Next, I'll show you just how.

6

The Color of Indecision

Finding the right wall color

"CAN'T YOU EVEN *THINK* without spending money?" Dan asked. I was bringing in a box of eight quarts of paint to test.

"I guess that's your answer," I said, plopping the carton on the counter of our shell of a house, built now except for the finishes.

"You're obsessing."

"Am not."

Like many men, Dan's brain wiring skips the region that perceives color and jumps straight to the region that computes compounded interest. To him, every color from mauve to merlot is red, and everything from celery to forest is green. I, on the other hand, see nuances in color that aren't even there, obsess about choosing, then still get it wrong. For our new house, I knew I wanted something between butterscotch and honeysuckle.

The color needed to be perfect. Having the wrong color on your walls is like living with a permanent hangover. Plus, the wall color influences all other background choices.

"Some poets spend months looking for the right word," I said.

"That's supposed to reassure me?"

"I know exactly the color I want."

"What color would that be?"

"You know, a sort of warm buttery biscuity sand."

"Hoo-boy."

When picking paint, keep these tips in mind:

Color Selection

- **Color is fickle** and changes depending on your light. A wall color that looks great in your friend's house could flop in yours. Don't go just from the paint chip, which is actually ink, not paint.
- **When you decide** on a general color, say a robin's egg blue, or a marigold, get several quarts to test. Some companies, including Ralph Lauren, sell little test bags of color, which are cheaper than quarts.
- **Paints with low levels of VOCs** (volatile organic compounds) are environmentally friendlier than traditional paints and don't cost much more. Although they sometimes go on a little runnier, they won't give you a headache from fumes.
- **Consider using** exterior paints inside. Their pigments are often more intense.
- **Test the paint** in the room where it will go. Use two coats. Ideally, you should test the paint on large (roughly 16" x 16") pieces of drywall that are the same texture as your walls. You can get these for just a few dollars (sometimes for free) at your local home improvement store. This is better than painting test patches on your walls for several reasons. If you paint test patches on the walls, the patches, particularly if the color is dark, can ghost through the final paint and haunt you for years to come. Using panels lets you move the colors around so you can see them in different lights and on different walls. Panels also let you place carpet candidates near the panels to see how they look together.
- **Before deciding,** observe the colors at different times of day.

He didn't even know what I'd been through to this point. At the paint store a few days earlier, I had seen The Perfect Color immediately. But, knowing how deceiving those little swatches can be, I pulled twenty paint chips similar to The Perfect Color and

---

("When picking paint, keep ..." continued)

Sheen

Lisa LaPorta, host of HGTV's *Designed to Sell* and spokesperson for KILZ paints, offers these tips for selecting the proper paint finish:

- **Semi-gloss or high-gloss** finishes are good choices in kitchens, bathrooms, laundry rooms, and mudrooms because they offer protection against moisture and an easy-to-clean surface.
- **Eggshell** finishes are good for bedrooms and bonus or playrooms because they are durable and washable. They are particularly good for children's areas.
- **Matte finishes,** as the name implies, have no sheen, so they are sophisticated solutions for more formal living areas, such as living rooms and dining rooms.
- **Satin and semi- or high-gloss** paints emphasize the architectural elements of woodwork and still hold up to frequent washing, so they are a good choice for woodwork, including doors, windows, and trim.
- **Deciding factor.** Though higher sheens are easier to clean, I always like to go with the lowest sheen possible, or no sheen. Personally, I'd rather repaint than live with shine.
- **Special effects.** Play with the many textures and washes available. They're easy to apply (really), and can add loads of character to a room.
- **The Fifth Wall.** Don't forget the ceiling. Some say leaving a ceiling (called a *lid* in the biz) white makes it seem higher. I say it makes it look ignored. You don't have to match the ceiling to the walls, but do tie it in by painting it either the same color or a shade slightly lighter.

brought them home to look at in my home's light. I then bought one quart of The Perfect Color, plus seven more test quarts, which I thought was prudent.

Dan stared into the carton of quarts. The guy at the paint store had helpfully dropped a spot of paint on each can lid to indicate the color inside.

"They're all the same," Dan said.

"Are not," I pointed out. "This one is more caramel. This is more toasted wheat. This . . ." I looked up and saw that he was walking away.

"As long as you like it," he said. Note to husbands: This is an excellent line, and you should use it often if you wish to stay married or at least avoid excessive bruising.

Using 99-cent disposable sponge brushes, I applied two coats of each color to large scraps of drywall. When the paint dried, I moved the drywall planks around the new house like stiff dance partners to view them in different lights.

Yikes! The Perfect Color turned pink. Its weaker cousin turned gray. Another was too taupe, several others too yellow.

"What is it you're looking for?" the man at the paint store asked when I returned for the third time.

"You know that sort of a honey, lemon, cafe au lait, butterscotch wheat." He nodded sympathetically and sent me home with two more quarts. I painted and numbered two more test panels. I was getting warmer.

"Don't you ever get on your own nerves?" Dan asked when he saw me testing yet another two samples.

I made blends: 30 percent of #2 with 70 percent of #6 to create #11. I solicited opinions shamelessly. Passersby, neighbors, even the UPS man were dragged in to put a pencil tick by the one they liked best. My kids voted. Dan abstained. Some wiseacre started a game of tic-tac-toe.

Once you've chosen your paint, you're ready to tackle the job. Here's how:

- **Consider Using Professionals.** Hiring a professional painter is a luxury, but it is usually affordable and worth it. If you decide to do the job yourself to save money, don't forget to factor in the cost of your time and the supplies you'll need to purchase: tarps, ladders, rollers, tape, paint trays, and brushes. Also factor in the aching knees, thighs, and arms you'll get from 800 trips up the ladder and painting over your head, and the 30 lost IQ points due to paint sniffing.
- **Prepare.** Mask all trim well. Move furniture to the room's center, then cover it and the floor with plastic or tarps.
- **Prime.** Unpainted drywall is thirsty. Use a primer first. The color will go on more smoothly. Because primer costs less than paint, you'll save overall. When going with a dark color, like deep red, have the paint store mix a color primer. If you have a lot of wall surface, consider renting a paint compressor (available for about $100 a day from a large home improvement store). It may be a hassle to clean when you're done, but it will save you time overall. If you're painting over already painted walls, ask your paint store whether a primer is recommended. It usually is for a darker color.
- **Paint.** Lay it on thick. Although compressors work well for primer coats, hand rolling two coats of color will produce the best coverage. Buy corner rollers to apply paint where walls meet. Be sure to open the windows to avoid breathing too many fumes.
- **Relax.** As home decorating mistakes go, choosing the wrong paint is one of the cheapest to fix.

TIP: A reader of my syndicated column gave me this excellent idea: On the back of your light switches, which you remove when painting, write the brand, color and sheen of the paint, alongside a dollop of the paint itself. That way, when you go to touch up the room, you'll know the exact paint you need. This is especially helpful if you use various shades throughout your home.

"You're obsessing," Dan said.

"Am not."

Finally, ten days later (because the painter was coming in the morning), I chose a 50/50 blend of #5 and #7. I took a swatch to the patient man at the paint store, told him how I achieved it, and asked for 20 gallons.

"Our formulas don't work that way, Miss."

"Just mix them," I said. His eyebrows went up to his hairline and his mouth made a doubtful seam.

The next morning the painter asked brightly, "Got your color?"

I pointed to the twelve panels. "Which one do you like?"

"This one," he said, pointing to the winning color, as if it were the easiest choice in the world.

"Good," I said, "because I have 20 gallons."

"Well, it's obviously the best color in this space," he said, the brilliant man. "What's it called?"

"'Poetry,'" I said, glancing at Dan. "It's called 'Poetry.'"

Okay, so maybe I did obsess. But, bottom line, getting the paint color right is worth trial, error, and agony, because it's the foundation for all the design decisions that will follow. You'd better love it.

When you've zeroed in on your wall color, move on to the finish that will likely cover the next largest surface area in your home, your carpet or flooring. It will also take a big chunk of your budget, so tread carefully. Of all the interior design decisions I made for this home, this one may have made me the most unpopular.

7

Floored by the Options

A sane person's guide to choosing carpet, pad, and wood flooring

"KERRY!" I HOLLERED. He turned, smiled sheepishly. "Got a minute?" The receptionist at the carpet showroom gave Kerry a sympathetic expression. By now all the employees knew to avoid the frazzled lady who asks five million questions, can't make up her mind, and leaves a mound of carpet samples on the floor so big that half the staff is buried underneath. And no one here gets paid enough to deal with that.

"Don't worry," I said to Kerry. "I know what color I want. I've got my paint figured out, so this will be easy." I pulled him into the showroom and kept talking.

"Except that," he broke in politely, "you really should choose your color last." I halt and fan myself with my paint swatch. Now, I've owned five houses and have chosen carpet for each. You'd think I'd have this down.

First, you need to pick the kind of carpet you want, he said, then left me with a bunch of carpet types and stepped outside, presumably for some fresh air, but I wouldn't blame him if he took a small flask. Meanwhile, I got that familiar vertigo feeling I always get when faced with an expensive design decision. But I stuck to his

The experts at Shaw Industries, the world's largest carpet manufacturer, offered this three-step formula for carpet selection:

Step 1: Know the Types of Carpet and Pick One

- *Plush:* Seen mostly in formal homes and less often today, plush carpet is cut all one length. Think mowed. Downside: It shows every vacuum track and footstep.
- *Loop:* Also called berber, loop carpets have uncut fibers and often go in contemporary homes. Avoid these if you have pets. Their claws can hook on a loop and pull a permanent run.
- *Frieze:* (pronounced "frizz-ay"): Meet the new shag. These high twist yarns are long, soft, and casual. The new fibers stand up better, so no need to haul out that old carpet rake. Not for those who lack creative courage, as they definitely make a statement.
- *Textured:* Because the yarn fibers are cut at different lengths, these carpets don't show tracks, making them a household blessing. Cut halfway between a plush and a frieze, the look is shaggy, but shorter and neater than a frieze. Textured carpets work in both dressy and casual rooms.
- *Pattern:* A blend of cut and uncut (or loop) fibers, patterned carpets offer subtle texture. Botanical motifs and square and lattice patterns are popular. These carpets represent the fastest growing segment in the industry.

Step 2: Pick the Fiber Type

- **Polyester**
  Price: Inexpensive.
  Durability: Not great. A good choice for apartments or rentals.
  Market share: 28 percent.

  Footnote: Can give best color intensity.

- **Nylon**
  Price: Moderate.
  Durability: Good. Tried and true.
  Market share: 70 percent

  Footnote: In recent years, much softer versions (like Tactesse from Stainmaster) have come on the market.

recommended plan and chose style, then fiber, then color. And it worked. In the end, I went with a textured, nylon, caramel beige in the informal basement areas and a botanical patterned carpet in the same color for the upstairs and bedrooms, which was just what I knew I wanted all along.

Carpet Pad:
The Skinny on Thickness

When the men in white coats come to put me in a padded cell—and if I keep building houses like this that day will be soon—I want it on the record that I expect *density*. Got that? It turns out that density—not thickness—counts most in padding. And in my padded cell, I want the best.

"Regardless of thickness, an 8-pound pad is always better than a 6-pound pad," my carpet installer, who's been doing this for

---

("The experts at Shaw ...Step 2..." continued)

- **Wool**
  Price: Expensive
  Durability: Excellent. Will wear forever.
  Market share: 2 percent.
  Footnote: A status symbol.

Step 3: Dial in Color

- **Biggest mistake:** Going too light. A light carpet looks beautiful day one, but soil and traffic patterns show up fast. Plus, it's just stressful.
- **Know that** carpet looks lighter rolled on the floor than on the swatch.
- **Neutral colors,** like realtor beige, golds, and muted greens, are most popular.

eighteen years, explained. "If the pad is thick but not dense, the carpet will flex too much underfoot and break down faster."

I was trying to process this, but getting hung up figuring out how you weigh carpet pad, which comes in rolls as big as golf greens. What I learned is that if you chop up a 6-pound carpet pad and

Besides investing in a good carpet pad, be sure to get a good installation. Here are some tips my installer, Terry Hoppe, of Littleton, Colorado, recommends for both:

- *A lower profile carpet*, like a Berber, works best with a 3/8 inch pad. A short shag carpet works best with a 1/2 inch pad. Both should be dense.
- *Don't get hung up* on how plush a carpet feels. Ninety percent of foot feel comes from the pad.
- *Ask the installer* whether he uses a power stretcher, which makes carpet lie more evenly. The stretcher should have poles for leverage, not spikes, which can damage carpet.
- *Ask for a layout* of your job and note where the installer plans to place seams. Good installers make seams run perpendicular to windows when possible. Seams running parallel to a window show up more because of the way the light hits.
- *Get more than one bid* to compare yardage. Getting a layout also lets you calculate whether someone (like the builder) is selling you too much carpet. When we were buying carpet, the builder's carpet supplier said we would need 410 yards. Our installer, Terry, recalculated and found we only needed 350. (See Chapter 10 for other ways builders gouge.)
- *Check tightness.* A good job should have no visible ripples or bubbles and should pass the pluck test: When you pinch and pull the carpet in the middle of the room, it should lift no more than an inch.
- *Inspect seams.* Even the best installers can't make seams invisible, but they can make them less noticeable. Seams should be flat and not look frayed.

stuff it into a box that measures a cubic square foot, the contents will weigh 6 pounds. An 8-pound pad in the same container will weigh 8 pounds. The same wonks who came up with that wrote the tax code.

"But you wouldn't believe how many people put expensive carpet over cheap pad," he continued.

"Not me!" My carpet wasn't expensive. But since I was focused on color, texture, and price, I didn't remember ordering pad, so I nervously asked, "Did I buy a cheap pad?"

"You're good. You're on half-inch 8-pound."

I sat up a little straighter. "Good thing I knew what I was doing."

"I picked your pad. You forgot to."

"Oh," I said, feeling dense and thick, which I often do as I blunder my way through remodeling. "So let me get this straight: My cheap carpet on this dense pad will wear better than any carpet on a lighter pad."

"Right."

"So it's like fat and muscle," I said, trying to make this relevant.

"Huh?"

"You can be the same size as someone but weigh more and be stronger because you have more muscle, which is denser than fat. See, there's this girl at my gym. . . . "

"Something like that," he said, and went back to pounding tack strip.

As I mulled this, I picked up a scrap of pad, which is made of sweepings from the floors of mattress, tire, salami, tennis shoe, and chewing gum factories. The remains are put in a compost heap with disposed ashtray contents, homogenized, run through a large pasta press, and sold for $2 a yard.

Carpet feels nice underfoot. However, for the most lived-in rooms of my house—the kitchen, family room, dining room, and office—I went with wood floors, a good choice if you want flooring that will last 100 years.

Wood Floors to Stand the Test of Time

At the design center for the third time, I introduce myself to the unlucky rep who's stuck working with me to select my tiles and a stain for my wood flooring. I tell her I've gotten as far as choosing the paint and carpet. I show her my samples. "Starting with the

---

The National Wood Flooring Association, in St. Louis, Missouri, offers these pointers to consumers trying to select wood flooring:

- **The variety.** With fifty species of wood to choose from, even the most decisive home designers get stumped. If it helps, oak is still the wood of choice, making up 70 percent of what's sold and 90 percent of what's grown in the United States.
- **Plank widths.** In general, a strip floor (of 2 1/4 inch plank) works best in contemporary settings; wider planks (3–6 inches) lend themselves to country looks. Most species come in clear (ultra-pure), select (less pure, but nice), and distressed (rustic).
- **Finish.** Both water-based and oil-based urethane finishes wear equally well. The key difference: Oil bases yellow over time (which you won't notice on brown woods) but give more shine. Water bases won't yellow but won't shine as much.
- **Trends.** Parquet and patterned floors are out. People want floors laid straight or on the diagonal. Adding borders in a different species from the main field floor material is also popular, though in general, the more gimmicks there are in the layout, the greater the chance future buyers won't like it. The trend in stain colors is toward natural wood tones. Overall, people today want more simplicity as they realize that the texture, beauty, and grain of the wood is enough.
- **Biggest Mistake.** Being too unique. Most wood floors outlive their owners. You may think that inset medallion of a golfer is swell, but will the next homeowner?

wrong color base is like heading out on Highway 10 when you wanted Highway 15. You wind up in Riverside instead of Las Vegas," I tell her, trying to impress her with my knowledge of choosing backgrounds, but in fact confirming her suspicion that I'm a California psycho.

She nods, then excuses herself to bring us some coffee, and probably to slip a Valium in mine. She returns and we head toward the wood flooring.

This should be fast because the builder and I have agreed on wood floors downstairs. The builder's crew is already installing the 2 1/4 inch red oak floors, which look fine. I just have to pick the stain.

But as I look down on the acre of options, I feel a familiar waver: "Maybe there's something better?" whispers the voice within. My eyes wander from stain samples to floor samples. Suddenly, the generic 2 1/4 inch oak wood floor being installed seems less appealing. Besides oak, there's cherry, walnut, mahogany, and chestnut salvaged from old barns. (Imagine, floors that can talk! Moo!) Plank widths vary from 2 inches to 12 inches and can be laid straight, diagonally, and in patterns like crazy quilt. Stains go way beyond basic browns to include every shade from ivory to ebony. I'm dazzled to delirium.

"Excuse me, Ma'am?" the rep breaks through my daze.

"How much would it cost to rip out the floors and start over?" I ask.

"Ouch," she says. She gives me quotes for two floors I like. The cheapest doubles the cost of the floor going in. It's still oak, but quartered, rifted, and distressed, so it looks rustic but could be dressed up, and it has varying plank widths of 3 to 5 inches. The most expensive (the reclaimed barn version) costs as much as the house. I choose option one.

Around lunchtime, Dan calls to see how I'm doing.

"I'm over budget, and I haven't even gotten off the ground."

8

Set in Stone

The fine art of picking tile, granite, and other stone

LIKE MOST WOMEN, I've often dreamed about having the chance to select all my kitchen and bath surfaces. But when my moment came, I froze like the North Pole in January.

"I want something unique, that won't hurt resale," I told Karlie and the rep at the design center. "Something timeless that also feels fresh. I want a kitchen worthy of a magazine photo. I want distinctive bathrooms that make my daughters feel feminine, my guests feel pampered, and my husband and I feel like royalty. I want humble yet elegant, sophisticated but not stuffy. Oh, and it has to be in stock and in the budget."

"No problem," they said, at home with the task. Together we tackled each room; the designer laid out options in keeping with the big picture, while I zeroed in on ones I liked best.

After a grueling day picking tile and designing bathrooms, I got to the point where every time I closed my eyes I saw fields of grid work. Then I learned that we still weren't done with hard surfaces. Although, like most design centers, this one had granite samples, we couldn't pick the granite for the kitchen and bar here. This job required a field trip. Because there's so much variation in the natural stone, you need to actually pick your slab. I wasn't doing this alone. The next day, I grabbed Dan, and we went to a large granite warehouse.

The warehouse was bigger than a Wal-Mart and colder than a morgue. Before we even went in, our granite guide handed us orange vests to match hers. "Put these on," she said.

"What for?" I asked, slipping my arms through.

"Safety."

"So they can find us in the rubble?"

She didn't answer.

On that mortal note, Dan and I entered the warehouse to find a slab.

"What type of granite are you looking for?" the guide asked.

Here's what I learned about selecting hard surfaces, along with a few tips from the design pros at Daltile, in Dallas:

- **Choose your main (or field) material first.** This could be ceramic or porcelain tile or natural stone. Keep function in mind: Avoid white tile in a high traffic area, or a super-slick surface in a room that gets wet. When deciding between ceramic and porcelain, know the only advantage to porcelain is that it won't crack (as ceramic will) when used outside in a climate that freezes.
- **Decide on size.** Most materials come in squares with sides measuring from 1 to 18 inches. Some natural stones—such as granite, limestone, marble, and travertine—also come in solid slabs (see next section). The trend now is toward really large (16" x 16" and larger) and really small (1" x 1" or 2" x 2") tiles. Don't overlook the odd sizes, like 12" x 8" or 3" x 6", which can make interesting brick effects.
- **Add accent.** A trim, border, inset, or backsplash is the spice in your design. Consider whether you want it to blend or contrast, or add textural relief. The same tile but smaller and set on a diagonal can create low-cost interest.
- **Bring it home.** Before committing, put your tile finalists in the light of your home, against the paint you will be using, the flooring, and other

("Here's what I learned about ..." continues)

I answered with my typically succinct, "Uhhhh."

"I see." She looked at her watch. It was only 9 AM, but I could tell she was wishing it were lunch already.

I'd come armed with my bag, which had my carpet, paint, and tile samples—my guiding lights.

"Well, I don't want anything that looks like a cross-section of organ meats," I offered, pointing to a slab that looked like a lung cancer biopsy.

"No Baltic Brown," she said, making a note on her clipboard.

"Or that makes me seasick," I added, pointing to a swishy pattern that looked like a cresting wave.

"No movement," she jotted.

"Not that I'm against pattern," I clarified, "just not ones that cause vertigo."

("Here's what I learned about ..." continued)

selected finishes. Be sure the color and scale look right. Look for bad copies. When choosing a tile with a lot of variation, particularly one that's trying to mimic real stone, lay out no fewer than four pieces to see if the pattern repeats too often. A good and economical choice can be a tile made to look like stone. Many mimic the real thing so well that even discerning eyes find it difficult to tell the difference. But watch for these two signs of poor imitations: a veining or marbling pattern that repeats too often, or a visible dot pattern left from the printing process. If you notice either, bring home another tile.

- **Select grout.** The current trend is to make grout disappear. Consumers are picking grout colors that closely match their tile, and they are going with thinner grout lines. However, thicker grout lines, particularly with a distressed tile (one with chipped edges, called *clefting*) can add a casual or rustic feel.
- **Be brave.** The biggest mistake people make with hard surfaces is being too conservative. They make a bland selection, which is understandable considering that this decision really is set in stone.

"That's too much information, honey," Dan said, shushing me.

"But I don't want the stone to look as if it came through the food processor, either. So nothing too homogeneous. And nothing

---

These pointers from Earthquake Granite Fabrications, in Denver, will help you with your next slab stone selection:

- **Feel:** Don't just look at the stone, run your hand over it to feel for pitting.
- **Homework:** Walk a stone yard to get familiar with what's out there, what you like, and pricing.
- **Variation:** Don't just pick the type of stone you want, pick the actual slab. Stones in the same vein can vary a lot.
- **Edge detail:** Basic edge cuts, such as waterfall, bull nose, flat polished, and simple rounded, are usually included in the price, so try to fall in love with these. Upgraded edges include hand chiseled, ogee, double ogee, and rope. The edge detail can make a huge difference in the final appearance—and price—and dictate whether your space looks more contemporary (flat polished), masculine (bull nose), European (ogee), or rustic (hand chiseled).
- **Pattern:** Rock aficionados like marble or granite with lots of what they refer to as movement, so it makes a statement. However, most people like a more homogeneous stone, with more consistency and less variation, and still others want stone to fade into the background. These preferences are highly personal. In general, a heavily patterned stone works where other backgrounds are subtle. A quieter stone won't limit décor as much.
- **Thickness:** A 3-centimeter slab may cost more than a 2-centimeter slab, but working with the thinner slab will cost more in labor if fabricators have to sandwich slabs to get a good thickness.
- **Price:** Most installers want you to select the material before they quote a price for installation, because price often varies depending on your stone.
- **Biggest mistake:** Working with someone who doesn't understand the properties of stone. For example, many designers steer clients toward absolute black, which is beautiful, but it's like your soul: It shows every flaw and smudge.

too common. I don't want all the neighbors to have it. I don't want the cheapest, or the most expensive."

She sighed. "Well, that narrows it down."

The granites we zeroed in on had names that made me want to go on the kind of vacation where you need shots: Typhoon Green, Moscarello, Espirito Santo. Soon, they all became a blur.

After two hours, we dragged six heavy samples and an eye-crossing headache back to the house. We stood back and waited for one to raise its gritty hand and say: "Pick me!" We arranged the samples from favorite to least favorite. The showroom faxed the prices. Salespeople don't give you these prices in the showroom because most granite employees aren't trained in CPR. Prices range from $60 to $200 a square foot installed, which increases the appeal of Formica. We rearranged the samples based on price, which reversed the order based on favorites.

Over our years of chronic and obsessive home remodeling, Dan and I have selected several granite slabs. Every time, I think, How hard can this be? The answer is hard. Rock hard.

TIP: Know the order of what gets installed first, and factor in lead times. Getting the timing wrong is why so many home projects, particularly kitchen and bath remodels, take longer than necessary. Here's the ideal sequence: Paint the drywall. Then pre-paint the baseboards and moldings and install them. (If the moldings are in, you can paint both at once, but painting drywall before molding is in will give you crisper lines.) Next, install hard flooring (wood, stone, and tile), then cabinets, then countertops, then appliances. Carpet can go in last. Because you often have to order cabinets twelve weeks in advance, choose those early. And don't push your installers to go out of order. A good granite installer shouldn't even cut the granite until the cabinets are in. And you want to set cabinets on top of flooring, not cut your flooring around the base of the cabinets.

9

Cabinets Are Like Cabernet

The more you know the more you spend

RULE #87 IN HOME DESIGN: Choosing home finishes is like buying wine; the more you know, the more you spend.

Which brings me to choosing cabinets.

Before I launch into my cabinet debacle, because you know I have one, here's a cabinet primer. Cabinets will likely be one of the biggest line items in your budget, even if you go with the least expensive ones, and they will define—or, if you're remodeling, transform—your kitchen, or any room they go in: office, bathroom, bar. So do some homework before plunging into this decision.

Just like homes, cabinets come in three basic models: production (readymade and off the shelf), semi-custom (modular units you can order with more options for details and storage features), and custom (a cabinetmaker comes to your home and custom crafts cabinets for your space). I've listed them in order of expense, which can range from $75 a linear foot to $1,200 a foot (which can add up to as much as some houses). You can achieve a good look at all price points.

Besides being the lowest priced, production cabinets have another big advantage—delivery time. You can take a truck to the home improvement or cabinet store (IKEA has a nice selection), load up your cabinets, and have them installed immediately. Semi-custom cabinets, which I chose, require a long lead time, often eight to twelve weeks, but offer a wider selection and more storage options. Custom cabinets are a lovely luxury that I know nothing about because I have never been able to afford them and never will.

I went with semi-custom because my builder had a deal with a cabinet company he trusted. The product looked nice, so I went along.

Designing and choosing the cabinets for the kitchen, bathrooms, and office, I thought, would take thirty minutes, max. The amount of time mattered, because once again I'd asked my $100-an-hour designer, Karlie, to help. I thought of every twenty minutes we spent together as the cost of one yard of carpet installed. However, I'd learned the hard way that paying for her decisions was cheaper than paying for my mistakes. It also beat fretting for a month over a decision she could make with certainty in three minutes. To get Dan to agree to pay this design fee, I just reminded him of the time we had brilliantly ordered a sleeper sofa for the upstairs guest room only to learn that the piece couldn't fit through the room's door. Ouch! Still, whenever Dan knows I'm out with our designer, he gets a facial tic and worries a nervous hole in his pocket lining.

Because I already knew the cabinetmaker I wanted to use, all Karlie and I had to do was pick a door style and a finish. How hard could that be?

Super hard.

In the cabinet showroom, I telegraphed my expectations to the designer: "This should be simple," I said. "We just need to decide on the door style, pick a stain, and we're done." I hoped this said: *Make it speedy.*

The owner of the cabinet company handed Karlie a spec sheet featuring assorted cabinet legs and feet. Turns out they have bun, apple, tulip, and tapered feet, legs turned in several fashions, and half legs. Who knew? Then the two of them started this tango of a conversation during which I felt completely out of step. Did we want any glass fronts, under-cabinet lighting, brackets under top cabinets to make them look like hutches? And then there were the options for treating side panels.

Karlie saw that I looked puzzled: "You don't want plain cabinet sides, do you?" she asked.

"No, of course, not," I replied, though, truthfully, I'd never thought about my cabinet's sides. I was, however, concerned about the time. We'd been in the showroom for over an hour—the equivalent of three yards of carpet—and hadn't even looked at door styles or finishes. Meanwhile, she and the manager were sketching designs to illustrate which cabinets would recede, which would jut out, and which we could put on a diagonal with a drawer front supported by legs. To make me feel useful, they handed me a booklet filled with drawer pulls and knobs.

"See what you like," Karlie said. I looked. The choice should have been simple, but doubts swarmed me. By the time we finally moved on to the door fronts (fifteen choices) and the stain (thirty choices), I was slouched in a corner sniffing menthol Chapstick so I wouldn't lose consciousness. It turned out that choosing the door style (Windsor) and the wood (distressed maple) was the easy part. Choosing the finish (nutmeg) didn't take long either, because I'd already chosen my wood floor finish and carpet. I chose a finish that went nicely with those colors. (It's true that the first decisions are the hardest; the later ones get easier because you have context.) Now came the hard part.

As usual, now that I'd been educated, my taste had become more expensive. I suddenly couldn't live with cabinets that weren't rich in custom detailing. Which brings me back to Rule #87, and its converse, Rule #88: *Ignorance in home design is not just bliss; it's cheaper.*

Three hours later, I was home with a migraine. I collapsed on the sofa and put a package of frozen peas on my forehead. This was how Dan found me. "What took you so long?" he asked nervously.

Here's what I learned about cabinets, but read this disclaimer: If you pay more for cabinets as a result, don't blame me.

- **Before you select** cabinetry, measure your space and create a cabinet layout. (Here again, graph paper is nice.) Decide where you want cabinets, both upper and lower, based on your storage needs. Eventually, you'll want a professional to remeasure, but at least you'll start shopping with a rough layout in hand.
- **Next,** study the options for the types of doors and colors available. Know how raised panels differ from flat panels and the difference between doors that are square, arched, or ribbed. Review magazines for a look you like that complements your home's architecture and style. Know whether your look is contemporary, rustic, country, traditional, or sleek chic. Wood tones can be natural, stained, colored, or painted, or you may choose a laminate. Production cabinets will offer a smaller selection, which can be a good thing. Prepare to be stymied if you start looking at semi-custom or custom options.
- **Inquire about storage options.** Again, production models may not have as many features, but other lines will offer pull-out shelving, lazy Susans, wine racks, vertical dividers, and roll-out drawers for trash bins. Know what's available and decide what's important to you. If you choose stock cabinets that don't offer these features, you can add some later by purchasing storage products through stores like The Container Store.
- **Look for durability.** Cabinets will take a lot of use and abuse. Be sure that frames are solid, joints are well constructed, hinges

"It took forever to pick our cabinets," I said weakly. "It's so com-plicated."

"Complicated? How hard could it be? You pick a door, you pick a stain: thirty minutes, max."

("Here's what I learned ..." continued)

are sturdy, drawers pull out smoothly, and the backs are closed (so the mice can't run off with the egg beater).

- **The secret** to creating a custom-cabinet look is to vary the cabinets' profiles. Cabinets that are flat all across the front, or all the same height, look like production work. Have some jut out, while others recede; let some rise higher than their neighbors. The exception is in ultra-contemporary kitchens, where you want a sleek profile.
- **The magic** is in the details: Corbels, brackets, rope trims, crown moldings, feet and legs, knobs and pulls—these extras turn cabi-nets from shelves with doors into furniture.
- **Think finish.** Most cabinetmakers offer a wide choice of stained and painted cabinets. You can add dimension to either by adding glaze or antique finish. These extra touches cost more, but once you see the difference they make, you might not want to turn back.
- **Glass or Solid.** Be careful. Glass-front cabinets, especially those with lighting inside, can look lovely—or not. Much depends on what you put in them. If, in general, your cabinets look better closed, get solid-front cabinets. You could, as I did, put glass fronts in only one or two cabinet doors, if you can commit to an artful display within.
- **For help** finding a stock, semi-custom, or custom cabinet dealer near you, use the "Find a Professional" search option at the National Kitchen and Bath Association Web site, www.nkba.org.

10

Buyer Beware

Avoiding builder gouge on upgrades: A word from the wary

IN JOURNALISM SCHOOL, I had a hard-boiled editing professor who taught doubt. "Journalists must be suspicious," he ranted. "If your mother tells you she loves you, check it out."

As it turns out, this is also good advice when purchasing carpet, or really, any major home improvement, from a builder. If you're working with a builder to build your new home, beware. Many home builders make more profit off the upgraded finishes they sell you than they do off the base home price. This isn't to say that buying the upgrades from the builder isn't a good way to go. Sometimes it is. Other times, however, it is wiser and less expensive to buy upgrades directly from the source—if you can. Let the following tale of rip-off and woe be a warning, whether you're buying flooring, cabinets, counters, or fixtures.

When the builder of our new house said I had to buy carpet through his source, I was suspicious. When his source, whom we'll call Gougers R Us, quoted me a per-yard price (with pad and installation) $17 higher than my direct carpet source for the same carpet, I became more suspicious. When I double-checked the yardage calculation of 410 yards and found I only needed 350, I got mad.

Like most people, I'm often torn between saving money and taking the easy way. But when easy street gets expensive, I go the cheap route. I called my low-cost carpet guy, who confirmed that if I purchased the 350 yards through him I'd save $5,000. For that kind of money, I'll fight.

"I believe I'll purchase and install my own carpet," I told my builder.

He said that I could only do that after escrow closed, when I would legally own the house. However, he added, the house needed carpet to close escrow, because it needed carpet to pass building inspection, so his installer had to do it. This sounded so unlikely that I figured it had to be true.

"Why?" I asked, feeling like a character in a Joseph Heller novel.

"Our insurance only covers our contractors."

"What if I buy the carpet, but you install it?"

"We can't work with materials we don't purchase."

"So," I say, counting to ten, "my only choice is to pay you 50 percent more than I should?"

"Or you can install our cheapest, base-grade carpet for $17 a yard, rip it out, and reinstall what you want after closing," he said, not joking.

So I'd waste good carpet, spend what I'd save, and have installers ding up my baseboards twice. Plus, my husband would probably think the cheap carpet looked fine, and we'd be stuck

Note: If you're buying a house that's been lived in, this won't apply, as the house probably already has carpet, cabinets, and fixtures, which you can change without a middle man. But egregious markups are common when buying a new house from production, custom, or semi-custom homebuilders.

New homebuyers should know that homebuilders often make 30 percent of their profits on upgrades. Knowing this, buyers have three options:

- **Buy the standard house** minus the upgrades and add upgrades later. Pros—You don't feel gouged. You can shop for price and selection. Cons—Demo costs can offset savings and create construction havoc in the home.
- **Go for builder upgrades.** Pros—The headaches are the builder's. You get what you want the day you move in. You can finance the upgrades in your mortgage. You don't have to live in the house during later demo and install work. Cons—You may overpay, and your builder's selection may be limited.
- **Ask the builder** if you can buy materials direct and have his team install them. This is often the best alternative, but it depends on the builder.

When buying your upgrades directly:

- **Find what you want online** or in showrooms, then scout for a source that sells the same product at the lowest price.
- **When possible,** buy materials directly from the manufacturer. Request that materials be side-marked, or tagged for customer identification, with your name, not the contractor's.
- **If you go through a middleman,** and sometimes there's no way around that, don't pay more than 30 percent of the job, or more than the cost of materials, up front. Ask the contractor to show receipts before he starts work to prove he really bought the materials.
- **If you buy from a store,** don't feel obligated to use a store's installers. You can save money by finding an independent installer.
- **Consider buying pricey materials** out of state to save sales tax. You will pay shipping, but that can be much less than sales tax.
- **Never pay in full** until the job is done. The best con artists can concoct amazingly plausible stories as to why you need to pay them in full sooner.
- **Check references,** preferably both commercial and private.
- **When possible,** pay with a credit card; it gives you recourse. Don't pay with cash or a cashier's check.
- **If your builder tells you** it can't be done, check it out.

with it. "Forget it!" I hung up steamed, determined to find a way around this Catch-22.

"Check it out," a voice from my past whispered. I called the building department and asked whether I needed carpet to close escrow. "We only require finished flooring in kitchens and bathrooms," the top inspector told me. My kitchen and bath floors were wood and tile, so closing didn't involve carpet.

"What!? I don't have to have carpet?" I made the inspector repeat this until he thought I was a moron.

I ordered my carpet directly through my friend, Kerry, at the carpet showroom, whom you met in Chapter 7. It was beautifully installed the day after escrow closed. In a victory for carpet vigilantes, I saved $5,000 and chalked one up for my professor, who was right: It pays to be suspicious.

In a perfect world, you would have all your backgrounds done before you ever moved into your home. In reality, of course, we often need to live in the home during these messy installations. Anyone who has ever had a baby arrive before the nursery was done, or been offered their dream job in another state and had to move pronto, knows life isn't always so tidy.

Regardless of backgrounds, if you are moving from an old house to another, consider this your chance for a fresh start. Before you haul a bunch of stuff that won't be a good fit in the new place, take this chance to reevaluate everything you own, and then purge. Before we talk about acquiring new furniture or household accessories, let's deal with what you have.

11

Moving Pains

What to pack, what to let go of, and how to put your old stuff in a new place

I'M JOGGING WITH MY FRIEND KATHY, who has more money than I do. Otherwise, we have much in common: We've known each other since seventh grade, have children the same ages, run a plodding ten-minute mile, and . . . we're both moving in two weeks.

As we jog, we talk about packing. At her house, she has packers—professionals currently dismantling her home in an orderly fashion, systematically filling and labeling each carton. Two kinds of people get professional packers: those with money and those in the military. I'm neither, and I'm jealous.

At my house, I *am* the packer. Currently, nothing is packed. This is not denial. I simply can't get motivated to take everything I own and put it where I can't get to it. Though I yearn for someone to do this dreaded job for me, I'm also grateful. We almost didn't have movers! For a delusional moment, Dan, whose middle name is "Save," actually contemplated doing the move ourselves.

"Save the money!" I cried. "What about our backs? Our marriage?!"

"It won't be that bad," he said. "I'll rent a U-Haul and call my brother."

"Honey, you're not in college anymore. You're married and have kids. It's not just you, your Yosemite placemats, and that ugly blue sofa."

"Kids?! We have kids?"

"And a household!"

"Movers cost more than kids or college!"

"But not as much as the mental institution I'll send you to if you go through with this!" (Talk about denial.)

"Hey," he said. "Where are those placemats?"

I called three moving companies. The estimates were sobering. We weighed nine tons! I hadn't been so shocked since I'd stepped on the scale after the holidays.

"That's it," I told my cowering family. "We're going on a diet."

Packing to Move: This House Needs a Diet

There's nothing like a sobering estimate from a moving company to get you to evaluate what you really need and what you can live without. The less you move, the less you pay movers. We got serious about letting go. Deep down I welcomed the opportunity to really think about how my existing furniture would transition into my new house, what I could use and build on, and what I really didn't want to haul with me. I also consulted some resources to help me decide what to cut loose, and I gave my family strict orders.

When we were almost done packing, I looked at Dan, then took a good look at myself. I wondered how my friend Kathy was doing. Dan and I were both wearing dirt-smudged skin and baseball caps. We had dark circles under our eyes and armpits, and scraggly cuticles. We'd given up showering because it was futile. Somewhere along the way, we'd packed our good hygiene. We began to do things we would normally never do, like eating greasy pizza with filthy hands on the tailgate. I wondered if it was possible to move and be classy. I pictured Kathy on her moving day. She was probably well coiffed, wearing crisp linen shorts. I imagined her sweetly

---

Try this purge-and-plot plan to save time, money, and back strain when moving:

- **Toss, sell, or donate.** Send the kids to their rooms, and the man of the house to the garage, with instructions to make three piles: dump, donate, and otherwise deal with. I did the same in my bedroom and the kitchen. Rent a Dumpster. We filled ours twice. If you have the energy and time, have a garage sale or post items on Craigslist. Cash is easier to move than stuff and can go toward items for the new place. We made three SUV-stuffed trips to the charity thrift store and got a receipt for a fat write-off. We lost, literally, one ton, which saved us money in our move.
- **Plot the new space.** Look at each large furniture item and visualize where it will go in the new home. Create a scaled furniture plan. (Draw layouts of each room using graph paper, with each square equal to one foot. Start with the view from the top, drawing each room's furniture layout as if you were looking down on the room from a ceiling fan. For layouts of art and other items on walls, you can sketch elevated drawings—that is, drawings from the perspective of someone standing in the room looking at one wall.) Know where the armoire, pool table, and piano will go. Your goal here is to avoid paying to move something heavy only to decide to get rid of it on the other end. If something necessary that you have isn't a good fit for your new place, consider selling it and buying the right piece in the new town. For instance, if you have a rectangular kitchen table, but your new kitchen calls for a round one, sell the one you have before you move. You can apply the money you make, plus the money you'll save by not shipping it, to the cause of purchasing a new table. Then you'll have what you want for the new space from the outset, rather than wasting money to keep something you don't want anyway.

asking the packers to take care when boxing her Jay Strongwater collection. Then it hit me: Kathy not only had packers, but, at her new place, she would also have UNpackers! Now that's classy. And she's still my friend.

Old Stuff, New House

"Where are you going?" Dan asks as I slink out the door. I'm dressed a tad nicer than usual and he had actually noticed. Why is it men never notice when you want them to?

"To see James."

"Why?" he asks. "We're moving."

"That's why!" James Charles is an interior designer in California I sometimes consult. Whenever Dan hears his name, he feels our bank account draining. (Picture Steve Martin in *Father of the Bride*.) "I need him to tell me where to put our stuff in the new house."

"You have to pay someone for that?" His eyebrows shoot so high they threaten to become ceiling fixtures. "I'll tell you. Put the family room furniture in the family room, and the bedroom furniture in the bedroom. It's that easy!"

"Honey," I say, which I've learned works better than *you numbskull*. "This is our chance for *change*. James will help us be more creative."

"If he tells you to put the bedroom furniture in the living room, we're not paying the bill," he says and leaves, probably to freeze our bank accounts.

Besides creativity, another reason I need James's advice is certainty. For two weeks, I've been lying awake nights playing furniture leapfrog in my head: Put the leather sofa on this wall, the coffee table here, no! Switch the end table with the side chair, move the television, then, no! Room by room I play ceaseless rounds until my brain ties itself into a Gordian knot. If I do fall asleep, I awake in a sweat thinking: We must *angle* the sofa!

If you're part of the 14 percent of the population who will move this year, heed this:

- **Follow the two-times rule:** You need twice as many boxes, twice as much (2-inch plastic) tape, twice as many black markers, and twice as much time as you think to get the job done. (We ran out of boxes one night after all the moving supply sources had closed. I found myself in the desperate and unbecoming position of fishing for boxes in the Dumpster behind the local supermarket.)
- **Use unprinted newsprint** instead of newspaper to wrap dishes and other fragile items. Newsprint can soil and permanently stain some items. Your moving company can supply this, or you can buy it from a store that sells moving boxes.
- **Don't waste a box** packing blankets and beach towels. Use them in place of costly bubble wrap to cover pictures and mirrors before putting them in picture boxes.
- **Let pros pack anything big,** fragile, and expensive (Ming vases). If your mover packs a box and the contents break, the moving company pays. If you pack a box and the contents break, it's your fault, unless the box has visible damage.
- **If moving more than 150 miles** out of state, your household plants may need to be quarantined. Our neighbors' entire moving truck was delayed three days because it contained plants. We left everything green and growing behind for the new owners.
- **Know the going rates.** For short distances, movers generally charge by the hour. For long distances, they charge by the weight. We moved twice—first to a nearby condo, then to a home 1,100 miles away. To save time, we hauled boxes to the condo ourselves. The movers only had to move the big stuff, which halved our estimated cost. For the long haul, we saved using the dump and donate diet plan.
- **Check your inventory.** Though it seems tedious, be sure your expensive items are tagged and listed on the front end and that they arrive at the new house. Check them in at the new location, so that your fur coat and your mother's silver don't mysteriously disappear.

Such uncertainty brings out the worst in movers. I picture them on the threshold holding a 3,000-pound armoire, asking: "Where do you want this, lady?" Sweat drops large as trout are sprouting off their foreheads.

"Uhhh, let's see . . . here? . . . Hmmm, no . . . how about there? . . . Errr . . . maybe upstairs . . . ?"

I've heard that some movers have criminal pasts. Now I see why.

The third reason I need James is for the root problem. In my home, a piece lands, grows roots, and never moves again. (Which is what I plan to do when I get into this new home! Hear this: I'M NEVER MOVING AGAIN!)

I bring James photos of my previous furnished home and a floor plan of the new place. We don't have exact furniture measurements and can't see where outlets are or windowsill heights, but we nonetheless pencil out a plan, which looks good. (He moves the bedroom chairs into the living room, which I don't mention could jeopardize his payment.) Best of all, I start sleeping.

Move-in day: Two hours into the unloading process my assurance turns to doubt, then panic. Almost none of the plan works. Because James and I have chosen to float the furniture (that is, not press it against the walls, which always looks to me as if somebody has walked in and sneezed hard), the table lamp cords must stretch to the wall like jump ropes. We need floor outlets. A console we wanted beneath a window sits too high, the windowsill being 10 inches lower than the tabletop. A TV can't go on a designated wall because there's no cable outlet. I'm forced to rethink every room fast, and I realize this: You can only plan so much on paper. To know where to place furnishings, you or your designer must walk the house, know exactly where the outlets are, and measure how low the sills drop down, which James obviously couldn't do from 1,100 miles away.

Just as I'm about to tell the movers to dump everything in the front yard, I notice they have started placing the furniture without asking where I want it—probably because all I can say is "uhhhh." And it hits me: They're the experts! They move old stuff into new

---

Lauri Ward, a New York interior designer and author of *Use What You Have Decorating,* offered this advice for arranging furniture. (I liked this woman before we ever spoke just based on that title.)

- **If possible, get the shell**—floors, walls, blinds—finished before you move in. Backgrounds can pull a house together even when the furniture's not right. (What have I been telling you? See Chapter 4 on creating a design plan.)
- **When arranging furniture,** think of the three Fs:
  - *Flow.* Furniture should not be an obstacle course. Be sure people can enter and leave the room easily.
  - *Focal Point.* Arrange furniture around a welcoming visual. A fireplace, picture window, or television are all natural focal points. Or create one by arranging art over a table. Also bear in mind what people first see when they walk into a room. In a bedroom, for instance, a well-made and adorned bed can sit front and center.
  - *Friendliness.* A big mistake people make when placing furniture is to situate pieces too far apart or at awkward angles. Think about fostering conversation. Don't stick a chair off by itself in a corner. Place furniture so people can talk without shouting or twisting. A sofa and two chairs in a U-shape, or a sofa facing two chairs, or two sofas facing each other are ideal arrangements. Guests should be able to reach the coffee table without lifting their bottoms off the seat.
- **Bring couples together.** Keep pairs of matching lamps, chairs, or artwork in the same room.
- **Group collections,** whether baskets, dolls, or copper pots. Don't scatter them all over the house; instead, make one unified arrangement. (See Chapter 24.)
- **Go in with a plan, but** be ready to scrap it.

homes every day. I get out of their way and get a pretty decent arrangement.

Okay,˙ so we put the family room furniture in the family room and the bedroom furniture in the bedroom, prompting Dan to say: "So glad we paid for that furniture plan," though he doesn't add: *you numbskull.*

"It was a good investment," I say, defending myself.

"Oh?"

"It bought me some sleep."

12

No More Reality Television!

Covering windows with style

"Duck!" My husband yells. I hit the floor half-dressed. Our neighbor, one of only two we have so far, is walking his dog and has a clear view into our master bathroom, where I'm dressing. We needed blinds yesterday.

Finally, the walls are painted. Bathrooms are tiled. Carpet, wood flooring, cabinetry, and counters are in, and so are we. The hard finishes—and some of the hardest decisions—are behind us. But before we run to the furniture store, there's one more practical matter to address—privacy.

I consider basic window coverings to be part of the shell, or background, of the interior. I'm not talking about drapes—yet. We'll discuss those a bit later. First let's focus on blinds, shades, or shutters, functional window coverings that provide privacy and sun protection. Some people get to this point and thumbtack sheets over the windows. I totally get that.

According to Hunter Douglas, a large, New Jersey–based manufacturer of window-covering options, many people cover windows for reasons beyond mere decorating. Here are the other drivers:

- **Light control.** This is essential in media rooms and home offices.
- **Privacy.** Decorative drapes may look nice, but often they aren't functional, particularly if they're stationary treatments or sheers.
- **Camouflage.** The right window covering can mask an ugly or crooked window, or one that looks onto the alley or the neighbor's clothesline. If the window is out of square, or it's really small, or the molding is unattractive, installing an over-mount treatment can make the window look larger and mask architectural flaws.
- **UV Protection.** To help prevent furnishings from fading or deteriorating due to sun exposure, covering the windows is your best defense. Second best is window tinting, which we'll discuss in the next section. To best appreciate the sun-protection concept, think of it this way: Window coverings are like clothes, whereas tinting is like sunscreen.
- **Design Options.** Unlike thirty years ago, when the primary way to cover a window was with a cheesy pull-down roller shade, today's options really are almost limitless. You can choose from an array of woven bamboo shades, pleated verticals, wood blinds, fabric shades, and more, in all assortments of materials. The key here—and possibly the hardest part—is to choose something that fits your décor, whether it's traditional, contemporary, or rustic, that will also jive with your long-term design plan. If you plan to add a drape treatment or valance, be sure the covering you pick will go with the drape. If your covering is the final window treatment, you may (or may not) want to choose something a little less neutral. Scope out the Hunter Douglas and Smith & Noble Web sites for ideas.

Although blinds or shades are practically essential in most homes for light control and privacy, ordering them, as you'll see in the following scenario, isn't so simple. Don't feel too bad if you get stumped here, too. My forty-day fiasco is fairly typical. . . .

Four-Day Blinds? Hah! Try Forty!

Day 1: Blinds in Four Days! The glossy catalog chirped. Living in a brand new house providing 24/7 reality television to all the neighbors and workers around, I thought four days sounded too long. I needed blinds yesterday. So I grabbed the catalog and flipped straight to the order form. My mind froze as I faced the options. To choose something that provided privacy, sun protection, and the right aesthetic, I needed to know how I wanted to decorate each room. (You'll recall the importance of having a plan, back in Chapter 4.)

Day 3: After much paralyzing thought, I zeroed in on white painted wood blinds for the kids' rooms, natural wood blinds for the office, natural reed shades for the kitchen, family room, and dining room, and fabric balloon shades for the master. I made sure each window covering would go with the decorative drapes or valances I would someday be able to afford. The order form strongly advised sending for free swatches before committing. Even though I was impatient, this was the right thing to do. I sighed heavily and ordered twenty samples.

Day 8: The swatches arrived. I tacked them to walls and viewed them in different lights against my existing finishes. Finally, I decided on the ones that would give me the most latitude when later selecting draperies. Thus, I chose *not* the materials I loved most, but the ones I would least regret choosing, the ones with staying power, which also is not a bad way to choose a mate.

Day 11: Ready to order? Uh, no. First, I had to muddle through the catalog's "Easy, Step-by-Step" measuring instructions, where I confronted a formula that made finding the square root of pi feel easy: Inside or outside mount? Privacy liners? Pull cords or tilt wands? Each window covering needed its own flow chart. I measured each window three times then scratched a hole in my head. At this point I was almost willing to consider ordering blinds from a local company that would send someone to my home to do the measuring for me. The savings from ordering through the catalog, however, propelled me forward. If you decide to go local, another benefit is that the local firm can do the installation, and you might save shipping time.

Day 15: I called the 800 number to. order. The phone tree did everything it inhumanly could to discourage me from talking to a live person. The tree really wanted me to order online, but I prefer real

---

Before ordering blinds, you must make decisions about the following issues. Only then can you make that call (or place your order online). As soon as you begin, you may start counting to see if you can beat my forty-day record.

- **Inside or outside mount.** Whether you mount shades or blinds inside or outside the window molding makes a big visual difference. According to the pros at Smith and Noble, a leading supplier of mail-order window coverings, interior mount looks more custom, but you need to measure very carefully. Exterior mount can make windows look larger and downplay unattractive moldings.
- **Cord control.** Consider your furniture plan when choosing which side you want pull cords or tilt wands. You can also put one on each side. Putting both controls on one side looks cleaner, but I did that and regret it. I'm constantly untangling the strings. Go for tilt wands if you have small children.
- **Privacy liners.** Pro: These are good for rooms with televisions and computer screens. Con: They will darken the room and make the shade heavier.
- **Decorative edge.** Though the explosion of choices of tapes and borders can be tempting, be careful. Unless you know where your décor is going, you could easily end up with something that you will later regret. That leopard-print tape detail may seem fun when you have nothing else in the room, but it can be limiting.
- **Make a deal.** Ask for discounts, and check the company's Web site for coupons. If you or someone you know is a member of the design trade, you may be able to get a discount.

people in a case like this, so I stayed on hold. Five minutes later, a real person told me to fax in my order, which she'd confirm by e-mail the next day. This seemed suspiciously like online ordering.

Day 16: The e-mail confirmation arrived. I called and naively asked, "Will they come in four days?" The real person snorted and laughed, then explained to silly me that they make only *some* blinds, the most basic wood variety, in four days. Others take up to seven. Plus there's shipping: Add five business days. (Everyone knows that business days are to real days what football minutes are to real minutes: Yeah, sure the game's over in three minutes.) Unless I felt like liquidating the children's college fund to cover next-day shipping, I would have to wait. Because my order was approaching $5,000 for twenty-nine window coverings, I asked for a volume discount. This caused the order to fall into a dark abyss for three days while we negotiated this unheard-of request.

Day 19: I learned I would have to wait seven days while the blinds were made, and seven more days for five-day shipping.

Day 33: After I'd provided the neighbors with a full season of reality television, the blinds arrived, bringing a new problem. To get them on the windows, I needed an installer. Good installers need lead time. No self-respecting one will schedule an install until the product is on-site—for obvious reasons. But once you have the product in hand, installers are booked for a week.

Day 40: The installer began to hang the "Four-Day" blinds. But he could only hang a third of them, because the order-taker forgot to ask one crucial question. . . .

Impatient or Cheap? Install Blinds Yourself

The day the installer, Gary, came to install the Forty-Day Blinds, my cousin Murphy Law was here, too. We had a problem. Our windows are surrounded with thick wood moldings that stick out from the wall three-quarters of an inch. If you hang window blinds over these moldings, as one does in the case of an "exterior mount," which we requested, they get hung up on the moldings and won't open or close. Details, shmeetails. To prevent this, you need extension brackets. *Hello—all you window-treatment order takers out there: When a customer orders exterior mount, please add to your standard question list— before you jump to "Which credit card will you be using?"—this: Do you have a molding that will require extension brackets so the blinds can operate properly?* This small oversight explains why Gary left after installing only one-third of the blinds, the third that didn't require extension brackets. He said to call when the brackets came. AARGH!!

When the hardware arrived, I called Gary before the UPS truck had even left the street, and learned—he was what?!—rafting! Then, in a rare moment of husband-and-wife domestic synergy, Dan and I brazenly decided to install the blinds ourselves. In short, my impatience fused with Dan's cheapness. Who needs an installer? we asked confidently. (Will we ever learn?) While Dan headed to the hardware store for a drill bit—the only size we couldn't find—I started taking down the blinds that were installed but didn't work because they needed extensions. Standing tiptoe on a chair, I opened the little side "doors" on the head rail and gently tugged at the blind to release it, then, when nothing budged, tugged harder. Bam! The entire contraption crashed down on my chin, which soon became the size of two chins. Within twenty minutes I looked like a close relative of Jay Leno's.

Dan came home to find me holding an ice pack to my chin.

"What happened?" he asked.

"Domestic violence," I answered.

"And we haven't even started."

"It's not every day your house beats you up," I said, thinking, "I sure hope that Gary is having fun, wherever he is."

We pressed on. My job was arbiter of placement (higher, lower, left, right), lemonade fetcher, and person in charge of seeing that the proper blind gets affixed to its appointed window. Dan did everything that involved the ladder and power tools. He drilled so

---

If you're feeling plucky, impatient, and cheap when faced with installing window blinds, you may want to do the job yourself. Here's some advice from the experts at Smith and Noble:

- **Use a level,** not your eye, a ruler, or the ceiling line, to make sure blinds are straight. Hung crooked they'll give you vertigo every time you enter the room. Plus they need to hang plumb to work. So when hanging overmount shades, don't go by the molding unless it's level. Go by what the level says and mount to the wall. For inside mounted shades, this is tougher, but if the window is a tad crooked, fudge the top bracket, using a spacer if necessary, until the head rail is true to level. If the window is out of square, go with overmount blinds.
- **Mind the cords,** which can be a serious hazard: Children can become strangled by cords that accidentally get wrapped around their necks. Use wall fasteners to secure loose cords to walls. If you have young children, consider cordless blinds or tilt wands. Never place a crib by a shade with a pull cord.
- **Think function.** Be sure brackets extend far enough to allow blinds to fully open and close over moldings and window cranks.
- **Pre-drill holes** in shades by setting the shade on the mounting bracket and drilling through bracket holes before securing shades with screws. (Be careful not to drill through cords.)
- **Don't be intimidated** by installation. It is actually easier than you might think. Although the first shade can take up to sixty minutes to install, you get faster.
- **Know it's not over.** Because of some conspiracy among interior designers, shelter magazine editors, and window covering manufacturers, blinds are only half the battle. To "complete" a window treatment, you often need layers, as in drapes (see Chapter 13). But for now, I'm calling it curtains.

many holes trying to get the dang things level that I thought he had a woodpecker for an assistant, but I didn't mention this. Long into the night we hung blinds. The job took us five times longer than it would have taken any one person who knew what he or she was doing. (Gary!) After several ice packs, two Band-Aids, much cursing, and six hours of wrestling blinds to the wall, they were installed and operating. Our modesty was restored, and we were up the $300 we would have paid Gary, that loafer. We fell into bed shortly before sunrise to the delicious thought that with the blinds down we wouldn't even notice when the sun came up.

Do Houses Really Need Sunglasses?

The worst part about buying a brand new home is not the hassle of moving, or escrow, or getting the builder to finish. It's fending off all those pesky salespeople who flock to a new development like ants to a honey jar.

Which was why I was so hard on the window tinter. He was part of that annoying pack of pitch people who swarmed from the day we moved in. Landscapers, driveway pavers, pool service providers, indoor plant companies, even a meat purveyor all peppered our house with unwelcome knocks, business cards, refrigerator magnets, and cheap pens.

"Don't you get it?" I wanted to scream at these people. "Just because we bought a new house doesn't mean we have money? We've never had less money! Go away!" I wanted to pull the blinds, but I didn't have them yet.

One day, the window tinter caught my much nicer husband and talked himself into our kitchen. When I came in, he was in the middle of his spiel: "Prevents glare, so it's easier to watch television. Reduces heating bills. In winter it keeps heat in, in summer keeps it out." He was singing Dan's song (improve TV, save money) and knew it, because when he saw me he switched to the female pitch: "It keeps your furnishings from fading prematurely, and it's safer. When a window shatters, the film holds the shards together so no one gets hurt."

"Sorry, not today," I said, moving to show him the door.

"Honey, we probably need to do this." Dan had totally swallowed the sales pitch.

"Next they'll be telling us window tinting prevents fabric cancer."

"Ma'am, everyone in your neighborhood is doing it."

"Thank you. When I decide my house needs sunglasses, I'll call."

As a native Californian, I know about sun damage. I wear sunscreen faithfully and force it on my children. But I wasn't ready to believe that my new Colorado home needed sunscreen, too. And I was skeptical for other reasons:

- Window tinting seemed like the ultimate hoax, an emperor's new clothes kind of rip-off: You pay a grand or so to these con

---

Tips for those who tint:

- **Know your goals.** Products are available to reduce glare, cut UV rays, improve insulation (theoretically cutting energy bills), and add privacy. (Some let in light but not sight.)
- **Tackle the job yourself.** Having a professional install tinting is nice, but this task isn't too hard for the do-it-yourselfer. You'll need a helper for large windows. The job is about as easy as applying contact paper to shelves, only you have to take more care to prevent bubbles, which look bad and tell the world you did this yourself.
- **Study the numbers.** There's more to sun protection than UV rays. Almost all products claim 98–99 percent UV absorption, but visible light transmission, energy coefficients, and total solar energy rejection are actually more critical numbers.
- **Check your window warranty.** Some window manufacturers will invalidate the warranty on their windows if someone tampers with—or tints—them.

artists who will coat your windows with something only you will know is there.

- How could lots of natural light be something you seek in a home, and yet also be "evil glare"?
- I'd spent hours selecting exactly the right paint, carpet, and fabric colors for my home. Now some guy who couldn't match socks to slacks was telling me to cast all that in a gray-green light?
- I knew the cruel truth: Window tinting won't *prevent* fading, it just *slows* it. To completely prevent fading, you need blackout curtains. Here's the catch: The darker the film you get, the drearier the light in your home, BUT, the longer your furnishings last. Conversely, the lighter the window tint, the less bleak the light, but the faster your furnishings fade. Hooey. This made me think of those people who leave the plastic wrap on their lampshades to protect them.
- Finally, I prefer more conspicuous forms of consumption. If I'm going to drop that kind of money, I want people to notice. Paying for window tinting has the same thrill factor as buying insurance.

So I resisted and convinced myself this was nonsense. Then, a few weeks later, while visiting a friend's home, that changed. My friend had recently rearranged her family room furniture. The new arrangement looked nice. "But look," she said and pointed to her carpet, which had a suntan in reverse. Where the sofa had been, the carpet was darker.

"Wow! That's from the sun?"

"In only six months," she said. I hadn't been so disillusioned since I'd learned the fat content of cheese.

When I returned home, I got three estimates, and then I went for it. The day our windows got their tint, the house looked slightly dimmer, but now, in truth, I hardly notice. And as I gaze out the window, I realize how much homeownership is like parenting—a whole batch of decisions driven by paranoia, hearsay, and hope.

13

Calling It Curtains

Drapes from the sublime to the simple

Dec-o-rate . . . *1: to add honor to 2: to furnish with something orna-mental* . . . **syn** *see* ADORN.

I'm consulting Webster because my mate and I differ on the definition of "decorate." To him it means a La-Z-Boy, a table to put your feet and drinks on, a lamp, and a big screen. To me it means crown moldings, draperies, sofas, side chairs, fringed pillows, and, well, you understand.

This disagreement has been going on for our entire marriage. "No, honey, a mattress with box springs isn't the same as a bed." (I swear, if it weren't for women, men wouldn't shave.) The argument resurfaced when Dan said he wanted to finish the basement. I said we don't *finish* (whatever that means to him) the basement until we *finish* the upstairs, or he's *finished*.

And we both know what that means.

"The upstairs is finished," he says.

"Hardly," I humph. "We need to decorate."

"What's left?"

"Well, drapes for one," I start, though my list is long, and I don't feel like administering CPR.

"What are these?" He points to the bamboo window shades.

"Those are shades. We need drapes around them."

"Why?"

"Shades and blinds are merely for function. Drapes are *dec-o-ra-tion.*"

"Who says?"

"Blinds without drapes are like a dress without a purse and shoes."

"All right," he says, resigned. "Do the drapes, but then I get my pool table."

I seize the victory that comes with those three little words: *Do the drapes!* which hit me like a lit match hits gasoline.

I have been primed for this moment. Months earlier, having done my homework and created a plan (see Chapter 4), I had consulted with Karlie Adams, the Denver interior designer who had helped me pick backgrounds, about the drapes. She had given me a direction for drapery looks for each room. I knew the fabrics and hardware I wanted. A custom drape maker had measured my windows and told me the yardage and labor costs that my plan would entail. I had the creative equivalent of a remedial paint-by-numbers set for the home decorator. All I needed was a green light and a budget, which is pretty much all I ever need. But when I added up the cost of fabric, hardware, and labor, I needed smelling salts. The drapes, I realized, would have to take a backseat to bills, braces, and food.

Until now!

I was off like a hound dog. I found three of the seven fabrics at the local fabric store. The others, including two lead fabrics, I couldn't find. After visiting eight fabric stores, I learned that the two main fabrics had been discontinued.

At this news, I did the three things I always do in a crisis: I cried till my mascara came off. I called my mother. And I got tough. (My

Here are a few lessons I learned on choosing and hunting down fabric.

- **Create a fabric family.** When choosing fabrics for a room, or a home, don't pick one at a time. You need to pick a family of fabrics that work together. (See section on blending patterns in Chapter 26.) The fabrics in your living room, while they might be dressier, should get along with fabrics in the family room, and share a color palate with your kitchen valances. So your whole house flows and feels seamless. It's tricky, but important. In a particular room, say the living room, know what's going on the sofa and side chairs before you marry your drape fabric. Avoid using the same fabric for both sofa and drapes, which can look as if you took the easy way out. However, it's nice to pull the drape fabric into the room by putting it on a sofa pillow or using it to skirt a table. Key point: You can't, or shouldn't, choose your drape fabric without knowing what else is going in the room or home.
- **Go tactile.** If you want to add interest, go tactile. Texture is one of the main tools in the decorator's box, yet people don't do enough with it. Texture has its own language: Shiny says fancy; dull or heavily textured says casual; floral prints and botanicals say approachable.
- **Hunt down deals.** You can get many fabrics supposedly available only in designer showrooms (which sell only to the trades) in stores open to the public. The only difference is that in the stores, the cost is actually much lower than in the showrooms. (After the showrooms and designers include their mark-up, the price can be double or triple what you could buy the fabric for elsewhere.) I paid $14 a yard at Calico Corners for fabric the design showroom was retailing for $37.
- **If it's right, snag it.** If you find a fabric you love that works in your home, and the price is too good to be true, get it, even if your project is months away. If you're not sure how much you'll need, guess and round up.
- **Ask for a discount.** If you're buying a large quantity, you might be able to negotiate a better deal. The store price for the silk I wanted was $59 a yard. Because I was buying a lot, they gave me 20 percent off—but only because I asked.
- **Confirm stock.** Once you pick your fabric, don't get your heart set on it until you confirm that enough is in stock. Have a back-up choice.

Just because a store has a sample doesn't mean it's available. Stores aren't always aware when fabrics get discontinued or go on back-order, which means you have to wait either until the next blue moon, or until you and your partner agree on the meaning of "decorate."

Of course, finding the fabric is a major victory, but it's only one piece of the multistep drape process. When choosing a drape treatment for your home, use this checklist:

- **First, choose the treatment.** You can't believe how many types of window dressings are out there until you look. There are literally hundreds of ways to hang fabric around your windows. Flip through books of window treatments and shelter books and magazines. Copy styles you like. In general, you want side drapes that fall to the floor in dressier rooms, living rooms, dens, libraries, some family rooms, and master bedrooms. These long drapes can layer over a sheer, shade, or blind and have a top treatment (a valance), or not. You'll need to decide if these drapes need to operate; that is, do you want to be able to open and close them, or are they stationary, for looks only. Valance-only treatments are great when you don't want fabric to get in the way of the activity in the room. Use them in kitchens, baths, and kids' bedrooms.
- **Get good measurements.** After you know what treatment you want, have a fabricator out to measure your windows and tell you how much yardage you need. It's best to have a fabric sample in hand, in case there's a repeat. Show this person the hardware you're considering so he or she can verify how much you need and double-check the specifications (like making sure the drapes will fit the rod).
- **Fabrication.** After buying all fabrics and trims, hand the job off to a good fabricator—unless you are a super sewer. (I often ask for referrals from local fabric stores.)
- **Gather your hardware.** While the drapery maker is making the drapes, purchase your hardware. Allow for plenty of lead time. This task can take time, while you weigh the mind-boggling options. (Who knew!) It's frustrating to have the drapes all made and be waiting on the hardware order; I've been there. Depending on your treatment, hardware can include rods, brackets, rings, tie backs, and finials. Some

("Of course, finding the fabric ..." continues)

great-grandmother was a terrier.) I called mills. I called stores across the country rumored to have carried the fabrics. I called France. The more the fabrics eluded me, the more none other would do.

Then, a victory. A local sleepy fabric store had one of the discontinued fabrics at 30 percent less than I'd been quoted! Now I only needed one more, a silk. I found one similar to my sample, but it was twice as expensive, which ate up the savings from the deal. I fretted, cursed quietly, rationalized, then bought it.

Just because you've made all these tough decisions doesn't mean you're off the drapery hook. You might be, but many of the best drapery looks have accent fabrics and trim. These are often what differentiate an off-the-rack drape from a custom drape. Of course, some lovely, understated treatments don't incorporate second fabrics or trim, but don't omit this step because you lack creative courage. To kick your drape treatment up a notch, consider adding trim, even if it's only a cord and a tie back. You'll soon find that the world of trim is a world of its own. . . .

("Of course, finding the fabric ..." continued)

drapery treatments mount to a board or box, which your drape maker will likely build. When selecting hardware, you need to decide three things: material (wood, iron, etc.), finish, and size. Be sure to consider the context. Choose the material based on the other finishes in the room. You don't have to match. Mixing—say, using an iron rod in a room with stained wood moldings—can look better than matching, or in this case using a wood rod.

- **Installation.** It's best if your fabricator is the same person who measures and installs your drapes, or at least coordinates the installation. Someone who has spent years successfully fabricating and installing drapes will be able to fix the problems that will inevitably arise.

On the Fringe

"Remember, you need three things," said Karlie. I can still see her, my guidance counselor, holding up three fingers to cement this into my bewildered brain. "Lead fabric, accent fabric, trim." With these parting words, my designer went off to—the nerve!—have and nurture a baby, leaving me alone to navigate the perilous world of finding fabric and trim for my drapes.

Granted, she'd given me photos of what the drapes should look like, along with suggested lead fabrics. I needed the accents. In the fabric store, I stood dazed by the prospects. I felt lured and seduced by the rolls of silk, damask, linen, and faux suede; the rows of fringe, braids, and tassels. Here I was in this virtual Vegas of opportunity, and I had to be faithful to my swatches. To stray in a place like this would mean I'd pay the ultimate price: I'd never get my drapes.

"Focus, breathe," I told myself.

I held the fabrics from my designer before me like a design compass. "Lead me not into temptation," I muttered.

"Can I help you?" said a friendly looking saleswoman.

"Do you have the forbearance of cast iron, the wisdom of Dumbledore, and the pure-driven purpose of a migrating whale charting the arctic seas?"

"Well, I was just about to take my lunch," she said, "but help yourself to some samples." She handed me scissors—though she could assume that a person in my mental state shouldn't possess a weapon—and beat a hasty retreat.

I snipped samples until the manager looked at me like I was some cloth-eating insect gnawing at the edges of her inventory. After finishing up there, I went to seven other fabric stores. When I came home, my husband said, "I thought you were only going to be gone for an hour." I dumped the bag of possibilities over his head, then gathered my notions and tried to piece together a vision from this hapless patchwork. The plaid with the paisley with the tassels? No. The stripe with the floral with the braid? No.

When I finally decided on two complementary fabrics (see Chapter 26), the trim put me in a bind: Shiny, matte, long, short, thick, thin, patterned, plain. I hadn't felt this much pressure since I tried to figure out what to wear to my high school reunion (and almost stayed home).

My husband returned to find me on the fringe of crazy. I laid out the trim problem. Then he said something infuriatingly brilliant: "Skip the trim."

Noel Francis, sales assistant for M&J Trim in New York, offered this advice for those picking fringe for home furnishings:

- **Bring samples.** To be sure you get the right color, bring samples of the room's fabric, wallpaper, and paint. Don't count on your memory. It's easy to be off. Rust, for example, can lean crimson, terracotta, or melon. Greens go toward olive, forest, or teal.
- **Beef it up.** When you see luxurious trims on pillows or drapes in showrooms, the trim has usually been doubled to add thickness. Great looks often involve layering trims or putting a cord or braid along the edge of a fringe. In other words, you buy double trim.
- **What's hot.** Feather, leather, wood, and bead trims.
- **What's not.** Skip the feathered boa look, and rickrack is still out, out, out.
- **Best tip.** Apply trim with a hot glue gun. (Read on to discover even more glue-gun drapery fun.) I always thought you had to sew it in! But you don't have to sew trim on, insisted Francis. Using a glue gun makes applying trim fast and easy. If you don't like it or want a change, you can pull it off without tearing a seam, glue on new trim, and use the old trim somewhere else.
- **Go for it.** Trim really does make the difference between common and custom.

Skip the trim! Why didn't I think of that? Not only is it hard to choose, it's expensive. On a project like this, the trim can cost more than the fabric. And for what? An afterthought. If I could forget the trim, I would save the money and the headache!

I called my drapery maker: "I have my fabrics, but I'm skipping the fringe."

"You can't skip the fringe!" she cried. "Fringe makes the difference between a custom drapery and something that looks as if you bought it off the shelf."

I didn't say that off the shelf was sounding pretty good right now. Heaven forbid we'd create something I could have picked up at Pottery Barn. If I was going to go to all this trouble, I might as well make myself miserable.

Then I saw my designer's three fingers: fabric, accent, trim.

Sigh. I went back to the fabric store, gathered my best picks, and laid them on the cutting counter. How much? The woman asked.

"Twelve yards," I said, and gulped.

She poised her scissors and said, "You sure?"

I nodded. She snipped, as if cutting an umbilical cord. And I knew there was no going back.

Once you've finally made all these decorating decisions, you'll be excited to see the final product, but don't push your fabricators too hard. It's a good idea to make this a general rule. Whether you are waiting for

---

TIP: When choosing fabrics for a room, follow this basic design rule: Every room should have a light color (such as cream) and a dark color (perhaps black), something shiny (a framed mirror), something dull (a suede chair), colors that complement each other (for example, lavender and lemon), plus one spike. A spike is the surprise in a room, like a zebra-print pillow.

custom drapes, bedding, a sofa, or some custom-ordered piece of furni-
ture, remember that it's better to be late and right than to be early and
wrong. Quality takes patience. Learn from my tale of woe. . . .

You Need It When? Hah!

"Can I get this before the holidays?" I asked my overbooked drapery
lady, who, like everyone in the home furnishing business, gets asked
that question more often than Santa gets asked for bicycles. Whether
it's a holiday party, a baby shower, or a visit from the in-laws, it seems
there is always some big event that makes me feel driven to request a
crash-and-burn deadline from my hardworking vendors.

In the big scheme of things, is it really so important to have the
bathroom drapes in before Christmas?

In a word—yes!

Thanks to every decorating doyenne from Laura Ashley to
Martha Stewart, many of us are programmed to believe our homes
must look a certain way before we can entertain. Our homes must
have beautifully furnished rooms, dolled up bathrooms, and fine
drapery. Why? To look good for your son's fourth-grade cookie ex-
change? The truth is, if the people coming really love us, they
don't care. And if they don't love us, drapes won't change that.

Even though I know this, I press for my drapes. "Well," the
drape lady stammers, "not before Thanksgiving, but maybe by
Christmas." I note the maybe, but don't push. This restraint is not
because I'm maturing—no way!—or because I've suddenly ac-
quired patience—though that's on my wish list. But because I've
learned the hard way.

A few years ago, in my former home, when all I had in my living
room was a glass coffee table and a fake ficus, I ordered new sofas. It
was late October, and despite the sofa company's normal ten-week

turn around, I asked if I could get them by Christmas. I explained about the coffee table and the ficus, and how they made a sorry background for holiday videos. The folks at the sofa company acted like they cared. I'd selected two matching six-foot sofas that would face each other across the coffee table. I hustled to select my fabric, had it air-shipped ($30 extra) to the sofa manufacturer, and promised them a fruitcake if they hurried. (Maybe that was the problem.)

Three days before Christmas, the sofas arrived. I still remember the men who carried them in. They both looked like the Grinch without the hair suit—eyes sleepless, expressions grim—ahh, the holidays. Wearily, they said they had fifteen more deliveries to make that day, probably to a line of equally manic women imposing deadlines as artificial as tinsel.

Here are a few other mantras to keep in mind when considering rushing some poor overworked fabricator. (Note: If they are busy and backed up they're probably good.)

- **Shoot high, expect medium.** If a company promises you'll have something by a certain delivery date, don't count on it. Expect disappointment, and you might be pleasantly surprised.
- **Try reverse psychology.** If you really want something by a certain date, tell the order taker it doesn't matter when you get it. He'll be so shocked he won't be able to forget you, and you'll get your order ahead of everyone else.
- **Ask, don't tell.** Most salespeople want to please, and many overpromise. I've learned not to ask: Can you have this for me by *x* date? But rather: When can you have this done? When the supplier—not you—sets the deadline, his or her chances of making it go up exponentially. Call every week or two to politely check on status.
- **Try the Zen Approach.** The timing of new furniture matters only as much as you let it matter. Stop caring, and a whole layer of pressure rolls away.

They unwrapped the sofas. As I stood back to admire, my digestive system had the urge to do everything it is capable of doing all at once. The company—in the rush—had upholstered the sofas with the wrong side of the fabric facing up.

"They're inside out!" I cried. I ran to get a piece of fabric to show them. I never saw two men want to leave a house so fast.

The sofas went back to the factory, where they were remade with the fabric right side up, and redelivered in January, when they should have been delivered in the first place.

Meanwhile, my living room was bare on Christmas, which was just fine with my kids because it gave them more room to ride their Barbie Jeep around.

Moral of the story: *Late and right beats early and wrong.*

Finally, if you're feeling cheap and impatient (I'm the queen of both), or if you shot your drape budget when you added trim and still don't have guest room drapes, before you call it curtains, grab your glue gun and make your own drapes—cheap! If I can, you can. . . .

Drapes Without a Stitch

Despite appearances, I am no Suzy Homemaker. For one, I don't sew. My lowest grade in school was in eighth-grade sewing class. I made a crooked orange dress. All the buttons fell off after the first washing. Worse, I had to model this monstrosity in a school fashion show. I'm still in therapy over this. Mrs. Lasansky, my home economics teacher, told me she was happy I was doing well in English and counseled me to pursue any career but homemaking. All through high school and college, I hemmed my pants with masking tape, which was not the only reason my mother called me a disgrace to the family. But all this was good training for my guest room drapes. By the time I got to them, I had no drape budget left. Actually, I had no budget period.

The story of my guest room drapes is a tale of what happens when a cheap, determined woman who can't sew finds a fire sale and a glue gun.

The guest room's large window had wood blinds, for privacy and light control, but needed drapes to look finished. The price of custom drapes is why many people get dressed lying down. Let's see, do I want drapes or a Hawaiian vacation? Point of fact: A friend recently told me that her interior designer gave her a bid for living room, dining room, and family room drapes. The bid was $27,000. "Is that too much?" she asked me.

Hack, gasp, wheeze.

Still, I was determined to dress the guest room window for next-to-no-money. I knew the fabric I wanted—the same coffee brown toile as the room's duvet cover, which I had folded at the foot of the mattelaisse-covered bed. And I knew the style—simple, no layers of frou-frou. These were bedroom drapes, not a baptism gown. When I saw that the catalog company, where I'd ordered the duvet cover, had put the discontinued matching sheets on fire sale for $29.99, I snapped up two full sets. I'd need two top sheets, one for each side panel. (Sheets are a non-sewer's best friend because they have four finished edges.)

At The Great Indoors, I found iron rods and rings that attached with clips. No sewing required! Talk about a company that knows its customer—the D home ec student! I got clips styled like black iron leaves, two tie backs, and brackets that would extend the rod more than 4 inches from the wall to clear the header of my wood blinds.

Back home, I hung the hardware myself, which made my family nervous. If I ever want complete solitude, all I have to do is walk through the house with a hammer and ladder. My husband gets an urgent business call. The kids go to their rooms and turn up their music, and the dogs dive under a bed.

Next, I clipped on the drapery rings, hung the drapes, and brought my family out of hiding to admire my handiwork. "Looks like you hung sheets," they said. In the honest light of day, the sun showed through, producing an effect not unlike that of a woman wearing a thin dress and no slip. My drapes needed to be lined. Crestfallen, I worried I might have to hire a seamstress after all.

But desperation spawned another idea: At a local bedding outlet, I bought two full-size flat sheets in ivory. I glue-gunned them to the patterned sheets using nickel-sized dots of glue every 6 to 8 inches across the top edges. I also put a few dots of glue down the sides of each panel. Amazingly, the dots were invisible. On the window again, the lining gave the drapes the body and opacity they needed to look like the high-quality drapes they're not. Total: $161.

If you're the crafty type and can sew, never mind. But if you can't sew and want to make an inexpensive window treatment, here's a recipe for Marni's Glue-Gun Drapes:

- **The panels.** Find sheets you like, twin or full, depending on how wide you want the panels. I like double gathered, so to cover 40 inches of wall, I'd get full sheets, which are about 80 inches wide.
- **The lining.** Get two flat ivory sheets and glue gun the backs of the ivory sheets to the back of the main sheets. To avoid puckering, use dots of glue, not stripes, across the top edges, and don't glue the bottom edges. Bonus: If you make a mistake, you can easily pull the sheets apart. The look is truly seamless.
- **The hardware.** Buy an adjustable rod, brackets, clip-on rings, and tie backs (optional). Measure and pencil-mark where screws will go. If drills make you nervous, tap a nail (use one slimmer than the screw) in the wall where you want screws, then twist the screw in. Hang your rods, and attach the drapes with clip-on rings.
- **Trim.** If you want to get fancy, glue on some fun trim. Then—brag!

(For you number types, here's the breakdown: sheets with pattern [two], $60; plain liner sheets [two], $12; hardware [rod, clip rings, tie backs], $89.)

Okay, so making drapes with a glue gun might seem tacky, like hemming with masking tape, but I'll bet if Mrs. Lasansky could see these drapes, even she would be proud.

Besides adding drapery, another great way to get pattern and texture on walls is with wallpaper. New designs mean you're not locked into grandma's florals anymore. Though wallpaper isn't for every home or room, it's definitely worth considering. . . .

14

It's Not Your Grandma's Wallpaper

The brave new world of wallpaper: For some it's a passion

FOR THREE WEEKS I'D BEEN lugging home wallpaper books (each weighs as much as a box of bricks), propping them around various rooms, matching them to paint and fabric samples, hemming, hawing, gathering unasked for opinions from my children, and changing my mind a dozen times. I'd had an installer out to measure, and I was on a roll, a wallpaper roll. When I finally zeroed in on my choices for our kitchen, the kids' bathrooms, and the office, I had that incomparable feeling of euphoria that only comes after one emerges from the migraine-inducing home-design jungle of choice with a decision. I showed Dan.

He wrinkled his nose.

"What? You don't like them?" I asked.

"I don't like wallpaper."

"Don't like wallpaper?!" This he tells me after fifteen years of marriage. To me, saying you don't like wallpaper is like saying you don't like food, or cars, or scenery. How can you dislike a whole product category with so much variety?

True, living in a room with bad wallpaper can feel worse than living a lifetime in Nina stiletto party shoes. I grew up in a home that had flocked wallpaper in the main bath, and I'm not trying to revisit that design experience. But the right wallpaper adds personality, texture, and tone to a room. It's like music at a party.

"What do you have against wallpaper?" I asked.

"It looks fake." Fake, he says, as if drywall is so natural. What does he want, mud bricks?

"Are you serious or are you just being cheap?" Dan's been known to issue objections as a stall tactic. When successful, he diverts me onto another twenty hours of ultimately futile home improvement research, which I've discovered is a male manifestation of PMS: Postpone Monetary Spending.

"I like faux painting," he said. This is the sort of diversion I'm talking about.

"So do I, but faux finishing isn't in my budget."

"You don't have a budget."

"Right, but faux finish is further outside of my non-existent budget than wallpaper is."

Then, because of federally mandated marital disclosure laws, I divulged what the wallpaper would cost. His eyebrows shot up to his hairline. "Then you have to pay someone to install it?" he asked.

"Well, that's the idea," I said. Or as our kids would say: "Duh!" He looked pained. So, being the sensitive wife that I am, I put the project on ice for ten minutes of deep reflection and consideration,

> **TIP:** An interior designer once told me the four ways to jazz up walls in order of price: Painted walls are the least expensive; after that, in order of increasing price, come wallpapered, faux-finished, and upholstered walls.

then, I headed for the wallpaper store. I ordered a lovely Ralph Lauren plaid in rose and celadon for one daughter's bathroom, a wide-striped Waverly in ochre and antique white for the other's, a fabulous floral for the kitchen, and two types for the office: a handsome paisley for below the chair rail, and a paper that resembles distressed leather, in a shade called "crocodile," for above.

I wanted to paper the guest powder room, too, but had to draw the line on the expenses somewhere. A while later, when I did finally muster the resources, I discovered that you can shop for wallpaper online, a revolution more exciting than iTunes. This took away all the pain but for the choosing.

Wallpaper Shopping Minus the Hernia

For two years I had envisioned the powder room walls covered in rich crimson damask wallpaper. I wasn't afraid of going bold. The powder room is a place where you can gun it since it's a room you don't live in. But I couldn't find the time to shop for the wallpaper, an ordeal on the order of acquiring citizenship in a foreign country. I couldn't face hauling all those sample books home again. I worried that carrying them too much might stretch out my arms bit by bit until I looked like our hairy ancestors. In fact I believe the great apes may have developed their long arms and stooped backs from carrying wallpaper books to their caves. Moreover, before the store grants you the privilege of carrying these books home, you have to check them out with a credit card and a guarantee to return them in three days or face a stiff prison sentence.

Every time I thought of going through this, I panicked. I still had six long-overdue fabric samples checked out from a sofa store. (Gasp!) I expected the sample police to haul me away any day. I imagined this scene happening on a busy sidewalk, people staring.

"Excuse me, Miss," the officer would say. "I understand you have fabric samples you were only supposed to keep for one week." I could try to defend myself then and there, explaining how I just

Because wallpaper is more expensive than paint and involves choosing both color and pattern, I called Paula Berberian, creative services manager for Brewster Wallcovering, and Stacy Senior, marketing director for Thibaut, a company that has been making wallpaper since 1886, for some advice and encouragement. They offered these ideas:

- **Why paper?** There's no better way to add color, pattern, and texture to your walls all at once.
- **Look at trends.** In the 1980s and 1990s people put pattern everywhere. Then the trend became no pattern, no color. Now we're back to loving interest, detail, and texture, but the patterns aren't so busy. Today people are buying papers with softened metallics (not the foil of the 1970s), textures that resemble alligator skin, and tone-on-tones, like damask.
- **Choose your style.** Selecting wallpaper is tougher than picking paint, because you're picking color and pattern. Start by making a design board. Include pictures from magazines that will inspire the room, colors you'll be using, and any finishes or pictures of furniture. Once you've established a mood and direction, picking the right wall covering gets easier.
- **Get samples.** When you find a paper you like in a book, order a sample. If you shop online, ask your wallpaper resource to send you good-sized samples of your top three to five favorites.
- **Live with them.** When the samples arrive, resist the temptation to order twenty rolls right away: First you have to live with them. Tape the samples to your wall for a few days. Walk them around your house and see if they feel at home with the other rooms. You want a sense of belonging.

("Because wallpaper is more expensive ..." continues)

couldn't decide between the caramel sand and the coffee mocha, or between the chenille and the tweed, but he wouldn't understand. Before I knew it, I'd be handcuffed and taken in for questioning.

So my powder room walls stayed a benign buttery beige. Until I learned I could shop for wallpaper online. By chance I found www.thibautdesign.com. (Other sites feature wallpaper, too, but this was the one I stumbled onto. I found it easy to navigate, and it had a well-edited selection.) I browsed by collection—stripes, florals, tone-on-tones, etc.—and viewed papers up close and in rooms. I tagged my favorites and e-mailed them to my wallpaper supplier. (You can go through a designer or wallpaper store. The site offers a store loca-

---

(*"Because wallpaper is ..."* continued)

- **Consider durability.** For kitchens and kids' baths, pick a paper with vinyl. Other rooms can handle paper wallpaper.
- **Feeling timid?** Choose a classic pattern like damask, a tasteful stripe, or toile. Papers that look like a faux finish are also safe. Or express yourself. Theme papers featuring everything from light-houses to tango dancers to Harley Davidsons are plentiful. (Being a dog lover, I once covered a bathroom in paper peppered with dog breeds, which I never regretted.)
- **Play.** Walls don't have to be completely covered, and borders can go places other than the top of the wall. Try hanging borders a foot from the ceiling, or around a door. Mix patterns. Consider papering the ceiling, too.
- **Don't know where to begin?** The best rooms to paper are rooms without soft furnishings. Dining rooms, bathrooms, kitchens, and laundry rooms are great places to start.
- **It's not forever.** Gone are the days when it was easier to take out the wall than remove old wallpaper. Today's wallpaper is easy to apply and remove. If you don't like what you picked in a few years, no big deal.

tor.) The supplier sent samples to my home. I got mine in less than a week and never had to return them! I easily eliminated those that were too rust, too rose, too gaudy, or too bright. That left two. Then I asked the ultimate authority, my housekeeper, to choose, and I ordered, all without getting a hernia or risking jail time.

Wallpaper Installers Need to Have Passion

Call it woman's intuition. I knew instantly that Tom Johnson, of Littleton, Colorado, was the guy to install my powder room wallpaper. The day he came to bid, my six wallpaper choices remained taped to the powder room wall. Whether to torture myself or test him—I'm not sure—I asked which he liked best. I'd already ordered the non-returnable paper, so odds were five to one this would end badly.

He pondered a moment, then pointed. "This one would look great in here." The brilliant man reached out to the very sample I had ordered, a deep crimson damask print. At this point, he would have had the job even if he smelled like yesterday's lunch and chewed tobacco, which he didn't.

"Great!" I said. "I've ordered twelve rolls."

"Great," he said, "except you'll need sixteen."

"But I measured!"

"So did I."

I almost started arguing, then thought: Whom are you going to trust? Me, who got my measuring instructions online, or Johnson, who's been hanging wallpaper for twenty-nine years? I rush-ordered four more rolls.

For the record, a second wallpaper installer who bid the job also said I needed sixteen rolls. But he had no opinion about the wallpaper.

As Johnson started hanging, I pulled up a stool to watch him work his craft. Then I got him to share trade tips:

- **Measure correctly.** I first used an online wallpaper calculator. I multiplied the room's perimeter in feet by ceiling height. I divided that by 25, the number of usable square feet per single roll of wallpaper. I calculated eleven rolls, and ordered twelve because wallpaper usually comes in double rolls. But I needed sixteen. The catch? The paper had an 18-inch repeat. Also, the room had a double inset niche on one wall, and, over the commode, the ceiling dropped 2 feet and formed a barrel ceiling. The repeat plus these architectural features meant more paper. My point: Have a pro measure.

- **Address surface issues.** Textured walls are more common in homes today than they were in the past. If you apply wallpaper directly to textured walls, your wallpaper will look bumpy. To smooth walls, installers can skim-coat them or hang wallpaper liner. Skim-coating costs less than hanging liner, but it creates dust, and with skim-coating, if you ever decide to remove the wallpaper, you will likely need to repair or replace the drywall. With liner, when you take the paper down, you can either repaper over the liner or strip the liner to recover the original walls. Many people skip this wall-smoothing step to save money. (You pay an installer as much to hang liner as you do to hang wallpaper—ouch!) But they may regret that decision once they see the result.

- **Use sizing.** Wallpaper comes pre-pasted or non-pasted. Both require the installer to add an adhesive to the paper. However, your paper will adhere better if you also coat the wall with sizing, a glue-based sealant. A wall coated with sizing holds paper better and aids later removal.

- **Set up the room.** A good wallpaper-hanger will know where each panel will fall, and where the final seam will be, before he starts. The final seam, which will most likely not match up, should go in the least visible corner.

- **Cut corners.** Many amateurs wrap wallpaper around interior corners. When paper dries, it draws away from corners, forming a curve. For a sharper look, cut paper into the corner, then continue with a fresh cut on the returning wall. Do, however, wrap paper around exterior corners. Don't place cuts there, or you may have the paper peeling away at the edges.

"You chose the guy because he liked your wallpaper?" Dan asked. I thought he was going to feel my forehead.

"I like a little passion in my contractors."

"Who was cheaper?"

I shrugged. "Can't remember."

"That's no way to go through life. Next you'll be choosing contractors with Tarot cards."

On hanging day, which sounds ominous, Johnson bounded in, saying, "I dreamed about your bathroom last night!"

"Why, I don't think anyone has ever said that to me before," I said, flattered.

Dan lurked in the hallway, rolling his eyes.

"I kept seeing the paper laying out in different ways," he continued. "All the way driving here I was talking to myself about different options."

"Told you he had passion," I whispered to Dan, who just shook his head. Johnson headed toward the powder room, whisking me along. "Let me tell you what I'm thinking." He rolled out the paper. "To get the pattern to match," he began, then promptly lost me as he started walking me through wallpaper layouts so complicated they made calculating interest on an adjustable mortgage seem easy. "Which would you prefer?"

("As Johnson started hanging, I ..." continued)

- **Hide seams.** Johnson buys a 2-ounce bottle of acrylic paint, in a shade closest to the paper's dominant color. After he's hung the paper, he dabs the paint onto seams with his finger, then wipes it off with a barely damp sponge. Seam lines disappear. A week later, you may need to touch up seams that pop up after the paper—especially dark paper—has dried.
- **Find a picky installer.** Price matters, but I'd go for passion any day.

"Uhh," I hesitated, not wanting to admit he'd lost me around the first bend. Finally, I responded: "Do it however you dreamed it would be." I looked around for Dan, who surely thought I was nuts, but he had faded from the scene like old wallpaper.

Before we leave the shell of our home and start to focus on furnishing, I want to address the matter of character. This is one of the few advantages that come with age. New homes, like infants, might scream fresh start, but they don't exude character. Giving a house character takes time. Short of waiting fifty years, here are some things you can do to put your new home on the character-acquiring fast track. Or you can invite my kids to stay for a month. That will age any home fast. . . .

15

Character Development Begins at Home

Building character one doorknob at a time

"**What are you doing?**" Dan asks when he hears a hammer banging. As you know, he gets nervous when I'm wielding a hammer.

"Building character."

"Your character is fine."

"Not mine, the house's."

"What's wrong with the house's character?"

"It needs more. I've given up developing character in you and the kids."

"Why, because we still make sounds with our armpits?"

"I'm putting my character development energies into the new house. For starters, I'm taking out this new mirror and putting in this old one."

"I'm confused," he says. "When we had an old house, you wanted it to look newer. Now you want our new house to look older?"

"It's the curly hair, straight hair dilemma," I say. "Have one, want the other."

True, everyone's idea of character differs. Even mine has changed over the years. When I was younger, my mother used the word to describe the unredeemed, as in: "You're not still dating that character!" Later, the word described an upstanding person, as in someone who did right when no one was looking, and did not mess around with interns. Then, character became something someone had when they'd reached a certain age, had crow's feet, a religious position, and Preparation H in their bathroom drawers. Today, however, when I think of character, I don't picture Tommy Lee or Billy Graham.

I picture houses. Some have it. Some don't.

To me, a home with character has a timeless, classic appeal with custom touches. The home doesn't have to be old, but that helps. The first house Dan and I bought, a fifty-plus-year-old California bungalow, oozed with character: real wood-burning fireplaces, plaster walls, wood ceilings, and a stand of fifty-year-old trees just outside. But the roof leaked as if it had been sealed with cheesecloth. The floor had more waves than the Pacific. And the wall rats had pedigrees dating back to their ancestors who came over with the pilgrims. When we bought the place, the real-estate agent said: *It has so much character.* Now I know that's shorthand for a place with old plumbing, small rooms, and dinky windows. I spent the next five years restoring it for the twenty-first century. We expanded the kitchen and master, raised the ceilings, updated the baths, and turned one bedroom into a closet, which is what I thought it was in the first place.

Our next home was so new that when we moved in it still had stickers on the windows. I spent the next five years trying to age it. Unfortunately, in the process, I aged more than the homestead. (Here I pause to give thanks to Retin-A, Clairol, and pink lightbulbs.) I added wood beams and moldings and faux-finished the walls so they looked as if they really needed a coat of paint. My

---

Here are a few character-building tricks I've stumbled across over the years:

- **Plant mature trees**—or at least one. Nothing screams new home louder than trees on sticks. Even though big trees cost more, they help a home look established. For the same price, one big tree offers more gravity than three small ones. Be sure to work with someone who guarantees their trees and knows how to transplant, or the large tree will be a dead tree (see Chapter 31).

- **Revisit the driveway** if yours is just cement. Repave it with stone pavers or cut in a border of used brick to soften the starkness.

- **Be different.** If you live in a production home, chances are good that everything from your mailbox to your mirrors matches your neighbors'. The less you match, the more your home looks like a custom home that evolved over time. Pick a style—say modern, rustic, French, Mediterranean—then change light fixtures, faucets, doorknobs, and drawer pulls to fit. Frame production mirrors with custom tile work or remove and replace them with framed mirrors.

- **Add moldings,** baseboards, and wainscoting where you can. If you have small 3-inch baseboards, change them out for ones 5 inches or larger.

- **Change flat doors** to raised panel doors, and sliding glass doors to French doors.

- **Make your fireplace an original.** Old homes often have great hearths. The fireplaces of new homes tend to be from molds. Go to an antique store and buy an old mantel to retrofit to your home, or faux-finish the existing white plaster to look like stone, or cover it with a veneer of stone or ceramic tile.

- **Take your time.** The cheapest way to add character to your home is to wait fifteen years. In our case, by the time we can afford to implement all these age-enhancing changes, our home will be that old anyway.

kids contributed their own patina by running their hands up the wall every time they climbed the stairs and carving their initials into the banister.

Now in this home we're trying to add an aura of establishment, which is difficult when you're surrounded on three sides by bull-dozers. Meanwhile, I'm still working on that other brand of home character, hoping that some day my kids will tell the truth when I ask who stuck the chewing gum on the counter, and my husband will honestly prefer spending Sundays at church instead of with the NFL.

When doing home improvements, whether painting, hanging wall-paper, laying tile, refinishing doors, changing a plumbing or light fixture, or adding character, a lot of folks are tempted to save money and do the job themselves rather than hire a pro. I'm all for it—depending on the job. What we've learned the hard way is that there are jobs you do yourself, and jobs you hire out. The following tale might help you next time you're trying to decide between DIY or hire a guy. . . .

16

Honey Do, Honey Don't

How to know when a home improvement job is for someone else

BOB IS HERE. I LIKE BOB. Bob has no idea how much I like him, nor how long I've waited for this day. Dan has some idea, but it's better if we don't talk about it. We inevitably wind up in that devil's triangle of male ego, do-it-yourself home improvements, and other men. Which brings me to this essential question: If women don't mind admitting they need a housekeeper, why do guys have so much trouble admitting they need a handyman? Anyone?

It's not that Dan's unhandy. Later on you'll hear about a terrific outdoor deck he built, and wainscoting he installed in the mudroom. He's also painted walls and put in light fixtures. But when it came to refinishing the oak front doors, uhh, let's just say, I'm glad he has other ways of making a living.

Although we wanted parts of our home to acquire character and lose that just-moved-in look, the front doors were aging at lightning speed. Probably because of the brutal southern exposure and the cheap stain job they initially got, they had blistered and peeled; in short, they needed to be refinished before the elements ate a hole clear through them.

Unlike men of yore, like my dad, who could take apart a car and a garbage disposal in the morning and have them both back to-

---

Here's what to consider before deciding whether to do a job yourself or hire a pro:

- **The grief factor.** Why spend your free time doing something you're not good at? If you pay a pro, there's no cursing and no twenty trips to the hardware store.
- **The trade-offs.** If you do a job yourself, you will save money in labor, but you will likely pay more for materials, which a professional can get at a discount. And, since the pro will get the job done right the first time, he won't have to duplicate any of these purchases. Keep in mind that with a DIY job you might need to buy special tools. Appealing as that might be to anyone who drools over tools, the reality is that these may be tools you'll never use again. Finally, the learning curve dictates that you'll spend more time than you ever thought possible trying to get the job done, if it indeed ever does get done.
- **The OK.** Find out whether your project requires city approval. Many small changes, like switching certain light fixtures, or adding decks, require a permit.
- **The know-how.** If you want to tackle a job yourself, like tiling or installing a ceiling fan, check with your local home improvement store. Many offer free courses on DIY projects.
- **The credentials.** Be sure the contractor is licensed for the work you're hiring him to do. (A flooring contractor may say he's licensed, but his license may be for plumbing.)
- **The references.** Check them to see if former clients rant or rave. And, if possible, visit jobs so you can see the quality of the work.
- **The contract.** Have him put in writing the price, completion time, and penalty (usually a discount) should the job exceed the estimated time.

gether before dinner, modern men specialize. They're trained to do fewer things really well. Which is why today's modern woman sometimes needs two men.

Like many DIY home-improvement projects, this one started with a price quote that made Dan choke on his Pepsi. Last time that happened, I'd just told him I'd sold an article to a woman's magazine about our sex life.

"For that kind of money, I'll do it," he said. (And who among us hasn't lived to regret those words?) Armed with resolve, he pulled off the doors and began stripping, scraping, and sanding. I've since seen a chart rating home improvement projects by difficulty. Using a scale of 1 (a drunk can do it blindfolded) to 7 (you're out of your mind to try), refinishing paneled doors rated 6. "Not a job for novices," the cautionary note read. "Every imperfection shows."

Ain't that the unvarnished truth.

When Dan was done, the doors looked like me, distressed, which would have been great if that had been the look we were going for. That took a long weekend, and the doors still weren't done. They were stained, but not sealed. Meantime, we had to re-hang the doors because Dan needed to go to his real job Monday. As we struggled to maneuver the first slab back onto its hinges, which is like doing the two-step with a refrigerator, it slipped and took the nail off my left big toe. Then my children heard all the bad words I know, and a few I made up.

The doors looked as if they had measles. Stripping chemical had run onto the inside surface of both doors, taking off the stain there, too, which had been nice, plus it had eaten the finish off the brass-plated handles.

Somehow this wasn't the time to suggest we hire someone to do the job right. I made the most positive remarks I could without lying: "Well they are darker. We wanted darker." And I waited for him to suggest we hire help. And waited.

Months later, I got another bid, now more because the inside of the doors needed redoing, too, and we needed new hardware. I showed Dan the bid. He was silent. Then one day, when the stock market was briefly up, I said: "Honey, why don't you keep working out the problems of corporate mergers and stop depriving other men of their livelihood?"

He gave in.

When Bob was done, the doors looked fabulous. I'm happy. Dan's relieved. And though he won't hold back from many future household projects, we've learned: Doing certain home improvement jobs yourself can bring immense satisfaction, but some are best left to the pros, like Bob. I like Bob.

PART III

The Goods on the Goods

Furnishing your home: Copying good looks, using what you have, finding what you need, getting deals, buying quality

So you know your design style, and you have a plan. The backgrounds are in. Next on the divide-and-conquer approach to home design comes furniture. Your design plan will dictate the style of furniture you're looking for, which should be the style that will best suit you, your lifestyle, and your home. By keeping in mind whether your look is traditional, Old World, country, modern, ethnic, or a careful eclectic blend, you will give your shopping focus.

If you've moved furniture from another home, you probably already have many key pieces in hand. Don't be too quick to toss what you have; not only is it a reflection of your taste, it also reflects your past.

(*Of course, if it truly is an albatross, put it on the curb.*) *The best home designs evolve over time.*

To realize your dream home, you'll probably need to acquire a few pieces. Consult your room files to see the photos you've pulled from magazines that feature rooms you like. Study the furniture in them that gives them the look you love. Remember to consult your furniture layout to get the right sizes. Don't forget to figure in how high the furniture should be (measured against window sills and the like) as part of the equation.

This part of the book will help you use the furniture you have (recovering if necessary) to decorate a new home or redecorate your existing home. The goal is to add pieces that will work with what you have. We'll explore how to mix furniture successfully and how to find amazing deals and still keep our eyes on quality. Don't get hung up on the accessories yet. We'll get to that next.

17

What Do-It-Yourself Decorators Don't Get

Basic design advice from top pros

ONE OF THE PERKS OF BEING a journalist is that if you have a burning curiosity about something, you can get paid to ask people at the top of that field about the subject, using as your entrée that you are going to write a story. Such was the case several years ago when I asked one of my editors at the *Los Angeles Times* if I could interview some of the area's best designers to find out the answer to this question: What is it that do-it-yourself home decorators don't get? In other words, what do these top designers know that I don't?

Great-looking rooms look as if they somehow came together effortlessly, but we know that's not true. I've tried, and made my share of decorating blunders. I once bought an antique armoire that looked fabulous in the furniture showroom, but it didn't fit up the stairwell when I got it home. I once chose paint for my office in what I thought was a subtle shade of mauve, but it morphed into bubblegum pink on my walls. I've witnessed beguiling swatches of botanical print fabric grow into a jungle of despair on a sofa.

Meanwhile, I learned this: Unlike a fashion faux pas, which you can shed at the end of the day, decorating disasters tend to be big, expensive, and in your face for a long time. Which means that the seemingly simple task of picking a new chair can stymie the best of us. The decision involves a perplexing tangle of style, fabric, fill, stain, and size decisions. All of which just make me want to swallow a handful of Advil.

Adding to the pressure are home-decorating magazines, where the featured homes seem so perfect. Why does my house always fall short by comparison? I can't blame my limited budget. Many people furnish rooms beautifully on less than I spend a year on manicures. But as I kept looking at and analyzing the beautiful homes on home tours and in magazines, the same nagging question kept coming up: What is it we do-it-yourself decorators don't get? So, with the *Los Angeles Times* assignment in hand, I called some top designers and asked.

Get the Size Right

At first, each designer said the same thing: "Scale."

They weren't referring to the bathroom scale that ruins your day, but the scale of furniture proportions. I flashed on my last house. We had a painting that we had moved from our previous house, where it seemed huge. When I hung it over the fireplace in the new living room, which had a 20-foot ceiling, it shrank to the size of a postage stamp. I tried "enlarging" it by putting candlesticks on the mantle beside it, but then it just looked small and cluttered.

So I cried. "What's wrong?" Dan asked.

"Nothing fits anymore."

"But you wanted a bigger house."

"The only possession we have that's the right scale is Bogie," I said, clutching our beloved and since departed French sheepdog.

"If you're lobbying to buy furniture, forget it."

I cried some more, but the truth was, I wouldn't have known what to buy if I did have the funds. It's one thing to see a problem, quite another to know how to fix it. So we rattled around in a big house decorated with doll furniture, until we s-l-o-w-l-y filled the

---

Here's what the experts said to consider when evaluating proportions:

- **Test-drive a floor plan.** Create a room's furniture layout by making a poor man's floor plan, said West Hollywood designer Kevin Kolanowski. Cut newspaper in the shapes of the furniture you're considering, lay the pieces on the floor, and walk around to see if the furniture fits and the room flows. You might want to warn your family, though. The first time I tried this, my husband thought he'd stumbled onto a crime scene.
- **Visualize traffic flow.** Don't create an obstacle course, said Newport Beach designer Sheila Perrone. Make a scaled furniture layout on graph paper. Draw arrows on the floor plan to indicate how people and pets will flow. Don't make people walk into the backs of furniture or maneuver around pieces. Never mind that certain inhabitants at my house like having furniture in their way: My youngest, a gymnast, thinks every piece of furniture is either a balance beam or a vault, and my two bichon frisés use the house as their agility course.
- **Vary the heights.** A room where all the furniture is one height lacks interest, according to Tom Allardyce, of L.A.'s Hendrix/Allardyce, who has created dream homes for Rod Stewart, Kennie G, and Sugar Ray Leonard. He likes to vary furniture heights to fit the architecture and especially likes higher backed sofas. Los Angeles designer Reg Adams, who has created residential ambience for Marlo Thomas and Chevy Chase, offered this rule of scale: If you have 8-foot ceilings, don't use high-back dining room chairs. They're more comfortable in homes with 10-foot ceilings. Use low-back chairs in rooms with 8-foot ceilings. Likewise, if you live in a

("Here's what the experts said ..." continues)

gaps. We moved the painting to the master and got a larger painting for the living room. We didn't eat that month.

"What's for dinner, Mom?" the kids asked.

"Why, this lovely painting."

So I was reassured to hear that I wasn't the only one plagued by
the problem of scale.

("Here's what the experts said ..." continued)

small bungalow, don't buy a huge sofa. If you live in a starter castle, go ahead and get an armchair that would befit Goliath.

- **Spread the visual weight.** If a room in your home feels like the entry
to the Knott's Berry Farm's Haunted House, so lopsided you almost fall over in it, you probably have too much physical or visual
weight on one side, said Dolly Chapman, a Los Angeles design vet-
eran. Imagine a seesaw in the center of the room. If one side gets
weighed down, add something to the other side to pull the eye
over and even out the room. Try a piece of furniture, a large wall
hanging in darker colors, or a large dog.

- **Mix up shapes.** Don't make all the pieces in one room the same basic shape. If all the pieces are squares or rectangles, said interior
designer Gary Gibson, of Los Angeles, throw in an oval.

- **Remember: Less is best.** When placing accessories, the biggest
mistake amateurs make is having too many that are too small. It's
far more appealing to have a few substantial, well-chosen accessories on a mantel or shelf than to have fifteen small pieces that
collectively look like clutter (see Chapter 24). When in doubt, Perrone said, it's better to scale up (get something too big) than to
have something too small.

- **Scale pieces to your place.** Of course, you always need to consider
the size of your home when accessorizing. A 15-inch crystal vase
may be perfect in the entry of a small apartment but could look
ridiculously lost if displayed in a large home.

Matching Is for Amateurs

After addressing scale, the chief advice from top designers—besides hire a designer—was to be perfectly imperfect. Easy shmeezy.

Beverly Hills designer Luis Ortega, whose work has graced many architectural magazines, said, "I'm always looking to make the layout simpler, to make the approach more welcoming. I want to take away color, pattern, and the number of pieces." But the best rooms aren't perfect, he added. "There's an art to being off on purpose."

Well, that's a relief. But how off?

"A room looks better when colors don't match but blend," agreed Tom Allardyce. "One sign of an amateur is someone who makes everything match. Houses and rooms should look as if they evolved over time." Whew! Our house is definitely evolving over time, since we can only afford about one lamp a month. We're on the ten-year installment plan. And at the rate things fade around here, soon nothing will match.

Gary Gibson said that most people don't understand that what they're after is not perfection, but ambience. "A great room is about the essence that happens when things get put together." And just what would that essence be when you blend a frugal husband, two slovenly children, a pair of overindulged dogs, and me, a mildly obsessive domestic maven with the creative courage of the census bureau?

In addition, said Gibson, whose more illustrious clients have included Paula Abdul and CBS President Leslie Moonves, DIY home decorators need to think outside the box more. "Don't get locked into your home's format. I've made living rooms dining rooms and dining rooms living rooms." Throw away borders and design with your needs in mind." Well, we've done that. Take our bathroom. To some who live here, it's the library or the dog-grooming parlor, and for me personally, it's a phone booth with a lock.

Whether you get help or make all your design decisions yourself, you still need to educate yourself about current design and be aware of what's possible. Before you start buying furniture, seek inspiration. The best way—and it's fun—is to take every opportunity to see good design, and take away the parts that will work for you. If you know your style—traditional, modern, country, whatever—you can focus on those publications or model interiors that are good examples of that style. Touring design homes, looking through home-design magazines and books, and watching home makeover shows on television used to just depress me. However, once I got over that, I learned that you can train your eye to get more from these resources than a bad feeling. You really can light on ideas that can help you with your plan.

18

Four Places to Find Inspiration (and Rip Off Ideas)

What to take away from home design books, shelter magazines, TV shows, home tours, and the color conspiracy— and what to ignore

Rip-Off Source #1: Looks from Books

I OFTEN SPEND MY LUNCHTIME flipping through gorgeous home-design books and magazines while eating my well-balanced lunch of nonfat yogurt and peanut M&Ms. I ooh and sigh over decked-out kitchens, master bedrooms, and great rooms. It's my guilty pleasure. House porn I call it, because these publications always stir feelings of desire mixed with hopeless longing. I'm hooked.

"Why do you keep looking at those?" Dan asks.

"For the articles," I say defensively. He knows they demoralize me.

The reality is, much as I look, and much as I would like to copy what I see, I've never lifted a look from a magazine page and applied it to my home. I wouldn't know where to begin. Plus, I lack two key ingredients.

First, I know that much of what succeeds in these stylized rooms has to do with context. No one item—lamp, rug, sofa—makes the room. If only it were that easy. What makes the room is the fact that these items sit in a Tuscan villa, or a $4 million cottage in the Hamptons, or Oprah Winfrey's penthouse. Picking up one or two accessories like the ones you see in the photo won't transform your place any more than getting a new shade of lipstick will make you look thinner.

Second, these featured homes involve money. Lots of it. You get the definite sense that the owners furnished the whole place without borrowed money or bounced checks. Everything in the house is paid for, as is the home itself. What's more, the owners still have money in the bank and time on their hands. I never see a place like mine: a newly built house that has a big mortgage; needs furniture and paint; and has more unrealized dreams than a Little League team.

So why drool over homes you can never have? Beyond the fantasy factor (maybe I, too, could someday live like this) or the voyeur factor (so this is how the other half of half of 1 percent lives), glossy shelter publications must offer more than frustration. But what?

Studying the Sources

For answers, I call Betty Lou Phillips, of Dallas, who has written seven gorgeous home-design books, including *Inspirations from France and Italy*, which I lust after, and I ask: What can the average person take from the pages of books like hers and really use?

"Imitation," she insists, "is not the sincerest form of flattery. Home design books should urge readers to create their own dazzling empires."

"But how if you're not starting with a handsome eighteenth-century château, or a fabulous vintage farmhouse?"

Here's what Betty Lou Phillips says to look for in home-design publications:

- **Harmony.** It's much more important than conformity. Rooms are more interesting when the elements complement each other rather than match.
- **Details.** Pay attention to them. The contrasting welt on a chair, the way a drape hangs off its rod, the textured throw tossed across a small sofa, all create interest and ambience. "When scouting a house to use in one of my books," Phillips says, "I strongly favor the home with the unexpected detail that raises it above the fray."
- **Elegance mixed with the familiar.** Phillips likes blending the humble and the grand. The crystal decanter beside the aged wooden bowl. A collection of old birdhouses alongside a stark contemporary painting. The point: Don't replicate the still life on the page, but take away the idea of mixing old with new, fancy with plain.
- **Style.** Know yours. When looking at a fashion magazine, you can appreciate a great new style (boots with short skirts), and also appreciate that it's not for you (not even in my casket). You have to know yourself and your house. A lot of home design is great—for other people (see Chapter 4).
- **Balance.** We often respond positively to photos of lovely rooms because they have balance. Whoever put the room together knew to place a large oil painting to balance the heavy armoire across the room. "It's one of those factors you don't notice right away, but it's there if you look," says Phillips.
- **Spareness.** Memorable and inviting rooms tend to have fewer but finer things.
- **Life.** And there's one more secret. In her book *The French Connection,* Phillips includes photos of rooms with newspapers lying on the floor and children's sneakers strewn across the rug. "Rooms look best when they look lived in," she says. If that's true, she'd love my place.

But it's important to be realistic when drooling over the eye candy in magazines. Don't be taken in. Even editors admit that much of what they put on those pages is an illusion.

"Train your eye so you look beyond how to copy a room, and instead study why it's working," says Phillips. "If you can master the why, not the what, you'll be on your way to doing something fascinating yourself," she promises.

Separating Fact from Fiction

Even though these design tips give me a big leg up, that doesn't change the fact that when I flip through the pages of home design

---

While shelter magazines do provide inspiration and decorating ideas, don't turn to them for reality. Here's what they won't tell you:

- **Rooms that fall together beautifully** look deceptively simple. To really appear effortlessly elegant takes hard work.
- **Great design involves blood,** tears, heavy drinking, cursing, more money than you think, counseling, antidepressants, charm school, and chocolate. If we knew that going in, we wouldn't get so frustrated.
- **Just like models in glamour magazines,** rooms featured in these shelter books are staged, airbrushed, and shot at just the right angle. Proof: Look closely next time and tell me if you see a lamp cord, or a waste can with even one scrap of paper. In her latest book, *Inspirations from France and Italy,* Betty Lou Phillips wrote (and I love her all the more for saying this) that when preparing to shoot photos for her gorgeous books, her crew removes telephones, televisions, and computers from the rooms and uses Photoshop to edit out recessed lights, thermostats, and wall switches.
- **Magazines are in business** to serve readers and please advertisers. If they revealed how truly difficult most remodeling projects were, readers would be too discouraged to remodel and the gig would be up.

magazines I still feel like Hobo Kelly standing on the threshold of the Ritz-Carlton. All those pictures of perfectly decorated rooms alongside that fluffy copy make me want to eat Tums by the roll. The stories usually start out something like this: "When Christie and Rich Perfect first laid eyes on that five-acre parcel in Martha's Vineyard, they knew in the very marrow of their bones that this would be the place to build a modest 18-bedroom ranch home, where they would nurture and adore their three Yale-bound children, who are also Ralph Lauren models, and their eight Dutch Warmbloods." I think it's hopeless.

Well, several years ago I started writing for some of these shelter magazines. I learned firsthand why you can't take these books too seriously.

Here's how they operate. These magazines tease you with photos of gorgeous interiors. The writer interviews the designer and owner (often one and the same), who gush about how easy the project was, how the flow of both inspiration and funds were endless, how everyone involved got along like honeymooners, and how their only regret was that the project had ended, because it was so much fun. (Pass the barf bag.) The narrative also lures the reader into believing this look is attainable. The copy is just nonspecific enough that impressionable readers will get hooked on a dream and then have to seek out and pay experts (read magazine advertisers) to really get the job done. This is how the magazines stay in business.

However, these magazines are to reality what politicians are to truth. What they will never tell you about are the hiccups in every project: the tile mason with the drinking problem, the carpenter who only showed up every third Thursday, the landscaper who left the country with the owner's five-figure deposit, the kid who rebelled because she wanted to put a climbing wall in her bedroom, the stratospheric costs that exceeded the initial quote exponentially, and the shipwreck of a marriage left at the end. Now that would be a good story.

That, dear readers, is reality.

Just for fun, I asked Renee Aragon Dolese, former editor in chief of Colorado Homes & Lifestyles magazine and now a freelance editor for shelter publications, if the homes she features really are that gorgeous. "Good design is good design, but how a room is photographed makes the difference between a nice-looking room and one that takes your breath away," she said. "No home gets shot as is."

When she shoots a house, she brings an art director, a stylist, and a photographer. Bigger magazines have even larger teams to direct a shot's composition, lighting, and styling. But once again, I'm encouraged. I believe, at least for the moment, that with just the right light, from just the right angle, with just the right props and a great photographer, any one of our homes could look gorgeous. "Remember," says Dolese, "our job is to sell fantasy and inspiration. We're given a look, but we create an image." So books and magazines offer one source of inspiration, but nothing quite illustrates good or bad design better than seeing it in three dimensions. . . .

Rip-Off Source #2: Home Tours

The Allure of Seeing the Bad, the Ugly, and the Dated

"You've got to see this house," my friend said. She was on the phone telling me to meet her quick at a rundown multimillion-dollar house that was so dated it belonged in the 70s wing of a museum. "It wouldn't be any fun to see this place if I didn't have anyone to dish with," she said. Well, she called the right gal. I never turn down an opportunity to see bad decorating. It's the only kind of decorating that makes me feel better about mine.

The home tour was to preview a house that designers would soon transform to benefit the local Junior Symphony Guild.

Two-inch shag carpet, with yarn thick as earthworms, covered the floors, and some walls, and even crawled up the deck surrounding the Jacuzzi tub. The carpet was mostly an earthy sage, but you could tell from the few unfaded spots where furniture had been that it was once a brilliant avocado. That was in its heyday, a day when Gloria Gaynor was topping the record charts (remember records?) with "I Will Survive." But this décor did not survive.

"Can you say 'gut'?" my friend whispered.

"I feel like I'm having a bad flashback."

Later, I did a little digging to find the scoop on this place. As I expected, the former owners were members of high society. When they built the house, they decorated it with first-class style du jour. With that task off their list, they busied themselves raising a family, tending business, traveling, and entertaining the well known and well to do. By the time they looked up again, twenty-five years had gone by, and their home, once a showplace, looked as dated as a macramé plant hanger. These owners had now moved on. And the 5,000-square-foot house was ready for a change as well.

As my friend and I were touring and gasping, design teams were working every room, tearing out mirrored bars, three-pinch pleated curtains on traverse rods, and disco-style light fixtures. Each crew had a vision, and one design diplomat had the delicate job of coordinating these visions to make sure they would flow together while keeping each designer's ego intact.

"He's putting purple feathers next to my leopard print!"

Though knowing what styles today will look dated down the road is tough to predict, Gibson offered several ways we can hedge our bets:

- **Start with colors from nature.** Consider pulling colors from your immediate landscape. Nature is always in style. Subtle earth tones such as green, brown, beige, and putty make a wonderful backdrop. (For more color tips, see Chapter 18.) The sage green shag carpet in the 70s house looked bad because of the style of the carpet, which was outdated, and because it was worn and faded, not because of its original color.

- **Build on those neutral backgrounds.** Put neutrals on walls, counters, and floors. If you pick up a trendy color or pattern, keep it in the accessories. You can afford to change pillows, art, and area rugs more easily than you can afford to change the backgrounds.

- **Choose classic fabrics.** Linen, silk, and leather are good choices. Leather is great for furniture because it often looks better with age.

- **Keep up with the times.** To avoid having to do a complete overhaul, change outdated appliances or furnishings a bit at a time. Hint: If the last time you painted, Watergate was making headlines, it's time.

- **Decorate with a period in mind.** For example, early craftsman and Old World European are classic looks that stand the test of time. Most people recognize the craftsman style (also called *mission*) by its straight lines and slats, exposed joints, and hand-hammered hardware and by the absence of carving or ornamentation. Hallmarks of Old World European design include a comfortable, broken-in look, distressed finishes, textured walls, and old tapestries. For a great overview of forty design styles, go to www.HGTV.com and search for "style glossary."

- **Remember, old often becomes in again.** "When you're working at the forefront of creative design, you have to borrow from history," said Gibson. "The trick is to draw from a past era and reinterpret it." Shag carpet is back, for instance, and metallic wallpaper is trending up. Today's shags, however, don't climb walls (or shouldn't) and are made of finer and better cut yarns, so you never need a rake. (Thank heavens!)

"Her pomegranate paint is clashing with my tangerine."

A few days later, I told Gary Gibson, my Los Angeles designer friend, about the house. "Where do you begin in a case like this?" I asked him.

"If you've let your décor go that long," he said, "I'd do as these designers are doing and strip the house back to its bones." Then I asked the better question: How do you avoid having a dated home to begin with? Most of us can only afford to decorate once or twice in our lives, so timeless design is partly about economics.

Snooping—Voyeurism Has Its Place

"The lights are on at lot 47," my husband announces. I race to the window and see he's right. We share a look. We know what we must do.

The timing is perfect. It's our date night. The sitter is here, and I can't think of a better way to start the evening than by scoping out how our soon-to-be neighbors have decked out their home.

The front door is unlocked. We enter like sleuths, slip off our shoes, and head in different directions to explore. This would feel criminal, except that the new owners don't technically own the house yet; it belongs to the builder until escrow closes. And the neighbors did this to our house. I know because shortly after I moved in and met my first neighbor, she told me how much she loved my entryway light fixture.

"When did you see it?" I asked, realizing I hadn't yet had her over.

"Oh, I looked, before you moved in. We all did."

As it turns out, snooping is common sport in our developing neighborhood. We've all been in each other's bedrooms, but most won't admit it. When almost everything is in the home except the new owners and their stuff, the builder leaves the lights on. Lights are the builder's way of guarding against vandals. (Not us!) But to the neighbors, lights say: Open House! Fortunately for us spies, those who work on these homes never lock the doors.

Besides checking out finishes and fixtures, these sneak previews give us insight. Are the new folks modern, old-fashioned, sophisticated, or rustic? How much did they upgrade? Did they spend more than we did? Did they copy us? Do any of their windows look into ours?

After all, it's human nature to yearn to know what our neighbors have that we don't. Okay, maybe not for Gandhi or Mother Theresa, but I said *human* nature. I'm curious. I want to know if I still like my choices better than theirs. Whether relieved or jealous, I always leave these self-conducted tours feeling that I know the new owners a little better.

Take the people who moved in to lot 53, another home we previewed. The décor was mountainy. The owners had selected bath tiles with fossil-like impressions of elk and bear. The kitchen cabinets had pinecone pulls. These people, we correctly deduced, were liberal naturalists who had more than one dog and ate a lot of whole grains.

"I feel like Gladys Kravitz," I say, recalling the snoopy neighbor on *Bewitched*, as I tiptoe past Dan in the hall.

"Be glad you don't look like her."

The to-be owners of lot 47 have chosen white travertine floors and black cabinets. I sense New York, or possibly Asian roots, definitely sophistication. Whatever, I feel relieved they are decorating in a different vein. (I had gone with natural slate and distressed wood floors because when I put my kids and dogs in the same room with anything white, my blood pressure goes up.) The secondary bathrooms at lot 47 are finished with ceramic tiles in Dodger blue and black, which tells me their children are boys. The upgrades are minimal, not over-the-top like the empty nesters on lot 27, who actually have discretionary income because their kids are on their own. Nope, like us, this family is starting with the basics.

Upstairs, Dan and I meet briefly in the master and momentarily covet the city views. Our curiosity satisfied, we start to leave. Just then I hear the front door open. I consider the possibility of slipping out another door, but what about our shoes? My heart beats quickly. I hear voices, a man's and a woman's.

"I think someone's here," the woman says nervously.

I come out, feeling as if I should put my hands over my head. When the other couple sees us, we laugh. It's the neighbors down the street, of course, doing the same thing we are.

If you're like me, always trying to deconstruct good home design, touring finished but unfurnished homes offers a great education. Here's why I spy:

- **Feel for flow.** You can look at floor plans on paper all day, but there's no better way to feel a home's flow or get a sense of its bones than by walking through it empty.
- **Reality check.** Unlike model and design homes, where designers have pulled out all the stops, these homes are designed by regular people who faced the same choices I faced. It's informative to see what they've chosen and how their backgrounds work together before the furnishings arrive.
- **Test drive.** These tours let you see how other finish combinations work—"So that's how blond bird's-eye maple cabinets look with limestone and ebony floors and persimmon pull-trowel walls"—in case you want to do a similar combo someday.
- **Before and after.** Once the neighbors move in, you can see how their furnishings work against that template. This time, you will have to be invited. Tip: Housewarming gifts or plates of cookies can get you an entrée. Just remember not to say, "I love the floor in your master bath," when, as far as they know, you've never been there.

Rip-Off Source #3: Reality TV Shows

"How do you do it?" I plead. I'm on the phone with Evan Farmer, host of TLC's *While You Were Out*. I'm torn between begging for advice and giving him a piece of my mind.

While some say these shows inspire people, they make me feel inferior, because the smallest home improvement at my house takes ten times as long, costs ten times as much, and looks half as creative as the projects on these shows.

"You spent as much on our living room drapes as these guys spent on a whole living room," Dan will point up.

"Why did our bookcase take, like, half a year to finish?" My daughter wonders. "Theirs only took an afternoon!"

Besides the warped sense of time and money these shows portray, the flamboyance factor creates more problems: "Why can't we wallpaper the wall in feathers?"

Hold me up to one of these shows and I come away looking like an unimaginative, disorganized spendthrift.

For instance, in one episode, the *While You Were Out* crew completely redid one couple's master bedroom. They tore out carpet, installed hardwood floors, added white wainscoting, sewed curtains and bedding, built and mounted shutters, beefed up moldings, painted the walls and trim, built a bed, refinished the armoire and dresser, and, oh, cooked up homemade spa products to adorn the master bath—all in two days for under $1,500.

That's when I picked up the phone and got Farmer on the line.

"So, Evan," I say and launch into a tirade of questions.

"Well, we do have a few advantages the folks at home don't," he confesses.

"Cough them up."

First, the show's designer gets a three-week lead to check out the room and design a solution. Then, the day before the shoot, the whole crew meets, sizes up the project, and goes shopping. All that happens before the two-day clock starts ticking. At show time, a whole team of pros works at once. This kind of teamwork only happens on reality decorating shows and sometimes at NASA—like when those rocket scientists brought Tom Hanks and Apollo 13 safely back to earth using only the supplies in the conference room. Anyway, real people like us have the electrician in, then wait two weeks for the carpenter, then wait two weeks for the tile guy, and two more weeks for the painter.

The TV crew is also fully equipped. "Our truck has every tool we need in easy reach, so no three trips to the hardware store," says Farmer. "Plus, we have a clean-up crew." At my place, we are the clean-up crew.

Though reality TV home-design shows reflect reality about as much as shelter magazines do, I do admire the clever solutions these crews come up with for design problems. Before we hung up, I got *While You Were Out* host Evan Farmer to share some redecorating rules he's learned from doing the show:

- **The power of paint.** Too many people are trapped inside white or beige walls. Nothing transforms a room more than paint. It's cheap and easy.
- **The 90/10 rule.** The team always starts by taking everything out of a room. In the end, only 10 percent goes back. Most stuff doesn't belong or is clutter.
- **Focus.** When the room is stripped, designers look for a focal point, such as a view window or fireplace, or they make one, such as a waterfall on the wall. They arrange the room around that.
- **Cutting chaos.** Before you demo any room, have your ducks in a row. Have the design complete, all your materials and tools in hand, any permits you'll need, and the appropriate contractors chained to your property.

So that's how they save time, but how about money? The $1,500 budget, Farmer insists, is real. Sort of. His team goes to Home Depot and pays the same price as anyone else, even though Home Depot is a show sponsor. Other companies, however, particularly fabric or accessory sources, donate merchandise in exchange for the exposure on national television. Ahh, I'm beginning to see how this works.

Of course, having all the tools and receiving donated items save a lot. But the real reason these show makeovers sound so cheap is that nobody adds in the cost of man—or woman—power. If they did, the budget would go way over $1,500. Labor, industry experts say, can account for 30 to 60 percent of a job's cost. On top of that, big-ticket items, like sofas or dining-room sets, the show throws in as a quiz prize, which also isn't included in the $1,500. The couple wins this prize if they correctly answer some obvious question— like, What's your address?

So see? I feel like saying to my family. "I'm feeling better," I tell Farmer as we wind up my peeve session. Then he gives me one more reassuring dose of reality. He's remodeling his own place, he tells me, a 286-square-foot apartment in New York City. "I have no budget. That's the luxury of living in a closet. I've been at it a year and I'm still not done. I work, you know."

I do know. That's reality.

Rip-Off Source #4: Color Forecasts

If You Feel Manipulated, It's Because You Are
I first noticed that lime green was back without apology two springs ago. Clothing, tableware, wallpaper, iPods, even parking tickets were suddenly all coming out in that citrusy green. The color was everywhere—except in my closet. Which meant one thing: This color was *in*, and my wardrobe was *out*. I immediately

bought a skirt, capris, T-shirt, blouse, two sweaters, and sandals in varying shades of this had-to-have color. I hadn't been this green since I was pregnant. My husband said I looked like a parakeet.

Once again, I'd fallen victim to the Palette Patrol.

When I first learned about this small but influential group who knows what colors I'll be wearing, decorating with, and driving in before I do, I felt as if I'd seen Santa take off his beard. Hood-winked. The last time I felt like this was when I learned that movies splice their films with subliminal ads. A frame of an ice-cold soda flashes on-screen, and viewers head like sleepwalkers toward the concessions stand. We're all being manipulated. Don't believe me? Remember all the combos of dark brown and silvery blue that suddenly started appearing in every home and fashion magazine and store a while ago? It's no accident. The Palette Patrol controls the interest rates of hue like the Federal Reserve controls the interest rates of money.

Here's how the color conspiracy works. Every year a dozen or more hoity-toity designers meet in New York, sequester themselves in a stark white room, and determine the *in* colors for the next year. To do this, they talk about what's going on in the world and how those events translate into colors people will want. Meanwhile, they throw darts at an elaborate color wheel. Conversations go something like this:

"What are people into these days?"

"A lot of people are drinking Starbucks."

"Put coffee browns on the list."

Darts fly at the brown section of the wheel.

"What are people talking about?"

"Global warming."

"We'll need a spate of solar oranges with some balanced greens."

Darts hurl toward these color sectors.

"What's happening in Hollywood?"

"Angelina Jolie's lips are everywhere. They stay in the room five minutes after she's left."

"Let's bring the lipstick shades out of retirement, but give them a new name."

"How about the Collagen Collection?"

"Perfect." Darts fly.

"What color is the bird flu? Anyone?"

And so on.

Then, the folks who make clothing, household goods, and cars get the group's color forecast and join in lockstep to create everything to match.

Here's how to use the color forecast, and not be abused by it.

- **Be aware.** Notice what colors are cycling up and which ones are trending down. As with any trend, you don't have to slavishly adhere to current color fads. But knowing what's in and the forces behind that trend will help you be a more conscientious consumer.
- **Count on neutrals.** For an up-to-date look that won't drain your bank account, choose neutrals for large or expensive items, and select less expensive accessories—pillows, towels, rugs—in the splashier trend shades.
- **Resist.** Don't let the market dictate a direction that's not right for you. Back in the 70s, my mother, who loves blue, finally had a chance to redecorate her living room. Somehow she wound up with an avocado green sofa and carpet. For years, I heard her say, "Whatever possessed me to buy that green?" Well, now we know. Today, her home is done in blues and corals, as it should be. Some homes look best a certain color because of their period or architecture. I wouldn't paint the columns on an old colonial anything but white.
- **Interior colors coming in.** At the time of this writing, forecasters were saying that in 2008 the hot colors would be earthy browns and brownish grays; more complex blues, like purpled navy; slick reds with names like ribbon and lacquer, which would be complicated

"I don't believe it's a conspiracy," says Margaret Walch, director of the Color Association of the United States, which has been furnishing color forecasts for nearly 100 years. "We don't dictate what colors will be in so much as we foresee what's coming."

This gets me thinking of that chicken-and-egg riddle until my brain hurts. Either way, these forecasts have a big upside. Sure, new colors in the marketplace make us buy more stuff, but the fresh shades also satisfy our craving for change. Aren't you glad you're not still wearing those emerald greens, royal blues, and fuchsias from the 80s? Think how boring life would be if colors didn't cycle.

("Here's how to use the color forecast ..." continued)

reds, not simple ones like stoplight red; new greens emphasizing the yellowed greens of nature; and yellow in all its hues (even whites will be buttery). To know what future forecasts will be, watch the news, or ask designers who subscribe to the forecasts to tell you. The two main forecasting groups are the Color Association of the United States (CAUS) and the Color Marketing Group (CMG).

- **Trending down.** Wimpy colors, including anything pastel. My sister-in-law just replaced the sea-foam green carpet in her home with carpet in cola brown. That move, Walch said, is a classic example of the times.
- **Biggest change.** More multicolored contrast looks. Interiors will mix a dark, a bright, and a light color, like brown, red, and cream. No more beige on beige. "These looks are more difficult to create," says Walch, "but the look is high-end and sophisticated."
- **Helpful to know.** While fashion colors cycle every few years, interior colors last from seven to fifteen. Thank goodness, because decorating is expensive enough.
- **You're in luck.** If you love a certain color, and it's trending up at a time you happen to be decorating, count your blessings. Whether you are picking fabrics, carpet, wallpaper, or towels, finding choices you like will never be easier.

Also, because manufacturers are in cahoots, when you're remodeling you can find fabric that goes with your new carpet and wallpaper; plus you can find a laundry basket, towels, a sweater, and nail polish to match. But good luck trying to match a ten-year-old bedspread.

Finally, color cycles help certain stodgy types to bust out of their ruts. Those still living with avocado green appliances and rust shag carpet will eventually have to replace them. And, thanks to the Palette Patrol, they won't be able to buy anything new in an out-of-date color. This alone provides an important public service.

To those who pooh-pooh all this and say they don't care about color trends, Walch has a few choice words: "If you don't have relevant color, you don't have a relevant space."

And your belt's ugly, too.

Just because you feel inspired, know your style, and have a folder full of ideas doesn't mean it will be easy for you to make that first big purchase. But it's better to do the thinking and research before you spend. Maybe you'll relate to the woman I describe in the next chapter. . . .

19

Pulling the Trigger

Why furniture shopping is so hard, and how to start

I'M HAVING LUNCH WITH several women from the neighborhood. As often happens among women, the conversation turns to home decorating.

"Do you have your dining room set yet?" One neighbor asks Lisa.

Lisa hangs her head shamefully and stops eating her rigatoni.

"No," she says to her plate. "I couldn't decide."

We all give a moment of respectful silence. Who hasn't been there? Paralyzed into a state of indecision while a room lays bare.

"We may never have dining room furniture," she continues, as if exposing a deep character flaw. "It's just such a big decision."

Like the rest of us, Lisa has swallowed society's dictum that a home is a mirror of the woman within, a sword we live and die by. What's more, thanks to years of indoctrination by Hallmark specials and *Better Homes & Gardens*, we all have a vision of the ideal dining room. This is the room where memories will be made. The table will serve as centerpiece during celebrations of holidays and family milestones: graduations, engagements, releases from jail. If the table isn't right, the occasion and all those potentially warm memories will be marred by bad taste.

In other words, this is not just a table. It's The Table.

"I finally find a table I like," Lisa continues, "but I don't like the chairs. Or the table doesn't have leaves and I want leaves for my grandchildren." No one points out that since her kids are only four and seven, grandkids might be a while.

"I know what you're going through," one neighbor says. "Legs straight, curved, carved, or tapered? Table round, rectangular, or square? Glass, wood, or iron?"

"And the style?" chimes another. "Contemporary, traditional, French, or Italian? The chairs? Ladder-back, Windsor, Parsons, Chippendale, or Queen Anne? It's enough to make a woman eat standing up for the rest of her life."

We shake our heads in collective understanding. Indeed, these decisions do seem momentous. I envy those homes where you sit at a table and the hostess says in passing, "Ahh, yes, this was Grandma Jacobs' table. All us kids used to sit around it in our high chairs with matching hand-loomed bibs."

The only story I know about my grandma's dining room table— and who knows where that wound up—was that all her kids were born on it. How about that for a conversation booster between the salad and the main course? "Oh, little Nancy popped out right where you're sitting."

"My husband doesn't know what's wrong with me," Lisa continues. "Every day he asks, 'Why don't you buy some furniture?' I feel so inadequate."

I nod sympathetically, though I can't recall a moment in my marriage when my husband ever said, "Why don't you buy some furniture?" That would be rather like letting a bear loose in a butcher shop. Instead I flash on the two long years our living room remained unfurnished, unless you count the Barbie Jeep and the fake ficus.

"It's so embarrassing," I said back then to my husband. "People think we have no money."

As my neighbors and I commiserated with Lisa, who was fretting with indecision about a dining room table, we tossed out names of helpful Web sites, furniture stores, and decorators. We also came up with this bit of collective wisdom, born of experience:

- **Don't cheap out.** For the main pieces of furniture in your home, often called *case goods* in the business, buy quality and buy classic. (That doesn't mean you shouldn't hunt for a bargain.) Big items are investments you ideally will make only once. Buy as if you want to spare your grandchildren the pain you're going through now.

- **Mix and match.** Don't fall for a set. This same principle applies to bedroom and living room furniture. The best dining rooms have chairs and tables that look as if they were meant to be friends, but not relatives. With a little ingenuity (and maybe professional help) you can create a custom combination that doesn't scream "set," but rather whispers "style." When selecting the chairs, sit in them to test for comfort. Sit down and wiggle to be sure they're sturdy. Then be sure they fit under the table, are low enough to let you cross your legs, and tall enough to let you dine comfortably.

- **Get the upholstery you like now.** But choose a frame with staying power. You—and future generations—can always update it down the road. When covering dining room chairs, keep in mind that prints are more forgiving of stains than solids. Avoid white unless you want to hyperventilate at every dinner. Also, while silk and linen are lovely, save them for the drapes. A fabric with a little synthetic in it will aid stain removal.

- **Leave elbow room.** Allow for a minimum of 3 feet between the table and the wall. Four feet is better, and 5 feet is ideal. You want someone to be able to walk behind the chair when someone else is seated.

- **Know the magic numbers.** As for the dining room light fixture, if you have an 8-foot ceiling, hang your chandelier so the bottom of it is 30 inches over the table. Add 3 inches for every foot of ceiling height, up to a maximum of 40 inches. Thus, a fixture would hang 35–37 inches above the table from a 10-foot ceiling.

- **Keep it in the family.** If you're ever offered an heirloom dining room set, grab it, so long as it meets the hand-me-down-wedding-dress criteria: It fits, you like it, and it brought the bride good luck.

"They're right," he said. Sometimes his realism really bugs me.

True, in some homes, rooms lay bare because the couple has the money but not the inspiration, as in Lisa's case. Other's have the vision but not the dough. We often lack both.

Chair Shopping

I was on mission impossible. My about-to-be-thirteen-year-old daughter wanted a bedroom chair for her birthday, a chair she "could chill out in." While I pictured her curled up reading *Little Women*, she envisioned herself wearing headphones and listening to the newest Weird Al Yankovic CD. That was clue one that our tastes were on a collision course. Shopping was painful.

"How about this one?" she said, heading for an enormous over-stuffed chair, right for, say, a country club lobby.

"Too big. You couldn't walk around it."

"I'll just climb on the bed and jump to it," she said, confirming my suspicion that my kids are more closely related to the apes than their parents.

"How about this one?" I redirected her to an antique vanity chair with a carved wood back and a velvet cushion. Her nose wrinkled up like a straw wrapper. "This one?" I pointed to a lovely rattan sun chair with a floral seat cushion.

"Eeww," she said, then made a beeline for a chair the size and shape of a satellite dish with a cushion that resembled a dog's bed. "Perfect!" she declared.

"When you have your own place," I said. And so we went. She wanted big and stuffed; I wanted feminine, small—and cheap. That was the other hitch. Decent upholstered chairs sell for be-tween $750 and $1,500, but my birthday chair budget was under $300. Like I said: mission impossible.

Which is where Kobe Bryant came in with a game-saving three-point shot in the final seconds. It was the eve of Paige's birthday. A clerk at the local Pier One store, who was trying to close and was legitimately worried that I might never leave, suggested I try a store called The Chairman. The next day, an hour before I was to pick Paige up from school, I went, knowing I had about a 2 percent chance that this store would have The Chair.

"Moving! Everything 50% off!" said the heartening sign on the window. (I later learned the same sign had been in the window for years.) Inside, chairs were everywhere, hanging, stacked, knocked over. In one room, 100 or so upholstered chairs were piled like cars in a junkyard. "Just got these in," said a man who looked as if he'd crawled out from under one. The price tags said $100.

"Only $100?" I asked.

"The hotel was getting rid of them."

Buying used furniture is tricky, but I called Terri Bowersock, owner of Terri's Consign and Design Furniture, which has sixteen consignment furniture stores across the country. She gave me these trade secrets to apply when buying upholstered furniture:

- **Do the scoot test.** When buying a chair or sofa, sit in it and scoot your behind forward, back, and side to side. The legs shouldn't wiggle. Look for frames of hardwood (oak), not softwood (pine).
- **Push your thumb into the seat cushion.** Watch how fast the seat bounces back. Quick rebound means good foam quality.
- **Unzip the back pillow.** Make sure the filling is muslin wrapped. If not, it won't hold its shape.
- **Don't buy planning to recover.** It's not cost effective. If it's soiled slightly, it will probably clean up. If it has a stain, forget it.
- **Ask where the piece came from.** It might have a story.

"What hotel?"

"The one where Kobe Bryant stayed and wished he hadn't."

"The Lodge at Cordillera? Where he was with that woman?"

He nodded. The upscale lodge is just outside Denver and not far from my home. Having lived most of my life in Southern California, I was used to odd brushes with celebrity, but chairs with a past?

"You mean one of these might have been in Room 35?"

"Might have." I had just read in the newspaper that the lodge was undergoing a $5 million makeover, so the guy was probably telling the truth. Whether the remodel was because notoriety had attracted a surge of visitors, or because management wanted a new look to erase negative associations, wasn't clear. But either way, I'd stumbled on a bargain.

Then I saw it. It had a rose background with cream lattice print and touches of green ivy. The fabric perfectly complemented Paige's room. Though fully upholstered, it was small, bedroom size. I loved it, but I was suspicious.

I decided to give it the Paige test: I took off my shoes, stood on the chair, and bounced. It was that kind of place.

"The frames?" I asked.

"Solid alder," he said.

"The fill?"

"Down-wrapped poly." My favorite. Pure down you're always plumping and all foam is so hard.

"Spring construction?"

"Eight-way hand tied." He pulled the bottom cover off one chair to prove it. "Wholesale these were $600 new," he said, "double that retail." I believed him.

With the chair in the back of my SUV, I headed to school. As Paige flung open the back hatch to toss in her backpack, she stood stunned at the chair facing her. Then she cracked a huge smile, jumped in, and plunked down as if at a tailgate party. I smiled, too. I'd gotten it: the chair we thought didn't exist.

Finding a Leg to Stand On

Much of what I've learned about home design, I've learned by eavesdropping. And so it was with furniture legs. I clearly remember the day in the model home. A decorator was talking to another decorator about legs. The two were tsk-tsking about the number, style, and color of legs in the room, as if the situation were an atrocity on the scale of Chernobyl.

When I first heard this, I wanted to go check into one of those hospitals that keep you from hurting yourself. Just when I thought decorating was doable, the game changed—again. I was just getting the hang of color, texture, and scale, and now I had legs to worry about. At times like this, you just wish someone would throw you a life raft. I made mental design note #897: Beware of clashing and numerous furniture legs. This notion came back with searing clarity as I stood in my office gazing at a just-purchased chair. I realized I had made the dreaded leg mistake.

After months of looking for the perfect chair to replace the dead chair in my office, I finally found it. It was a steal. The furniture store was going out of business, and the sign in its window said, "Everything 70% off." I was lured like a gambler to a casino. However, the sign also said, "All sales final." So I considered the chair carefully. The color was right—a sage chenille with a thin black stripe, dark mahogany wood. The style was right—classic, not too formal, not too bohemian. It sat well and passed the scoot test. It seemed to be the right scale, and the right price! I hauled it home, single-handedly, because everyone knows the same woman who can't open a jelly jar suddenly acquires Herculean strength if it means acquiring new furniture. At the right moment, I can also lift a sofa over my head with one hand.

I heaved the chair into the family car, then into the house and into my office after heaving the old chair out. I stood back to admire my acquisition, then winced. Something wasn't working. My ten-year-old stopped by and swiftly observed: "The chair looks fine from the doorway, but when you walk in the room, it doesn't go with everything else." This is evolution at work. She could instantly finger what I couldn't.

That's when I remembered the leg lesson. My desk is a French writing desk, with a medium brown curved carved leg. The chair's legs were slightly curved, but smooth, and a darker wood tone. The chair sat only a few feet from the desk, and the legs argued like my children. You could hear them.

"I was here first, and I don't like your legs."

"Hey, I didn't ask to be put next to you."

"Get lost."

"You get lost."

See, the old ousted chair was upholstered to the floor, and as conservatively dressed as a Primitive Methodist. The new hussy chair was upholstered on the back and seat, but it had legs. Legs that didn't belong. Then another thought came back to haunt me: All sales final.

That night I dreamt of armies of spiders on stilts. I awoke, frustrated once again at what designers know that I don't. So I could learn from my mistake, I asked my interior design friend James Charles to give me a leg lesson. He assured me that the question was good, the problem common.

While I had intended this new chair to replace my worn-out office chair, I, fortunately, had another old chair in the family room that also needed to retire. There the new chair worked. "Sometimes you don't see these things until a room is put together," said

Charles, trying to make me feel better. "The pros won't admit this, but it happens to all of us."

Of course, you won't make any bad furniture decisions now because you've taken all the right steps. You've created a furniture floor plan for each room and sketched it out on graph paper. You've cut old newspapers to create a to-scale outline of the furniture and laid it out on the

---

Those who know what they're doing can break the rules, but the rest of us would do well to follow these guidelines:

- **Know your legs.** Legs come curved, straight, tapered, and carved. They come in wood, chrome, and iron as well as in other materials. Start noticing the visual effect they convey. Most people don't pay much attention, but if you begin to notice, you'll appreciate the statement they make.

- **Avoid rooms on stilts.** Too many furniture legs in a room make the place look like a Rockettes' audition. Ground leggy furniture by setting it next to a barrier, such as a piece fully upholstered to the floor, a skirted table, or a chest.

- **Pair opposites.** Because furniture with legs looks best next to furniture without, a coffee table with legs goes well in front of a fully upholstered sofa. Likewise, a sofa with legs looks nice paired with an ottoman or chest.

- **Find a common denominator.** If you're putting several pieces of legged furniture in the same room, be sure the legs have something in common. They should share the same finish, style, or texture, for example. You can blend chrome and wood if both styles are contemporary. My new chair's legs had three strikes against them. They differed from the desk's legs in color, style, and texture.

- **Beware of too much matching.** Like the six-piece matched bedroom set, furniture that has matched legs shows no originality. To create a custom look, pair legs that have the same style but different finishes. "If I have a crackle finish on one piece, I'd pair that with something simple, like a smooth cherry, or iron," said Charles. "Too many people add another crackle, and that's a mistake."

floor. You've made sure the room has flow, taken care that it is not an obstacle course, and considered how the furniture can enhance the function of the room. It may facilitate conversation, for example, or provide a good place to work or to watch television. You've paid attention to detail, even added interest by including an oval or round element, if all the other pieces are square or rectangular. And because you've created a plan, have your backgrounds in place, and have a color scheme, you'll no doubt get the fabric right. Right? I sure hope so, because in the next chapter, you'll read the story of someone who didn't.

20

When Something's Got to Go

Dealing with furniture mistakes and deaths

TO KNOW MY MOTHER-IN-LAW is to know her red sofas. For six months they were all she could talk about. Every conversation led to them:

"So have you been exercising?"

"I would, but these sofas have been so consuming. What color could I put on the wall to make them work?"

Or: "How's your daughter's new boyfriend?"

"Fine, he came for dinner the other night, but we couldn't sit in the living room—with those sofas."

Talking to her is like talking to someone in a doomed relationship: "Do I just live with them? Try to make them work? Or dump them and move on?"

Buying a sofa you regret is a drag, much less buying two, and especially in her case. Like many devoted mothers, my mother-in-law put decorating on hold while she raised five kids. Now that they've moved on, the living room, like her, is tired and deserving. She chronicled her sofa saga in a string of e-mails to me:

Week One

"I ordered new living room furniture, a cranberry couch and love seat. Do you think two couches in that shade will be too dominant?"

What can I say? She'd ordered them. Though I'm thinking, *The only place two large cranberry sofas belong is in a bordello,* I write: "They'll be fine."

The Next Day

"After I placed the order, I didn't sleep. The gal at the store says they'll be great and even made suggestions for drapes and wallcoverings."

The "gal at the store" is a salesperson. She'd never been to my mother-in-law's home, which has Wedgwood blue carpet, off-white walls, and entryway tile in French blue and marigold. Cranberry? What was she thinking? I reply: "I'm sure she's right."

Ten Weeks Later

"Sorry if I seemed out of sorts last night. The sofas arrived. I went to bed with a migraine. In the small sample, the color looked ok. Should I go to a lot of trouble and make everything conform to the color scheme they dictate?"

I have no words except: "See a professional—as in designer, not salesperson."

Two Weeks after That

"I talked to a decorator. She could try to make the sofas work, and if I still didn't like the room, she would consider buying them for model homes. But I'd still be paying to decorate around sofas I may not keep. If I could just sell them without losing so much money, I would start over."

"Recover? Consign? Donate?"

One Week Later

"I inquired at the consignment store. I would take a big loss. Our couches cost $3,000. If I sell through consignment I would get $500, tops. Recovering them would cost nearly what I paid."

When you select fabric for a custom piece of furniture, choose wisely, because once you order it, it's yours, said Jim Calhoun, creative director for Norwalk Furniture, a national chain based in Norwalk, Ohio. But if, like my mother-in-law, you do get stuck with a sofa you can't stand, he said, you have four ways out.

- **Make it work.** Just how you make it work will depend on what you put around the sofa and how you cover it. To put the piece into the background, layer it with colored pillows and throws, then find an area rug that has the sofa color in it as well as other colors in the room to help it blend in. Calhoun said my mother-in-law could have incorporated her cranberry sofas into her light blue and white room by picking a Persian rug with those colors in it, throwing a tribal blanket over the sofa, then adding some Moroccan art and pottery.
- **Slipcover.** A slipcover can cost about half as much as the item new.
- **Recover.** This option will probably cost as much as the sofa did to begin with, but if you like the lines, that may be the way to go.
- **Donate to charity.** If the piece is new, you can take the full purchase amount as a tax deduction. To prove you donated a new item, keep dated copies of your original receipt and your donation receipt. Attach a photo.

"The sooner the sofas are out of your house, the sooner you'll stop flogging yourself."

One Month Later

My mother-in-law flies in from three states away, ostensibly to see my daughter, her granddaughter, perform in the school musical, but I suspect my father-in-law shipped her off because he was tired of hearing about the sofas.

"Do you think if I kept one, it would be okay?" she asks. We're standing in my kitchen staring at her swatches.

"If the sofas are wrong, half of wrong is still wrong," I say. Then I break it to her and tell her what I would tell anyone I care about who's struggling to end a bad relationship: "Let go." She hangs her head. After a respectful pause, I try to change the subject. "Your hair looks nice. Who's cutting it lately?"

She pats her hair absently. "My hairdresser once bought a sofa she couldn't live with."

"Oh?"

"She gave it to a person she couldn't live with—her ex-husband."

Six Months after Ordering the Wrong Sofas

"I found a sofa I like. I'm just waiting for the designer to go with me to pick out the fabric. The thrift store truck comes for the awful red ones next week."

"Great," I reply. I don't say: *Now can we change the subject?*

Giving up something new and wrong is almost as hard as parting with something old and loved. But home decorators have to maintain an objective eye and admit when something is past its prime. If you are mov-

ing into a new house, it's the perfect time to let the old stuff go. But sometimes you don't realize how bad a tried and true chair looks until everything around it looks fresh.

Furniture Funerals—When to Let Go

The funeral was a long time coming. For ten years, these two domestic servants had served useful and productive lives. But now the large stuffed chairs, both white in their prime, needed to go to chair heaven—a peaceful place where no one sits on you in a wet bathing suit.

"But they're so comfortable," my family whined each time I brought up the need to replace the chairs. One sat in the office, and the other, the more popular of the two, in the family room. "And the dogs love them."

"Which is half the problem," I said.

Ten years ago, when I decided to buy two pristine white chairs, I could not have foreseen the havoc that two kids, two poorly trained dogs, ten years of compounded newspaper ink, seventeen bouts of flu, and 2,957 cups of coffee would wreak. I have had the chairs professionally cleaned, but the remaining stains resist like cellulite.

The family room chair even had an ink stain where someone, who refuses to step forward, sat with a black felt-tip marker, then thoughtfully poised the pen so it bled into the fabric, leaving a Rorschach-like inkblot.

"It's a cat."

"No, a key."

"I see a new handbag."

"You're all wrong. It's the Dow falling."

Besides the stains, the fabric was so worn that feathers fluttered out whenever you sat down, as if you'd landed in a goose nest. I'd

I called Karlie Adams, the Denver interior designer I've worked with, who I'm convinced possesses pitch-perfect taste, and asked her about sick, dead, and dying furniture. As with the red sofa debacle, you have four choices, but they differ slightly from the four options you have when you buy something awful. In the case of old pieces that look like they just might be an insult to charity, you can clean, slipcover, reupholster, or replace. Here's how to choose:

- **Clean.** Success depends on the fabric and the damage. A white linen that's ten years old probably won't look much better after it's cleaned. But a sturdier tapestry fabric with some acrylic in it can refresh beautifully.
- **Slipcover.** If the lines of the chair are still good and not dated, and the scale still works in your home, then slipcovering or recovering can be a great option. Slipcovering costs about half as much as reupholstering. But do this only if you like a relaxed, shabby chic look, because slipcover fabric will never look as taut as an upholstered piece. This casual touch can look fabulous in an English or French Country home.
- **Reupholster.** Once people discover the cost of reupholstering, they often just buy a new chair. This option costs about as much as buying a midpriced chair. But if your chair still has great lines and was high-end to begin with—or belonged to your grandfather and holds fond memories—reupholstering makes sense. A good upholsterer can even refresh or replace the filling so chairs get their original shape and feel back. There's also the peace factor to consider. Karlie has a client whose family would have been furious if she had gotten rid of their favorite sofas and chairs. Even though recovering them was more expensive than replacing them, that's what the family did.
- **Replace.** If the lines of the chair don't work anymore, the chair wasn't too high quality to begin with, or you're just ready for a change, then tossing the piece and replacing it may be your best bet. Or, to save the dump fee, you could have a yard sale. Just be prepared to hang a "Free" sign on it if necessary.

considered slipcovers, but it would have creeped me out to sit down and think about what might be growing underneath. Meanwhile, I'd tossed throws over the chairs, so I wouldn't have to look at them, and pinned "Do Not Resuscitate" signs on them while I searched for replacements.

Dan didn't see the need for replacements. To him, the chairs looked as fresh as the day they arrived. He's the same way with his shirts and shoes. I've come to see this as a positive trait in a man. I figure if I look just as fresh to him as the day we met, well, I'm not messing with that.

But chair death must be reckoned with. I've overheard that the average life for moderately used upholstered furniture is seven years. After that, it's probably time for rehabilitation or euthanasia. After learning my options, I chose to replace the family room chair (see Chapter 19) and have the office chair slipcovered.

In the world of furniture, everything is negotiable. In fact, I can't recall the last time I paid full retail price for any home furnishing. But that doesn't mean I don't get good quality, just that I hunt for deals. So come along as I share some of my best furniture bargain tactics. Whether shopping retail for new furniture or at a consignment store or flea market for gently used treasures, my motto is: It never hurts to ask. . . .

21

Bargain Hunting

Finding deals, insisting on quality

"JUST BUY IT," SAID MY OLDEST daughter, who thinks my purse taps directly into Bill Gates's bank account.

"Not at that price," I snorted.

She rolled her eyes. Boy, did that feel familiar.

We were browsing through a nearby furniture boutique, and I had found a sink vanity I liked. I love the look of those old-fashioned chests with the sinks cut in the top. (Apparently, I'm not alone: The concept came out of nowhere in 2002, and within a few years these vanities had become a fast-growing furniture category.) But I don't always like the price. This one was a good antique reproduction; I had seen its likes in catalogs. It had a carved wood cabinet, claw feet, and a black marble top with an aged brass sink and faucet. It would glam up my powder room nicely, but it cost twice as much as I thought it should, which was why I was scoffing, and my daughter was embarrassed.

I flashed back to when I was a girl. My mother used to mortify me whenever she acted frugal, which was often. She was born in Scotland, so she came by this trait genetically.

"Forty dollars for an all-cotton blouse!" she'd exclaim in a voice that would turn my hair into porcupine quills. "It's not worth two!" She thought nothing of saying to a store clerk, loud enough for everyone around to hear: "What a ridiculous price! I can't believe the markup. I bet you only paid half that." You would find me outside hiding in the hedges.

When she hauled me out, I'd plead, "Mom, don't be so embarrassing."

"Embarrassing! They should be the ones embarrassed, charging those prices."

While Mom did teach me to question both price values and people's values, I also learned that how much something is worth

---

If price matters to you, try these tips when scouting for furniture deals:

- **Do your homework.** If you find a piece you like that isn't an original antique, learn who the manufacturer is. Then search for the piece online to see what it sells for elsewhere. Sometimes manufacturers list the retail stores that sell their furniture. Call stores near you and compare prices. They can vary widely.
- **Get an inside line.** Ask the salesperson to call you first when the piece goes on sale or has an additional markdown. Sometimes, to make quotas, salespeople will deal.
- **Let time be your ally.** Rushing a purchase can get costly. Patience pays. Even if the piece you're eyeing sells, the store can probably get it again.
- **Buy out of state or offer cash.** When you ship a piece from out of state, you can save sales tax. You will have to pay shipping, but, depending on the piece's price, you could come out ahead. Some store operators prefer cash because they don't have to pay the 2 to 3 percent service fee to the credit card company.
- **Don't be afraid to make an offer.** All you have to lose is your kids' respect.

isn't what matters. What matters is how much people will pay. A world of difference often lies between the two. Witness those $248 torn-up jeans at Nordstrom. "You're kidding, right?" I hold up a pair of the holey jeans and challenge the unsuspecting Nordstrom clerk, as my daughter does a half-gainer into the nearby clothing rounder.

But back to the furniture store. A few months later, my daughter and I visited again. The vanity was marked down 30 percent. We were getting somewhere.

"See," I told her. "It pays to wait."

"So get it already," she said, "then let's go." She wasn't so eager to see the powder room furnished as she was to get me out of the store before I humiliated her.

"Watch this," I said as the owner approached. She asked if she could help us.

"Not today," I said. "But if you ever mark this down 50 percent, call me. I'll buy it."

I looked around for my daughter. Poof! She'd vaporized like a genie, as if I'd mentioned chores.

The gracious owner took my name.

I found my daughter crouched behind the ceramics: "Mom, you're so embarrassing."

Several weeks later, the gracious owner called. The chest was now 40 percent off. Tempting, but 50 percent off was still my price. Then I hopped online and found the same chest on Horchow. It was $500 more and didn't have a faucet. The faucet cost an additional $430, and shipping was $115. Suddenly, 40 percent off with no shipping or wait time appealed.

I panicked. "What if someone buys it?" I worried out loud.

"No one's going to buy it," Dan said from behind the sports section. Dan can't believe anyone actually buys furniture, since that's the last thing he'd ever do.

"How do you know?"

"Because it's been sitting there for six months."

"But not at this price."

I called the gracious owner back and asked whether paying cash would make any difference. She paused, then said she could take another 5 percent off. In a victory for cheapskates, I had my car in front of her store faster than you could say *"It never hurts to ask."*

Sometimes the best finds are from used furniture sources. Consignment stores and Craigslist are two of my favorites.

Not the Confinement Store

Going furniture shopping with my husband is like going underwater diving without oxygen. He withholds the essential ingredient.

"It takes money, honey," I've told Dan more than a few times.

If you don't know what you're doing when shopping consignment, you can quickly become a junk collector. So again I called the queen of used furniture buying, Terri Bowersock, of Terri's Consign and Design, and got her advice.

- **Get educated.** Visit a high-end furniture store, a mid-range store, and a low-end store and see the quality differences yourself. When in the more expensive stores, note the brand names of the better furniture. Once you've done your research, you'll appreciate the value of a Chippendale table when you see one.
- **Look past the staging.** Retail showrooms make furniture look great. Don't let the trappings fool you. You need a discerning eye to spot the true gems lurking in flea markets, estate sales, consignment stores, and other hideouts for gently used furniture.
- **Don't buy a fixer-upper.** Never buy a used upholstered item with the intention of recovering it. That will cost you more in the long run.

"Not if you just look."

"What's the point of looking if you can't buy?"

"Then you'll know what you want when you can buy."

"And just when would that be? When the kids are out of braces and the college fund is full and the cars are paid off and I'm in a rest home where the furniture is all provided?!"

"Something like that," he says.

"Argh!!"

But I've learned, the one way to get this man to budge his billfold is to say the three magic words: *It's a deal.*

Which is how I've come to love consignment stores. These are stores where people who are downsizing, divorcing (probably due to a remodel), or tired of their furnishings—and really do have the money to redecorate—bring their gently used stuff to sell. Inventory also comes from model homes that have closed and from over-

---

("If you don't know ..." continued)

- **Be discerning.** Before you buy, apply the same five-step criteria Bowersock uses when deciding whether to accept a piece for consignment: (1) Condition: Is it good to excellent? (2) Age: Newer is usually better, except when scouting for original period pieces. (3) Style: Is it out of fashion? Does it fit in your home? (4) Brand: Is it made by a good manufacturer? (5) Color: Is the color dated or off for your home? And I'd add: Is it part of your plan?

- **Consider the price.** Find out what the item would cost new. Is this really a bargain? If you're a gambler, wait to see if the price changes. Most consignment stores mark items down further after they sit a while. While I've watched items I've had my eye on get sold from under me, I've also found that patience saves.

- **Visit often.** If you don't, you miss out. You never know when a great new item is coming in, and the good stuff sells fast.

- **Remember the rule for partners.** Buy now, explain yourself later, especially if it was a deal and you got miles.

stocked or closing furniture stores. The consignment store sets the price and typically splits the proceeds with the original owner, who generally feels that this option beats donating the item, dumping it, or giving it to their ungrateful children.

"It's a glorified garage sale," Dan said the first time I dragged him to a consignment store.

Granted, these stores don't have the cachet of stylized furniture showrooms, and some of the stuff I wouldn't let my dogs sit on. But you can find some great bargains among the riff-raff if you know what to look for—and you don't have impatient family members along.

"Not the *confinement* store!" my kids wail when they sense the car veering toward one.

They dislike furniture shopping even more than my husband does. In fact, sometimes, when my sadistic streak flares and we're on our way somewhere they find fun, like a water park, I'll say, "but first I want to stop at this consignment store."

"Nooooo!" they protest.

"Just kidding," I say, smiling.

Other times, when I do drag them along, I promise I'll be quick and will buy smoothies all around when we're done. This paid off last time. I scored a great dark brown leather ottoman with brass

---

TIP: TRADE SECRETS

- To tell the difference between a cheap mirror and an expensive one, put a quarter on the glass. If the quarter looks as if it's sitting on itself, the mirror is cheap. On an older, better mirror, the two quarters will look like they're ¼" or more apart.
- Bring a magnet when shopping for a brass bed. The magnet won't stick to a brass-plated bed, but it will to solid brass.
- When buying a chest of drawers, look to see that the drawers are made with dove-tailed construction, so parts fit like interlocking fingers and aren't just stapled and glued.

nail heads for the loft. It had come off the showroom floor of Woodley's, a well-regarded maker of leather furniture, so it was practically new. I knew it had retailed for over $400, and it was only $195. I smuggled it home, hoping Dan would think it had been in our home all along, and that the kids, bribed with the smoothies, would consider it too boring to mention. If Dan ever does notice, I'll tell him the truth: It was a great deal, plus we got miles.

Buying Furniture on Craigslist— the Pain and the Glory

We had come to a standstill. Well, one of us wasn't standing. He'd fallen over. In an odd bonding moment, four of us—Dan; Tom, the guy we'd bought the secondhand desk from; me, superfluous bystander; and The Desk were stuck together like a blood clot in our basement stairwell. On the uphill end of the desk, Tom was holding up his end of the bargain—literally. As part of the sale, Tom had agreed, probably to his regret, to help Dan move the desk from our truck to the basement. As they lugged the monster downstairs, Dan slipped on the nylon sleeping bag that someone—that superfluous bystander!—had put down to protect the wood stairs. (Forget the people, don't nick the stairs!) The desk was now on Dan. I pictured my husband, flattened like Wile E. Coyote at the bottom of a cliff beneath a boulder. I'd killed him!

A faint cry came from what sounded like the desk's file drawer: "I could use a hand here." I came to my senses and slid sideways between the stairwell wall and the desk, and hoisted the desk off Dan's leg. The rest of him was lying headfirst downstairs. He got up, brushed himself off with his remaining dignity, picked the desk up again, and limped onward with Tom into his office. All because this was a deal.

Let me rewind. When not traveling, Dan works in his home office in the basement, which is newly finished, but, until now, unfurnished. My office is one floor up. Lately, when I would venture

Apparently, Dan isn't the only one who thinks buying furniture on Craigslist makes sense. The San Francisco–based company has 450 Web sites in fifty countries and all fifty United States; and 20 million visitors stop by each month to shop for everything from mates to jobs and houses. In the furniture section, Craigslist publishes 1 million ads each month, said Jim Buckmaster, Craigslist president and CEO. I called him to ask what was behind this hot trend. Here's what he said:

- **Immediacy and convenience:** Craigslist facilitates buying and selling secondhand furniture so well because it's organized around small regions. Furniture is not usually something that people want to buy sight unseen. Most people want to see the piece in person and haul it away on the spot.
- **Low price:** Most sellers aren't trying to get the maximum price. They're trying to shift an item they no longer need. There's even a section on the site offering stuff for free.
- **Fun adventure:** The experience of buying and selling on Craigslist often leads to meeting people in your area, who may be interesting to you in other ways.
- **Caution:** Deal only with local people you can meet. Don't buy anything without meeting the seller. Don't wire money to the seller, and never divulge personal financial information. Requests for wire transfers are almost always fraudulent. Buyers can get into trouble when they become so fixated on scoring a bargain that they ignore common sense. If you are a seller, be aware that fake cashier's checks and money orders are common, and that banks will hold you responsible, even if a fake is discovered weeks later. By following these rules, you'll eliminate 99 percent of the risk of falling for a scam.

down to his office looking for a lunch date, I'd notice that he wasn't working, but shopping on Craigslist for used office furniture.

"Hard at work, I see," I'd joke.

"I'm working on working," he'd defend. "I can't get anything done until I get some furniture." He was working on three folding tables, smothered in computer equipment, cords, and mountains of paper. Because I'm a fan of neatness, productivity, and shopping, I helped him browse.

As usual, we had different furniture agendas. He wanted a U-shaped desk, with lots of cabinetry, for under $1,000. I wanted a traditional, Old World–style desk to go with the room's coffered ceiling. He was shopping Craigslist, because you can zero in on local sellers. Craigslist is the world's biggest online virtual garage sale. I was leery, but Dan insisted it was a great way to buy furniture. (This from a man who had suggested we buy our daughter's eighth-grade graduation dress from Wal-Mart.)

Postings ranged from hideous to hilarious and showed that more people should take photo classes. Weeks passed. We found a desk we liked, but it sold in three hours. We resolved to pull the trigger faster next time. Then a desk that seemed perfect appeared: cherry, U-shaped, with a hutch, excellent condition, for $1,000, and it was just twenty minutes away. A quick online search revealed that the same desk new would have cost $3,000. We were there within the hour. After a brief negotiation, Tom lowered the price to $850 and threw in the black leather office chair. Score!

Because we wanted a record of the business expense, we wanted to pay with a check. Tom, understandably, wanted cash. So we agreed to drive him to our bank, where he could cash our check, and, since we'd be near our house—how convenient!—he could help us unload. He looked as if he could move the desk alone with his jaws. This is how the four of us got into the stairwell jam.

That night I surveyed Dan's injuries: cuts on his elbow, two goose-egg bruises on his leg, and a welt on his back the size of a crow's wing. "Are you sure this was worth it?" I asked.

"Absolutely," he said.

Not quite a scam, but often disappointing, are home furnishing purchases made from catalogs. While catalog consumption is one of my favorite armchair pastimes, I've made ordering mistakes. Read on to find out how to avoid them. . . .

Catalog Victim

I come down the stairs in what I think is a pretty cute new sweat suit. My unsuspecting family is gathered around the breakfast table, which is what they do when they hope something to eat will magically appear on it. I'm hoping they'll notice the outfit, say something along the lines of: "You look nice. Is that new?" (Which, by the way, men, is a no-fail line you should try on the lady in your life at least once a week.)

"Where did you get that?" my husband asks.

"From a catalog," I say, twirling so all can admire.

"You paid money for that?"

I look down at the gray pants and matching jacket and reconsider.

"Lupe has an outfit just like that," my youngest daughter adds sweetly. Lupe is our dear, lovely housekeeper, who happens to be a grandmother. "Older housekeeper" wasn't the look I was going for.

"Maybe she'd like another one," Dan adds.

"It looked cute in the catalog," I say, feeling deflated. Then I get an unpleasant déjà vu feeling. How many times have I been hoodwinked by seductive catalog portrayals of fashion or furnishing only to be sorely disappointed when the items arrived? And when will I stop falling for this trick?

Before the sweat-suit mistake, it was the mirrors. I'd ordered two, one for over each sink in the master bath. When we were building this home, I told the builder not to install the flat plate production mirrors because I wanted to find my own. Along the way, I've learned two facts about bathroom mirrors:

1. An easy way to make a bathroom look more personal and custom is to replace production mirrors with handsomely framed ones.

To avoid future catalog calamities, I called Ruth Swan, director of merchandise information for Ballard Design in Atlanta, which publishes a popular French Country catalog. How could we consumers do better? I asked.

- **Look past the merchandising.** Just as when buying clothes, when buying items for your home from a catalog you need to factor out the marketing tricks. For clothes, that means the model; for home design, it means the setting. Focus on style, color, size, and quality. Is the item right for you and for your home? A lot of home furnishings are fabulous; most of them are for other people.
- **Order swatches.** When items get returned, it's usually because they're the wrong color, said Swan. Always order the free swatches for fabric or wood finishes before committing.
- **Know the quality.** One of the best ways to do that is to know the company. For instance, Horchow (Neiman Marcus), Crate & Barrel, and Pottery Barn all sell home furnishings in stores. So you can see their quality firsthand.
- **Check material content.** I once ordered an area rug from a catalog. The color looked great for my interior, and the size was right, but when it arrived, I discovered that the material felt like something I would use to scrub my sink. I had been envisioning wool, but sure enough, it was nylon. Some items that look like solid wood are actually veneered composite or painted resin. Ask before you order.

2. If a functional mirror is over the sink, my husband won't see the need to replace it. So it's best to do without until I find the mirror I want.

We went mirrorless for months while I shopped. Unfortunately, the mirrors I finally picked were poor reflections of their catalog-stylized selves. Plus, they fought with the fixtures. They were too small. Their frames were too thin, the detailing too decorative. They just looked scrappy.

("To avoid future catalog calamities ..." continued)

- **Be sure it's a fit.** One of the hardest variables for DIY home decorators to get right is scale. Check, don't ignore, the measurements. They're usually provided, but if they're not, ask for all dimensions. To envision how the item will fit, block it out in the space using a measuring tape and cut-to-size cardboard or newspaper, or mask out the shape in painter's tape. When in doubt, know it's better to go too big than too small.
- **Read the return policy.** Once the item arrives, keep the packaging until you're sure you're keeping the piece.
- **Know it's still a gamble.** Whenever you buy something you can't see, it's a risk. Knowing all this, I recently bought a small woven rug to put inside the kitchen door. When I set the rug down, I couldn't open the door over it. The rug was too thick. When I tried to return it, I learned that shipping would cost $12, half what the rug cost. Rats. I kept it and figured I'd use it somewhere someday. I'm still learning.
- **Ask for special offers.** Before you purchase, inquire about whether the catalog company is offering any promotions you're not aware of.

When I told Swan my mirror story, she empathized. "All of us in the catalog industry strive to keep returns down," she said. "One thing we constantly say around here is: 'Don't make the picture look too good.'"

"They're fine," Dan said, grateful I'd finally put up something he could shave in.

"I blew it," I said.

"How could you blow something you spent three months shopping for?"

"They looked great in the catalog! Those catalog companies conspire to defraud people like me all the time," I huffed. Dan rolled his eyes in the all-wrong mirrors.

I can still see that beautiful mirror in the catalog picture, hung artfully among other items that were in proportion, were the right motif, and didn't compete: an antique buffet, slender side lamps, and crimson wallpaper. I think back to the sweat suit model, six feet tall and waiflike. She'd look great wearing a potato sack. What was I thinking? I can't pull off a gray sweat suit no matter how fashionable my shoes and earrings are. On me gray sweats just look dowdy. And my bathroom, I now see, is not the place for delicate, gilded mirrors. Unfortunately, as with the sweat suit, in a fit of optimism I'd thrown away the packaging, so there was no easy way to return these blunders.

The mirrors are in the garage with my growing collection of catalog casualties—that too-fake ficus! That too-small table! And Lupe has herself a new sweat suit.

As much as I love a deal, I'm still a stickler for quality. If you can't find the furniture you want at the price you can afford, you face a choice: Buy lesser quality, or wait till you can afford the quality you want. In general, I opt for the latter, which explains why some rooms in my home are still empty. Here's what I mean. . . .

Quality Is Worth the Wait

Regardless of whether you're buying a dining room table, a bed, or a chair, or whether the piece you're purchasing is new or gently used, take a lesson from the French: Buy furniture as if it were going to be an heirloom. Sometimes that takes patience, and delay of gratification, as Dan and I learned recently when pool-table shopping.

We were in this pool-table store getting that uneasy feeling you get before you make a big purchase. Now that we had a home with a basement—currently finished but not furnished—Dan was jonesing for a pool table. He'd been going around the house playing air pool all week, shooting phantom cues.

We'd been to three billiard stores and seen tables ranging from $1,500 to $10,000. Though all tables have six pockets and do the job, they differ in expensive ways. Some are made of high-end mahogany, others from veneer-covered particleboard or vinyl. Some have rail sights made from inlaid mother of pearl, others use

---

You may not agree with French politics, but you can't argue with their taste and style. Betty Lou Phillips, author and Dallas-based interior designer, has made the study of French design her life's work. I asked her what the French know that we should. She gave me these French lessons:

- **The past must always be present.** "In America, when our parents give us furniture for our first home, as soon as we can afford to, we usher that old furniture out the door with a sense of satisfaction," she said. Not the French. They cherish what they inherit, so they keep the past present and build family history.
- **Quality is important.** Because the French buy quality in the first place, the following generations don't need to replace it. Unlike many Americans, the French invest in quality even if that means doing without for a while.
- **Patience.** The French don't feel the urgency to pull their homes together overnight, and they attach a stigma to those who do. The French are comfortable with empty rooms. "They don't apologize. When the price of what they want is out of reach, they do without rather than compromise their ideals."

pressed-on mother of plastic. Dan had decided on a lower-priced table, on special, and had moved on to selecting pool cues. He was also planning a neighborhood billiard party for Saturday.

"Way, way, wait a minute," I said. "Not so fast." I'd glommed onto the store's interactive video game of "Build Your Own Table" and found many features I liked—and that of course doubled the price.

Dan sighed and found a place to sit.

A salesman hovered nearby but wisely kept his mouth shut. Who needs a salesperson when you have me?

"So basically," said Dan, "we either get the table that's perfectly fine and on sale, or pay more than is comfortable and get a fancier table with features that won't make any difference when you're sinking a billiard ball into the corner pocket."

"When we're old, feeble, or gone, our kids are going to get stuck with this pool table. If we buy a cheap one, they'll have to sell it in a garage sale with the rest of our cheap stuff, or keep it as a reminder of how tacky we were. A nice one will become an heirloom, and our grandchildren will play on it and our grandchildren's children."

"How did a trip to pick a pool table turn into a discussion about our children's inheritance—or lack of it?"

"That's not how the French think."

"What do the French have to do with this?"

"Betty Lou says."

"Who's Betty Lou?"

"She wrote all those gorgeous French design books: *The French Connection, Unmistakably French* . . . and she says the French are patient and buy quality furniture that will become heirlooms."

"So because of the French we're not getting a pool table?"

"Yet."

PART IV

The Finishing Touch

Putting home accessories in their place

In Part II, "Decisions, Decisions," we talked about the importance of choosing and installing your backgrounds first, and adding accessories last. Remember, vegetables before dessert. Well, now that the furniture is in place, it's time for dessert. . . .

22

Home Accessories Are Like Dessert

It's not the first thousand dollars you spend that matter, but the last hundred

THE OLD SAYING I'VE USED for the subtitle of this chapter has been around for so long that in the home design world the numbers are off. The "last hundred" refers to the money you will spend on the finishing touches. The perfect piece of art, the coffee table accessory, the lamp: These are the grace notes that are going to make the room.

A common mistake DIY decorators make is to accessorize too early. Because they're afraid to make a big commitment to something like carpet, or drapes, or an armoire, they hit the default button and start buying picture frames, vases, and candlesticks. They hope in vain that these items will somehow pull the room together. But your love for a variety of random objects isn't enough to unify them in your home. They won't pull a room together any more than a necklace or purse will salvage an outfit that isn't working to begin with.

If you've stuck with the program, and you've put your backgrounds in, dressed the windows, and selected and placed good furniture that will serve as your backdrop, you can now add pizzazz.

When It's Time to Indulge

"Did you hear about the new store?" the ladies asked in hushed tones. "Do you know when it's opening?" A new home accessory store was opening down the street, and the neighbors were buzzing about it. Even as store workers stocked merchandise, women hovered at the door asking for sneak previews. I was happening by and thought I'd stumbled onto either a Brad Pitt sighting or a place handing out low-carb Danishes. The manager turned the women away with a smile and told them to come back opening day.

When accessorizing your home, follow these rules from the experts:

- **Consider accessories the finishing touch.** They're the hat, the shoe, the glove.
- **Subtract before adding.** Critically edit what you have and eliminate what's not working before adding to it. Try to see your home as a newcomer would.
- **Err on spare.** Remember what almost every interior designer and real estate pro says about homes today: They're too cluttered. They're right. Having larger, fewer accessories will help you avoid making a room visually noisy.
- **Rotate.** If you have too many accessories and can't part with enough to make your décor look clean and not cluttered, consider rotating the items. Put some away on a closet shelf and leave others on display. In a couple of months, when you want a change, pull some out of storage and swap them out. You will see the item anew and your eye will appreciate it more.
- **Play.** Add, remove, and rearrange accessories until the room feels right.
- **Consume in moderation.** When the temptation to buy strikes, remember: Accessories are like dessert, easy to eat, harder to lose.

I was conveniently having my hair cut across from the store the morning it opened, so I was among the first legitimate customers. I browsed. I drooled. I envisioned. I had a few all-out decorating fantasies. And I left. Empty-handed. My craving for an interior design fix was satisfied.

"I saw the new store," I told one of my neighbors that evening.

"Good stuff?" she pressed.

I nodded.

"Did you buy anything?"

I shook my head.

"Why not?" She sounded surprised, knowing how much my home could use.

"Not on my diet."

"What diet?"

"Home accessories are like dessert," I continued, tumbling into my two-cent philosophy. "They come after the meat and vegetables. I need drapes first, built-ins, more lighting, and a few more pieces of furniture. Then I can indulge in accessories. Plus, too many aren't good for your home."

"You're probably right," she said, sounding disappointed, as if I'd just told her the calorie count of cheesecake.

I learned such uncharacteristic restraint the hard way. See, I used to buy every home accessory that caught my concupiscent eye, until my home looked as if I'd run through the local home

---

TIP: To see how a piece of art, a sculpture, or a rug will look in your home, do what designers do—take the piece out on memo. Many of the better home-furnishing stores will let customers try pieces at home before they buy them. Just leave the kids and their electric scooters at home when making these arrangements with the store.

design outlet with a large butterfly net. I had candlesticks and picture frames, baskets and floral arrangements, vases, wall hangings, and sculptures. Visitors thought my home was the collection site for the neighborhood garage sale. So, when I moved into my new home, I tossed all but the most sentimental, which I put in a box marked "Trial Separation." I started with a clean slate and more self-knowledge.

I had finally learned that home accessories—tempting as they are—must come last. And, like skipping dessert, the delay of gratification takes discipline.

I have another neighbor who's like I used to be. She sees a home accessory she likes and buys it. But her home doesn't have drapes, wall treatments, or the most basic built-ins. It has stuff but no soul. "My husband tells me to stop buying all these chatchkes and start decorating," she confesses, "but decorating is so hard, and these are so fun."

"I know," I say, like a Weight Watchers counselor. "It takes more willpower than the dessert buffet."

That doesn't mean I don't love to walk through a tasteful home accessory store, absorb the ambience of the well-appointed space, and envision such an aura filling my home some day. But I also love the virtuous feeling of leaving without buying a scrap, of practicing a monklike abstinence akin to passing on the chocolate éclair.

Decorating the Coffee Table: The Pressure Is On

First I tried putting the candelabra on the coffee table with the bowl of lemons. That looked hokey. Then I tried the silk floral arrangement with the three glass paperweights on books. That looked worse. I tried a table arrangement using the lemon bowl

with the flowers. No. Books and candelabra? Possibly. I had potential coffee table accessories all over the floor. I kept trying them out
on the table, swapping them like partners in a singles club.

"What are you doing?" Dan asked on his way to surely something more meaningful.

"Creating a tablescape."

"A what?"

"It's an artistic composition, like a still life."

"Looks like you're putting a bunch of unnecessary stuff on that
nice table."

"We can't leave it bare."

"Sure we can. That will leave more room for food, drinks, and
our feet. Anything else is just in the way."

I went back to my arranging, which wasn't going so well. I set a
ceramic carousel horse beside a pair of brass candlesticks. Ugh.

Part of what makes accessorizing a coffee table so hard is all the
pressure. Here's this table, prominently positioned in the middle of
the room, basically saying, "Look at me. I'm on display. Whatever
you put on me is something you think is to die for." It's essentially
your taste—or lack of it—in 3-D.

No wonder it's paralyzing.

Making matters worse, I had been so confident of my ability to
arrange the living room coffee table that when the home was being
built, I'd had the electricians put in a ceiling spot to focus on it and
wash it—and the presumably tasteful art objects I would place on
it—in gallery-style lighting. Once again, I'd created my own problem, then put it in the spotlight.

My oldest daughter came by, looked at the stuff all over the living
room, and said, "I have more things for your thrift store donation."

"This isn't a donation. I'm accessorizing the coffee table."

"Just throw some books and flowers on it. That's what everyone
else does."

Since no one in my family understood the significance of coffee table décor, I called someone who would, interior designer James Charles. Even pros have to play with different arrangements, he said. "You don't know an object is right until you put it down. You have to play." Play? I would call it torture. Here's what he said the best tablescapes have:

- **Composition.** The individual objects are not as important as how they work together. The tabletop is like a canvas; you compose the landscape.
- **Variation.** Look at each object for its color, texture, height, and shape. You want a mix. The most important factors are proportion, color, and contrast. Pair shiny objects with dull, hard with soft, straight with curved. A tall, brightly colored square glass vase would contrast nicely with an oval wood platter, for example. Or put a short stack of handsome picture books (hard line) with a taller floral arrangement (soft edge).
- **Context.** Consider the room you're in and your table. More formal objects belong in the living room; studious objects in the den, less formal items in the family room. Wood objects on a glass table look more interesting than wood items on a wood table.
- **Passion.** Look for tabletop accessories that are not only artful but that also reflect your passion. For instance, if you're into photography, you could have a couple of great books of photography sitting beside an old antique camera. A stamp collector could display a pair of stamp collecting books along with his collection, opened to a page of preserved stamps, perhaps with a large magnifying glass and a small model of an old post office.
- **360-degree perspective.** Everything on the table should look good from all sides. So no framed pictures. That rule doesn't apply for mantels, or tables against a wall.
- **Patience.** Getting the right blend and balance takes some experimenting, said Charles. It also might require putting up with insults from your unappreciative family.

"It's not that easy. You know how, when you're wearing a dress, you change the necklace four times until you get just the look you want?"

"No, I don't."

"You need to hit the right balance of scale, color, texture, style, and relevance."

"Whatever floats your boat," she said, then breathed one of those only-my-mother breaths and left me to my obsession.

The two most expensive and probably significant accessories you'll likely purchase for your home are area rugs and fine artwork. In some cases, these do drive a room's or a home's color scheme. If you already have a great piece of art, or a fabulous rug, you can decorate around it. But if you're looking to acquire them, keep in mind Rule #1. . . .

23

Selecting Artwork and Area Rugs

Rule #1: Buy What You Love

I LOOKED AT THE DOG. The dog looked at me. He was longing and needy. I longed to be needed. There was chemistry. You could even say love. I resisted and walked away. His eyes followed me. I circled back, and back again. Each time the dog's face pulled me in. I called my husband and got no answer. Finally, because the place was closing, and I was leaving town, and I would never see this dog again, I bought the dog. I swallowed hard, knowing such choices test a marriage.

Now this heart-pulling scene didn't happen at a pet store or pound, but at an art show. The dog was oil on wood, a large-eyed Weimaraner-type, set deep in a linen-lined frame. The show was in Laguna Beach, the art capital of California. Dan and I were in town for his company's annual meeting. While he worked, I art-shopped. Usually, art shopping for me is not hazardous, because when I look at art, I react in one of four ways:

- They call that art?
- Nice, but not my style.

- Lovely, but I have no place for it.
- Perfect, for when lawyers realize Sam Walton included me in his will.

Thus, I enjoy myself, walk on by, and stay out of trouble. But ever so rarely, I have this reaction:

- Oh no! I love that! *And* it's my colors, my style. I have the right place. And money? What's money?

It's just as well Dan didn't answer his cell phone. I can imagine the conversation:

"There's a painting here I really love."

"How much?"

"I know just where we could put it."

"What's it of?"

"Well, a dog."

"A dog?"

"You have to see it."

"No I don't."

"What's my budget?"

"You don't have a budget."

Nah, just as well he didn't answer.

Instead, I consulted my internal panel of rationalizers. Ms. Opportunity told me I'd never have this chance again. Ms. Philosophy reminded me that we should surround ourselves with art from our travels and our origins. (Dan and I were born and raised near this art town.) Ms. Timing noted the upbeat tenor of the annual business meeting (all the wining and dining) and predicted that my husband's future held nothing but success. And so, I fell under the spell of love at first sight, mixed with the pull of homeland and a fleeting illusion of prosperity. I gave the art dealer my credit card and shipping address.

That night during a noisy dinner aboard a boat with a band playing, I hollered to Dan: "I bought a painting!"

"You're fainting?"

"I tried calling you."

"You're calling who?" Then someone interrupted to ask Dan if he golfed. I felt that between the attempted phone call and that trun-cated conversation I'd satisfied marital disclosure requirements.

Days after we got home, I kept thinking about the dog. Would he find his way to our home? Would I love him as much when he got here? And, most important, would buying him land me in the dog

---

Buying art is so personal: One person's masterpiece is an-other person's punch line. But a home without it feels sterile. For tips on how to be a smart art buyer, I turned to William Godley, a Chicago-based interior designer and art collector:

- **Only buy art you love.** What matters most is how you respond emotionally to a piece. "I see a lot of art that is well done, but I don't necessarily like it," Godley said.
- **Once you feel that emotional pull,** analyze why you like the piece. Be critical and look at the art's elements: the use of color, perspec-tive, line, light, and composition. This will either deepen or weaken your appreciation for it.
- **Learn about the technique the artist used** and how to assess its quality. Also learn about the artist's background. Do his or her cre-dentials in the art world warrant the asking price? In essence, con-sider this as you would any investment.
- **Use the Internet** to shop. The World Wide Web has improved everyone's access to art. While you used to have to go to art shows and galleries to see a limited number of artists, you can now view the work of thousands of artists with clicks of your mouse. Some Web sites let you see the art on different wall colors, or to scale on

house? Two weeks later he arrived. He came so alive in my house he practically licked my face. I hung him in the dining room.

"What's that dog doing in here?" Dan hollered.

"I bought him in Laguna."

"You paid money for that?"

"I told you on the boat, but you changed the subject to golf."

"How much did you pay?"

"I fell in love."

"You're always falling in love," he huffed. I took that remark as a sign of Dan's security.

Now every time Dan walks by the painting, he shakes his head at the dog.

The dog shakes his head back. I think there's chemistry. Maybe even love.

Art for Cheapskates

"I want the monkey."

"No! I want the monkey."

"Then I want the dragonfly."

("Buying art is so personal: ..." continued)

a wall. Find out the site's return policies before you buy. If you like an artist, search for his or her name in Google images to see more of his or her work. Note that the colors on the computer screen will probably not be exact.

- **If you and your mate don't agree on art,** rather than compromise and get art you're not passionate about, take turns. Have one partner choose art for one room, and the other for another room.
- **Tastes change.** People can grow into and out of certain kinds of art. And some you can love all your life. Like this dog.

"Fine, then I get the yellow bird."

Though I feigned distress at my daughters' arguing, secretly I was delighted. At issue was which of the eight nature prints I just framed would hang in the upstairs hallway outside their bedrooms. When I started this art project, all the members of my family, including the dogs, moaned and rolled their eyes. They anticipated the pain, inconvenience, and lousy dinners that usually accompany my home improvement efforts.

As you know from the dog story, I love fine art. But this time my goal was *cheap* art that I also loved. My budget—let alone my art budget—was and remains limited. If I'm going to drop a bundle on art, I'm hanging it publicly, not in the upstairs hall.

The hall wall facing my daughters' bedrooms has four large (two feet by five feet), recessed art niches, a detail the clever builder

According to Kelly Jaycox, wall décor buyer for Ballard Designs, in Atlanta, here's what to know when choosing, or creating, an art grouping:

- **Flexibility.** A set of unified prints often costs less than a large piece, and is more versatile. You can arrange sets in grids, side by side, up and down, or flanking a mirror.
- **Placement.** Small-scaled prints work well in intimate spaces, like hallways and powder rooms. Tight quarters don't allow enough distance to appreciate larger pieces.
- **Motif.** Fit the location. Put pictures of food in kitchens, maps in studies, wine labels in bars, wild animals in kids' areas.
- **Rules.** Images should share a theme, all photos of umbrellas or water colored scenes of France. Frames should match and not be bulky. Hang them meticulously. Grids allow no room for forgiveness. More advanced decorators can break the rules a bit, says Jaycox. For instance, they could get frames of the same color but not matching.
- **Mix.** Layer framed art with other wall décor, such as mirrors, shelves, or corbels.

thought would break up the space, but which just pressures home-owners. Niches grab you by the collar and say, "Look at me! I'm all about showcasing your art, so hang something fabulous here!" Thus, I was suffering from niche pressure *and* budget pressure.

The best solution, I decided, was a set of eight framed prints, two per niche. But whenever I found a set I liked, the price almost triggered an aneurysm. I spotted the solution in a magazine—a bedroom wall featuring framed squares of vintage wallpaper. Ding! I'd frame my own art.

Wall art doesn't have to be expensive to be good, says William Godley, interior designer and art collector. I've seen terrific wall art that costs next to nothing. A friend of mine who likes birds made high-quality colored copies of six birds from an Audubon bird book, framed them all in the matching frames, and hung the sextet in her guest room in a handsome grid. It looked great. Another friend, who really truly never has to worry about money, hung paintings her twin girls made in their second grade class. She put them in nice gold frames and hung them in her entryway. When a well-traveled gentleman came to visit, he inquired as to the name of the artist who created the fine art. So see.

("According to Kelly Jaycox ..." continued)

- **Do It Yourself.** Creating your own art lets you express your passions and can be much cheaper than readymade sets. You can make framed art sets from old magazine covers, calendar pages, photos of leaves, post cards of places traveled, pictures, pages from storybooks your kids loved, pieces of an antique map, sports memorabilia, unpaid parking tickets. Here's what mine cost: Dover Art Book with CD, $40; eight frames with mats and glass, $64; antique bronze paint, $8; archival paper, $6; Total $118, less than $15 a piece. Cheaper art you'd have to steal.

Inspired, I went to the bookstore and found a series of Dover Pictura art books filled with beautiful color illustrations and CDs to import them. I snagged the flora and fauna book. Untamed nature seemed a fitting theme for outside the girls' rooms. Back home I taped pages I liked to the wall, fussed with combinations, and chalked in frame sizes. The eye rolling started.

I printed images I liked on archival-quality paper. At Michael's craft store I found solid wood frames, flat black with precut mats and glass, for only $8 each. Score! Because the black looked too pedestrian, I bought antique bronze paint to rag on and add dimension.

That night, fortified with a dinner of dark chocolate and strong coffee, I turned my dining room table into Frames R Me. I dismantled the frames and rubbed paint on the wood with terry cloth. As I placed the art under the mat, my younger daughter stopped by and, sounding stunned, said, "They look so professional." I puffed up like a kid with a bee allergy.

That's when the fighting broke out. The older daughter came on scene. "I want the monkey."

"No I want the monkey."

Once you've chosen a masterpiece to bring home, the next question is often how to frame it. Few things in life, save maybe the cost of ski-lift tickets for a family of four, have shocked me as much as the price of framing. Whenever I get the estimate from the framer, I feel as if I've been framed.

The Art of the Frame

Nature hath framed strange fellows in her time.

—SHAKESPEARE

"Mom, look!" It's my youngest showing me her latest art project from school—a dragon etched and preserved in extra-strength aluminum foil.

"That's beautiful, honey," I lie.

"Can we frame it?"

"Uhh," I stutter, once again torn between the twin desires of bolstering my child's self-esteem and not having my home look like the halls of an elementary school.

"You never frame my stuff," she says in a voice that implies child abuse.

"Errr," I say. She's right. See, I know framing anything will greatly increase the odds of its assuming a permanent place in our humble art collection. It will never get thrown out, mainly because framing costs so much, and the Scot side of me won't let me give up the investment. "How about if we put it with the other treasures I plan to frame," I head to the stash behind the coat closet door.

"Mom!" she stops me. "Even you call that closet the Black Hole of Calcutta." She's onto me. It's true. Hidden here are the kids' first handprints, three yards of butcher paper covered with tracks from a tricycle rolled through paint, and glitter-covered pine cones.

I play analyst with myself and try to seek the roots of my hang up. I dig deep and uncover two painful memories that symbolize the reasons I resist putting art, however loosely defined, into a frame:

1. Sticker shock.
2. Triple black diamond difficulty level.

Now, however, the disappointment on my daughter's face tells me I must face my framing phobia.

Determined not to be hoodwinked again, I gather my resolve, my purse, my daughter, and her dragon and head to the local frame shop. The framer considers the art and pulls out some mats. I encourage my daughter to choose a mat color that goes with her room (so this won't hang in the entryway). She picks one in rose. Then the framer pulls out a cardboard backing that attaches to the mat and includes a paper stand. "I'd put this on," he says, "and leave it at that."

I called Paul Butler, co-owner of Art and Frame Express, in Costa Mesa, California, and one of the top framers for Laguna Beach artists. He told me I needed to work on my trust issues and establish a working relationship with an honest framer, which he insisted is not an oxymoron. Then he offered the following frugal framing tips so I could start to actually enjoy—rather than resist—the process.

- **Talk cost up front.** Tell the framer what you would like to spend and ask whether that's realistic.
- **Check stock.** Ask which frames or moldings the frame store stocks a lot of. Often, if a framer buys bigger quantities of one, he gets a volume discount that he can pass on to you.
- **Go for volume.** Frame two or three pictures at once. Using the same type of frame on several pieces not only saves money but can unify the art.
- **Size it up.** To cut costs, skimp on material rather than size. For example, opt for a larger rag mat over a smaller silk one.
- **Shop flea markets.** Watch for great frames at swap meets and thrift stores. Throw the art away and reuse the frame and glass.
- **Settle for plain glass.** Opt for regular glass (as opposed to the more expensive non-glare or invisible glass). Most of the time it's just fine, and much cheaper.
- **Dry mount.** If you know (or hope) your child's motorcycle or rock-star poster phase will be brief, dry-mount posters on colored Masonite, then laminate them. The hard protective finish is so durable that you could eat lunch on it. (And you never know with kids.) The cost is low and the result looks better than thumbtacks.

TIP: Forget hanging artwork at eye level. People's eye levels come in many different heights. Use designer Lauri Ward's 3-inch rule: Hold art where it looks good, then lower it 3 inches.

"What?" I say, shocked that he's not trying to oversell me. The total, including cutting the mat, is under $10.

"Not everything," he says, when my daughter's out of earshot, "warrants an expensive frame." And my faith in humanity is redeemed.

A Rug for the Cause

"Are you sure?" he asks.

"I'm sure," I say.

"I don't believe you."

"Believe me."

"Well, if you're *sure*."

So went the conversation between Dan and me moments before we bid on an area rug at a silent auction. The auction was a fancy affair held to raise money for our children's school. So when the rug about which I was so sure turned out to be so wrong, I consoled myself by saying at least the money went to a good cause.

Dan didn't see it that way.

Pass the crow. But this much was true: We needed a round rug for our entryway, something 6 feet wide with burgundy, green, and gold in it. This rug was all that. So I fell for it. Mainly because—I now see—I desperately wanted to avoid rug shopping.

Every time I face one of those daunting Oriental rug stacks—all those colors and patterns, the sales banter about machine versus hand tufted, grades of wool, quality of dyes—I have painful flashbacks of when I last bought a rug. I test-drove at least two dozen. I rolled each one up, stuffed it in the back of my car, then, once home, dragged it like a dead sea mammal into the dining room, where I unrolled it, stood back, and waited for a declarative voice to say: That's it! Which never happened.

Rugs that looked rust in the store turned rose in my light. What appeared elegant in the show room looked pretentious in my home. Prices were all over the map, and the merchants made me nervous. High-end dealers who hang rugs on their walls like museum art intimidate me. And the scallywags who triple their prices, only to reduce them 70 percent, and profess to be going out of business, I don't trust. Every time I leave a carpet merchant, I feel like counting all my fingers to be sure I still have them.

I did some research into how to buy a quality rug and avoid rug-trading scams. Here's what I learned.

- **Don't avoid buying an area rug** just because you're chicken. The right rug can be a huge asset, the defining statement of a room. Rugs add layered warmth and texture and can define a space and anchor furnishings.
- **Before buying,** try the rug in your home. Most rug dealers will let you, if you leave a deposit. Even if you're positive a rug is right in the store, that certainty can unravel once the rug is home.
- **Consider buying the rug first,** decorating second. This may be the one exception to the rule of accessorizing last. Many people start with an area rug, or have one they really like, and decorate around it. Finding furnishings to go with a rug can be easier than finding a rug to go with furnishings.
- **Look for hand-tufted wool.** Hand-tufted rugs are considered finer than machine-made ones, and the rugs that wear best are pure wool. However, many synthetic yarns are good looking, durable, and easy to clean, and many machine-made rugs look handmade. For good quality, expect to pay between $20 and $60 per square foot. But if you know the rug is just temporary, say for a college apartment, don't splurge.
- **Feel the difference.** Rub your hand across lower-quality wool and it sheds. Higher-end wools feel softer, almost greasy, because the wool has so much lanolin.

Having been through this painful, unfulfilling experience several times, I've started analyzing other people's rug selections, and discovered this: The most successful rugs fall into place yet don't perfectly match everything around them. Ah-hah! So . . . the goal is not perfection, but *perfect non-perfection.*

The auction rug, you see, had a good chance of being perfectly non-perfect in my home. Though the stated "fair market value" was $1,000, we scooped it up for a mere $500. When we got home, I put the rug in its place. Next morning, under the light of a new day, Dan caught me looking over the upstairs railing onto the rug.

"You don't like it," he said.

"It's not that."

"We shouldn't have done this."

("I did some reasearch into ..." continued)

- **Test color fastness** by rubbing a damp cloth over the rug in an inconspicuous spot.
- **When choosing size,** plan to leave 18 to 36 inches between the rug and the wall. Under a dining table, allow at least 4 feet all around the table to allow chairs to move in and out without getting hung up. Lay down newspaper when trying to visualize how a size will fit in a room. If you're between two sizes, get the larger one.
- **Old is okay.** Many rug investors pay more for old rugs that show obvious wear and sun damage. Why this adds value I can't explain. I just wish it held true for my complexion.
- **Consider the context.** Think of what will sit on the rug. In general, solid color furnishings work better on a patterned rug, and printed fabrics sit better on a solid rug. Varying the texture is also important. A distressed wood table will play well against a rug with a smooth, more refined texture.
- **You don't have to break the bank.** Of course, not all area rugs have to be Persian or precious. Woven sea grass and sisal can work in many interiors, and they are durable and inexpensive.

"It's so blue."

"It's as blue as it was last night."

"It's too non-perfect."

"You said you were sure."

"I *was* sure. *Then.* Just not *now.*"

He made a moaning sound like Lurch on *The Addams Family.*

A few evenings later, when Dan came home from work, three round rugs lay in the entryway like an invasion of flying saucers. "Where did these come from?" he asked.

"I found a rug store that does trades."

"You went to a rug trader?"

"He'll give us $500 for our rug."

"They're worse than used car dealers!"

"We'll recoup! If we apply the $500 to another rug, like one of these." My arm swept the floor Vanna White style.

"How much are these?" he asked nervously.

"Around $1,000, but really only $500 more because we can subtract the $500 credit from the auction rug. We would have spent $1,000 in the first place."

"We weren't going to spend anything in the first place!"

"We need an entry rug."

"*Need,*" he echoed.

"Half the money went to a good cause."

He rolled his eyes. "So which one do you like?" I point to my favorite. "If that's what you want," he said, with equal parts capitulation and exasperation.

We made the trade for a hand-tufted, wool Persian tabris, with no blue, that looked perfectly non-perfect. I counted my fingers.

So far we've dealt with the big stuff. But what about all the little stuff: the books, the dolls, the blue glass bottles? The next chapter will help you give your collectables a sure hand. . . .

24

Arranging Books, Collections, and Other Knickknacks

Turn a hodgepodge into an artful display

SO I'M AT THIS FASHION SHOW fundraiser, and this runway model sashays down the aisle with a skirt so sheer you can see her underwear—what there is of it. Another model wearing a head-piece with a pineapple and a canary follows. Somehow both models manage to look stunning.

Why is it that in fashion—as well as in home design—some stylish types can get away with moves that would make the rest of us look as if we were a few bottles short of a six pack? I mean, if I went around with a fruit bowl on my head and a see-through skirt, my kids would hide under the bed and my husband would dial 911.

For example, I once tried smudging eye pencil at the corners of my eyes the way I'd seen models do in a fashion magazine. All day people kept helpfully telling me my make-up was smeared. Some would just rub the corner of their eye to give me a hint. So much for cutting-edge style.

It's the same with home accessorizing. Some have a knack I lack. A top interior designer once told me she liked to put heads of raw cabbage in a bowl, mist them with water to make them look dewy fresh, and call that a centerpiece. I tried that once. When my dinner guests came, they walked into the kitchen carrying the centerpiece and asked if I needed help putting the groceries away. Another designer I know propped a black lacquered wooden ladder against a wall next to a long table. Though the ladder led to nowhere, the look was avant-garde, even existential. So I propped an old wooden ladder in my home, and the cleaning lady carried it out to the garage for me. I tried to explain to her the existential aspect of the design. She looked at me as though I didn't have all my chairs pulled up to the table and said, "Somebody might get hurt."

Determined to find the roots of my failure, I analyzed those homes whose owners have the collecting knack and uncovered these insights:

- **Place like items together.** A collection that is unified makes more of a statement than one that is scattered all around the house.
- **Context is everything.** When displaying a collection, put the items in the room where they belong. For example, put a collection of old maps in the study. Put perfume bottles on a bedroom dresser, and antique cooking gadgets in the kitchen.
- **Put collections in a defined area.** When encased in a cabinet, or on a designated shelf or bookcase, your would-be hodgepodge becomes orderly.
- **Group items that have a motif.** Pick a theme—like pineapples, turtles, or people with bad hair—and display representations, whether prints, photos, books, figurines, or woodcarvings.
- **Layer your display.** Put tall items in the back, and add variety by putting some items on a pedestal or a stack of books.
- **Don't go crazy.** Five—even fifteen—items make a collection. Fifty make a mess.

Thus I realized that what passes for style in some homes flops in mine. And probably yours, too. So I decided to study how some people can make everyday items look special. I thought about those people who raise collecting to an art form. They amass milk bottles, matchbooks, old magazine covers, sports memorabilia, animal brains in formaldehyde, and transform into art what would otherwise be trash. In their home a butterfly collection becomes a still life; in mine it looks like road kill. If I pull together a collection of anything, people either think I'm one of those crazy people who keeps dozens of cats or ask me when the garage sale is starting.

"Sometimes everyday pieces can turn into conversation starters," crows one home magazine in an article featuring people and their collections. I'll say. If I had baskets filled with dozens of rolling pins I'd start the whole neighborhood talking: "Poor Marni, she needs to let go."

Books vs. Beauty: Rivalry in the Library

Like most writers, I'm a reader. Like most readers, I have lots of books. Many are ugly. But books to me are like friends. I don't judge them by their covers, even if they do have red "USED" stickers on them left over from their college days. With books and friends, it's what's inside that matters.

Designers don't see it that way. To them, ugly is simply ugly. And ugly needs to go.

This philosophical clash recently played itself out in my home library. Two designers had their way with my sanctum, and I let it happen.

I first learned of this "service" while visiting a nearby home accessories boutique, another place where I love to look, but rarely buy. What looks great in the store becomes a white elephant in my home, I explained to the gal at the counter.

"We have a service," she said.

"Oh?"

She explained that the store owner, an interior designer, and her daughter, her protégé, would come to my home and, for $65 an hour, rearrange my accessories. They would also suggest others that might work. They could do several rooms in a couple of hours.

Sold!

They came armed with good taste and resolve. They briskly surveyed the house, then started in the guest room. They placed a wood-framed mirror over the bed between two sconces, dragged in a fake tree from the garage, put the television in the closet, and covered the sitting chair with a hand-woven throw.

Presto. In twenty minutes, the room went from ho-hum homey to haute hotel—with stuff I had all along! They worked their same magic in the family room. I was impressed. Then they hit the library, really a small loft flanked with floor-to-ceiling bookshelves, and skidded to a halt.

They looked at each other knowingly: "Are you up to this?" the mother asked her daughter.

"If you are," the daughter said.

"Are you up to this?" they asked me.

"Sure," I said. "Up for what?"

"We need to arrange your books."

"But they are arranged! Alpha by author and subject."

The two exchanged a knowing mother-daughter glance that I've used before myself. Translation: "This woman's nuts."

Now, I'm not the kind of person who is all function and no form. I've worn less-than-practical shoes because they looked better with my outfit. I've also put small kitchen appliances that I use every day inside cabinets rather than on counters because, even though they're less convenient, the kitchen looks better without the can opener and toaster in plain view.

But de-alphabetize my bookcases!?

The mother was already taking books out in stacks and handing them to her daughter. "We separate paperbacks from hard covers, then arrange by size," she said.

I must have looked horrified, because she added, "You can always put them back." She was on the stepladder socking away the paperbacks to the farthest back position on the highest shelf. As they passed stacks of books, they sorted them by spine height, tall to short like children lining up for choir. I watched as at a tennis match, mother handing to daughter, an old system giving way to a new order.

"Next, we'll group the hardbacks so they're more prominent," said the mother. I was speechless as I watched whole collections of my favorite authors, once meticulously grouped, now blown like pollen all over the room. I tried not to twitch visibly and periodically left the room to breathe. "Ideally, we would take the book jackets off," she continued, then paused and added: "But you probably don't want me to do that."

"What's wrong with book jackets?"

"Books look more handsome without them," she said.

"But jackets are like small talk," I defended. "It's a book's way of shaking hands and asking would you like to know me better?"

"I understand." She looked at her daughter. The look said: "A fruitcake."

Once the books were placed, the women gathered the family photos that I had randomly put on the shelves and grouped them onto one shelf. Then they added decorative items from around the house—some larger framed artwork, an iron church the size of a Kleenex box, and my daughter's handmade red papier-mâché cat. (Who would have thought that would make the vetting?) They employed a design principle I knew but had forgotten: When arranging objects of art, seek variation—the red papier-mâché, the iron church, the flat planes of glass. When they were done, the bookcases looked—I admit—artful. I may need five times longer to find a book, but I know this won't be the last time I sacrifice convenience for beauty.

Interior designer Lauri Ward devoted a section of her book, *Use What You Have Decorating,* to books. Her pointers for displaying them sound like my design duo's:

- **Separate paperbacks** from hardcovers and display hardcovers more prominently.
- **Arrange from tall to short.**
- **Put book spines flush** against the front edge of the shelf.
- **Don't mix photos with books,** put them on separate shelves. All books on one shelf, all photos on the next. Make frames the same material, say all silver or polished wood.
- **Place accessories** next to, not in front of, books.
- **Think in thirds.** If you have the space, arrange shelves so you have one-third books, one-third art objects, one-third open space.

One shelf space I have found to be even more challenging to decorate than bookshelves is that gap between the upper kitchen cabinets and the ceiling. Mostly, I've seen this done two ways: not done, or overdone. Not done works in ultramodern homes, where sleek and clean are the rule. But often that's not the case and not done just looks neglected. More often, I've seen DIY decorators put up more bric-a-brac than you see at a county fair. My goal was to divine an aesthetic balance between a sterile kitchen devoid of décor and one falling prey to collective clutter. Here's how I conquered The Gap.

Chicken in the Kitchen

The chickens inspired the breakthrough. This was apt, because I'd been a chicken when I faced the task of accessorizing my kitchen.

Unlike many people who can throw perfectly selected and well-proportioned knickknacks on kitchen cabinets and counters, I didn't get that gene. Whenever I arrange accessories in that odd space between ceiling and cabinetry, they look as appealing as last week's leftovers. In my last home, I didn't have this problem. My cabinets went to the ceiling. But here I have The Gap. After several failed attempts to decorate this space, I finally took every doodad off and went for that just-moved-in look.

Then I found the chickens. I bought a lovely 20-inch-tall ceramic rooster and hen and brought them home to roost on one of my upper kitchen cabinets, where they cackled: "You need to decorate the rest." This was a step, I told them.

"What are chickens doing in the kitchen?" asks my youngest.

"Laying eggs?" I suggest.

"Mom, they're not real."

"Shoot. Ripped off again."

"They look funny there."

"Shhh! They'll hear you," I whisper.

"Seriously, why are they up there?" she whispers back.

"To cry fowl when you don't eat your vegetables, or you fight with your sister, and to cluck at your Dad when he can't open the mayonnaise jar." I look at the chickens on their perch. They shake their beaked heads and cluck disapprovingly.

Dan comes in. "Why's everyone whispering?" he whispers.

Our youngest points to the chickens.

"What the heck?" he asks.

"We need to decorate The Gap."

"Why? We can't reach anything up there." Men.

Now, I'm not one of those women who need to fill every empty space. Some women use cabinet tops as a catchall and put every old jelly jar, milk jug, fake plant, and basket up there along with the house cat. That looks cluttered. But the other extreme—nothing—looks like a missed opportunity.

I wave my arm at our cabinet tops and try to explain: "I want enough but not too much, a few well-chosen items that together create a still life without looking affected. It should look as if it evolved and wasn't forced. The chickens are the first step." At this billing, the chickens puff their feathers and buck buck proudly.

Dan rolls his eyes and says, "Whatever you want." As usual, I take those words and run.

Only this time, I didn't get far. Pathetic as it seems, I needed professional help to put chatchkes in my kitchen. So I asked Karlie

---

Between the two designers, here's what I learned works best when accessorizing The Gap.

- **Use kitchen-related items.** Bowling pins, no. Rolling pins, yes. Art books, no. Cookbooks, yes. And, unless you're decorating a fraternity house, don't put up bottles representing every brand of beer you've ever consumed.
- **Go big.** As with other accessories, here, too, big and few look better than small and many.
- **Vary color, shape, and texture.** Put a smooth, curved ceramic object next to a roughly woven rectangular basket, and the basket next to something made of iron. Put round beside square, low beside tall. Fill with nice greenery.
- **Don't cover every surface.** Put accessories on a few cabinets, but not every one. Likewise, accessorize a corner of a counter and the kitchen island, but leave other surfaces bare.
- **Give items a lift.** If crown molding surrounds the upper edge of your cabinets, the top of your cabinets probably sinks several inches below the molding. To give objects a lift, use foam blocks, like florists use. It's light and cheap.
- **Go faux for plants and fruit.** Think low maintenance. Don't put anything on high that you have to water or that could rot.
- **Clean often.** But accept that whatever you put up there will acquire a layer of dust scum no matter how meticulously you clean the house.

Adams, the interior designer I'd leaned on before, to come up with a scheme. I sent her pictures of the gap, and she sent me a penciled schematic of the size, scale, and types of objects I should look for, a picture of a kitchen I should strive to emulate, and some tear sheets from a catalog to get me started. Her remedial kitchen accessorizing kit came with a reasonable bill for two hours of her time, or $200, which was worth it.

"Cheap," the chickens squawked.

With plan in hand, I sought and bought. My next challenge was placement. Again, I froze. I called my designer neighbor Sherrie Corbett, who refused payment but accepted lunch. Together we surveyed Karlie's pictures and my haul: two glass hurricane lamps, a large, low, oval painted planter with a dried dark green hedge, some fake lemons, a bundle of curly willow, an old iron dinner gong, an antique reproduction of a wooden egg crate, sheaves of wheat, a round wire basket, a tall ceramic urn the color of butter, and the chickens. I climbed up and down the ladder while she instructed placement. When we were done, the space looked balanced but not cluttered, professional but still personal, since all the pieces were ones I would have picked to begin with if only I'd known how.

A few nights later, I hosted my ladies book club. "I love what you've done on your kitchen cabinets," one guest oozed.

"Oh, that?" I look up as if I hadn't given the space much thought at all. "I just threw a few odds and ends up there," I said, winking at the hens. And they winked back.

Most designers agree that a room isn't finished unless it has some greenery in it. Mold doesn't count. Whether real or silk, plants and floral arrangements add a soft, natural touch. They also help unite the house and yard, provided, of course, the fakes are convincing (no phony colors) and the real plants are healthy. But should you go with live or fake? Or some combination of the two? How do you choose good fakes, and how can you have more success with the real thing?

25

Flowers and Houseplants

Getting good fakes, and helping what's alive thrive

AT MY GYM THERE'S A STICKER on the sound system that reads: "YES, THEY'RE REAL!" Then in smaller type below: "And so what if they're not?" I'd like to put a sign like this in my home. The defensive posture sums up my love-hate relationship with silk flowers.

The problem is, I agree with the snooty interior designers who think fake flowers are to the real thing what dime-store novels are to real romance. However, I also believe there's a point where one has to get real and buy fakes. While these highbrow types would never settle for charlatan botanicals, my home is full of falsies because I have a life and a budget.

See, I was once a purist. I scoffed at synthetic fabrics, fake jewelry, forged hair color, phony nails, and, yes, fraudulent florals. Then I got older and, if not wiser, certainly more practical. Those all-cotton 501 jeans? Traded out for jeans with a little synthetic stretch woven in. They move when I do and don't stretch out two sizes between washings. Cubic zirconias have also found a place in my life. And, while I'm not confessing to anything personally here, I also believe good arguments exist for hair color and acrylic nails.

Which brings me back to artificial flowers, which, like me, really have come a long way over the years. Now I know silk flowers don't smell like fresh rain, or gracefully drop a petal like a ballerina drops a slipper, or refract light as delectably as their real counterparts, but they have other considerable qualities: They never die,

---

If you use a floral designer to create a custom arrangement—as opposed to buying a pre-made arrangement or buying stems and arranging them yourself—don't do it the way I did. For an arrangement for my entry table, I consulted a designer at one of the top silk floral and plant companies in the area, and the results were disastrous. Here's what I learned the hard way:

- **Have the designer come to your home.** I met this designer at her store because she would have charged $65 an hour to visit my home. I brought her Polaroids. (Many floral designers will come to your home at no charge.)
- **Don't assume the designer understands your tastes.** Know what look you're going for and have pictures of it. Remember, the most beautiful arrangements may be wrong for your home. For example, an exotic tropical combo is a faux pas in a French Country setting. In my sorry case, the designer was going for a sort of Ritz Carlton look, which works great in the Ritz, but looked way too extroverted in my more humble home.
- **Agree on size and volume.** If it's a dining table centerpiece, is it important that seated guests be able to see over it? Don't let the designers oversell you. The arrangement I brought home was easily two times bigger than it should have been. To get around it,

("If you use a floral designer ..." continues)

are low maintenance, bend and come with generous stem lengths (allowing for more flexible styling), won't mar the furniture with water rings, and are economical. (Though you may pay dearly for good quality up front, you come out ahead when you consider the cost of repeatedly buying real flowers.)

Some of the newer silks and dyes make fake flowers look so real that last Christmas, when I put out silk poinsettias and garlands, my dogs actually watered them for me. Which proves that there is such a thing as too much realism.

("If you use a floral designer ..." continued)

you had to lean sideways, and it blocked all the views to the rooms off the entryway. A décor-savvy friend came over and started yanking out flowers while I yanked out my hair. After we'd plucked more than half of the flowers, the arrangement started to show promise.

- **Find out the store's return policy up front.** Know what recourse you have if you're not pleased. That was my next shocker. I couldn't return any of the flowers in my inflated arrangement, the store told me, because they had been cut. No refunds. No credits. No exchanges. So I had just paid $700 for $350 worth of usable flowers. (The designer did reshape the remains of my debacle for no charge.) I was furious.

- **Once it's home, keep it clean.** One designer told me she didn't mind silk arrangements, but she did mind that so many are dirty. Spiff them up often with a feather duster or with spray-on silk flower cleaner. Spray the plant or flowers and poof, the dust disappears. (Which reminds me of those hand sanitizers that don't require water: Where does all the dirt go?)

- **Keep food in the kitchen.** If an arrangement has dried fruit or vegetables in it, put it in the kitchen or dining area, not in the living room or a bedroom.

But to get this kind of authenticity, you have to choose well. Don't go for any flowers you wouldn't see in nature. That means no blue roses, and no chartreuse Gerber daisies, says floral designer Teresa Perry, of Dana Point, California. If you're not sure whether a color is botanically correct, visit a nursery, ask someone who knows, or look it up. Just a shade off—like a too-purple lilac—can kill any chance your guests will leave pondering: Does she or doesn't she?

Despite my traumatic experience, I still believe that silk flowers—well chosen and well done—have their place in today's homes. It isn't practical to spend the time or money it would require to buy and tend florals that die in a week. But, given the right occasion (sweethearts, listen up), nothing, nothing beats real flowers. You walk in the door with two dozen honest-to-God roses, and I guarantee, the love in your life will gladly stash the fakes temporarily and delight in the real thing.

When choosing between real and silk plants, consider where they're going. I like to put silk plants in high places, where greenery is needed, but where I'm not likely to go with a watering can. They're also a good choice for a dark corner, where a real plant would croak. If you're like me, however, and every live houseplant you buy winds up in the morgue, don't wallow in guilt. Here's what you need to know. . . .

Help for Serial Houseplant Killers

It's not my fault. I didn't kill my houseplants. They were most likely dying on arrival. This was the best news I'd heard since learning that genes—and not anything I do—dictate my fingernail strength. So I can stop flogging myself about the fact that while some people have a thriving indoor garden, I have a botanical death row, and lousy nails.

Julie Bawden-Davis, founder of www.healthyhouseplants.com and author of *Indoor Gardening the Organic Way*, reassured me that houseplants die shortly after people bring them home because of what happened to them *before* they came home. (Okay, so I didn't tell her about the time I went away for two weeks, didn't hire a plant sitter, and left the heater blasting.)

"Many store-bought houseplants have bad childhoods and are set up to fail," she said. Most plants start life in a perfect environment. Full-time tenders administer ideal doses of light, water, fertilizer, and humidity while controlling the temperature. Caretakers also ply the plants with chemical stimulants and growth hormones, so they reach a perky marketable prime fast. These spoiled and drugged plants then leave this womblike environment for the harsh real world. They're trucked in the dark for days, through temperatures more erratic than a menopausal woman's, before arriving at garden centers where they are overwatered and exposed to the wrong amount of light. Unaccustomed to mistreatment, they become stressed and prone to pests and disease. These ailments don't show up for several weeks, a point that usually hits shortly after you've brought them home. Then they collapse after too much partying, like Lindsay Lohan.

"The poor things," I said, dabbing my eyes.

"You can't just cut them off like that," Bawden-Davis said.

"It would be like someone suddenly boarding up every Starbucks at once, leaving caffeine addicts to dry out."

"Exactly," she said. "These plants need a proper detox program."

"At first people would be okay, but soon they'd start lying in traffic."

"So you can imagine how the plants feel."

Although I agree with Bawden-Davis and many interior designers who say that a room isn't finished unless it has greenery, I had given up on real plants. "Sunk money," my husband said every time I brought one home. Sadly, he was right. So, as I mentioned, I switched to silk plants. They're a compromise I make when faced with the alternative of dead greenery or no greenery. I explained all this to Bawden-Davis, who motivated me to give houseplants another try.

Because I didn't want to go on being a serial plant killer, I listened to Bawden-Davis's tips for plant-challenged folks:

- **Shop the right store.** At the garden center, take a good look around at the stock to see that it looks healthy. The seller should have houseplants in shade. Plants that have burn marks have gotten too much sun. Really long stems and few leaves indicate that the plant isn't getting enough light and is reaching for it. The combination of drooping leaves and wet soil may be a sign of fungal infection.
- **Pick the right plants.** Opt for hearty, hard-to-kill houseplants. Here are five of Bawden-Davis's favorites for beginners. All grow in medium to low light.
  - Pothos grows anywhere.
  - Chinese evergreens offer nice color variation.
  - Snake plants add architectural interest.
  - Corn plants, because they're tall, make great floor plants.
  - African violets are the easiest of all indoor flowering plants to care for.
- **Detox plants once they're home.** The best way is to repot them. Shake out the soil they came in, rinse the roots gently, and replant them in organic soil. Bawden-Davis likes soil that contains mycorrhizal fungi, a friend to roots. Or leach the soil by running water through the pot until water streams out. To help new plants overcome their chemical dependence, Bawden-Davis fertilizes them with liquid seaweed. "They may go through a little sad phase," she said, "because you've taken away their candy. Then they will perk up and thrive."

Her argument was convincing: Apart from looking nice, healthy indoor plants are good for your home because they make for cleaner air. "Green plants are the only things on the planet that absorb carbon dioxide and give off oxygen," she said. They actually help the ozone layer. Plants also absorb volatile organic

---

Julie Bawden-Davis assured me that even I could keep plants alive, almost effortlessly, and without a plant service. Here's how:

- **Soil.** Go organic. Use liquid seaweed fertilizer after replanting or when the plant is stressed. Feed regularly with organic fertilizer, which is longer lasting and better for the environment.
- **Light.** Don't buy a plant to fill a particular corner if the light's not right. At first the plant may do all right, because it will live off its light reserves. When those are tapped, however, the plant will drop leaves and likely die. Instead, place plants in the best light for them. Read the tag to determine the plant's light needs—low, medium, or bright. Then do the shadow test: When the light coming inside is at or near its peak, put your hand over a white piece of paper. If your hand's shadow is barely visible, you have low light. More discernible, you have medium light, and a high contrast shadow means bright light. (If the room has full-spectrum or fluorescent light, that counts.) Most houseplants thrive in medium light.
- **Water.** The chief reason houseplants die is improper watering. Water plants—with warm water—only when they need it. Regimens, like watering every Thursday, backfire. Plants need different amounts of water based on the season (less in winter, when growth is slower) and other factors. (Plants in heated or air-conditioned homes and hanging plants dry out faster than plants rooted in the ground outside.) Generally, houseplants should "approach dryness," before you water. They like to be moist, but not soggy. Test: Insert a wooden stick in the dirt (as if testing a cake). If it comes out clean, water.

compounds from the air and thrive on them. "Ideally, you should put plants wherever you spend a lot of time, such as near your desk or bed." I immediately thought of a few less fragrant places that would benefit.

"But," I asked, "what if the only plant life I can support is in the kids' rooms, where green mold rings float in old cocoa cups?"

"Not to worry," she said.

("Julie Bawden-Davis assured me ..." continued)

- **Humidity.** If a plant's leaves have brown tips or a plant isn't flowering, it may need more humidity. Boost the humidity level by creating a humidity tray. Fill a cachepot (a decorative style of pot with no holes) with an inch or two of marbles or chunky gravel. Put water in the pot until the water line is just under the surface of the rocks. Set the plant in its plastic container on that. When you water, runoff will drain into the gravel, collect, evaporate, and create humidity. Grouping plants also boosts humidity because plants draw moisture off each other.
- **Repotting.** When roots start growing out the drain hole, or when too many roots cause water to rush through the pot quickly, repot the plant in a container just one size bigger. Don't try the lazy idea (mine) of putting the plant in a much bigger pot to avoid future repotting. If you put the plant in too large a pot, the roots won't be able to absorb all the water and they'll rot.
- **Protecting furniture.** To prevent wet plant containers from marring furniture and floors, put smaller plants on an old towel after watering. When they're done dripping, set them back in their spots on cork coasters, which look better than tacky plastic saucers. Set larger pots on cork coasters, too.

TIP: If water rings have marred the wood on a piece of furniture, try rubbing mayonnaise on the ring mark. Let the mayo sit a few minutes, then wipe it off.

I was still skeptical. When I first bring home a houseplant, it looks so robust. It fools me with its insincere perkiness, like an insurance agent. Three weeks later, when I think the plant and I are coexisting nicely, it collapses, as if it has suffered an aneurysm. Then it defies all attempts for revival and stubbornly dies.

But I can't kid myself. Live plants, whether in an office, hotel room, or home, say *life thrives here*. So I got some more botanical advice and became determined to try my hand—and its brown thumb—at the real thing again.

PART V

Rooms for a Reason

Kids' rooms, home theaters, offices, guest rooms, laundry and mudrooms, garages

Up till now we've covered general interior design principles: discovering your style, creating a plan, choosing backgrounds, furnishing, and accessorizing. Now we're going to get specific. This next section delves into the hallmarks and hassles of decorating rooms dedicated to the varied acts of daily living, from raising children and doing laundry to parking the car and enjoying a good movie. . . .

26

Kids' Rooms

Where decorating and parenting clash

"MOM, YOU KNOW THAT CEILING at Rainforest Café?" We're driving and for some certifiably insane reason I'm letting my youngest daughter describe her ideal bedroom. "I'd like a ceiling like that, one that lights up with lightning. And you know those animals they have?"

"The gorillas and elephants that come roaring to life, making you choke on your mango smoothie?"

"Yeah, I'd like some like those in the corner."

Just when I'd conquered the decorator wars with my husband, I had to start dealing with my kids. By comparison, coming to an agreement with my husband was a cinch. Wise man that he is, he quickly saw the upside of leaving the home decorating to me. It was either that or domestic homicide. Our truce is modeled after the relationship between the U.S. Congress and the president. (Trust me, girlfriends, this works.) He gets executive privilege. (Be sure to call it that.) That means he gets veto power and final budget approval, *but* he brings no proposals to the floor or to the house (or to the walls or the ceiling, for that matter). That's my domain. I'm the Congress.

But who knew my kids would come on like a pack of noisy lobbyists?

"And I'd like a furry phone, like my slippers." My daughter has locked onto this taste-challenged vision like a heat-seeking missile. As she describes this phone slipper I get a flash of Maxwell Smart talking on his wingtip.

"I want my walls and ceilings painted like sky," she continues. "Only on one wall I want a large sun painted with a face on it, and I want gold lamps." For drapes, she wants dark blue panels with a moon on one, a sun on the other.

I'm trying to imagine how all this—the rain forest, gold lamps, furry phones, and touches of the universe—will blend in her room. I'm hit with a vision of Carl Sagan meets the Crocodile Hunter at Graceland.

At times like this, I appreciate my mother. Though strict, she pretty much let my brother and I—angels have mercy—decorate our bedrooms the way we wanted, which at one point involved a horrid combination of Indian tapestry, macramé hangings, and walls of black-light posters. I can still hear her sagely saying: "That's what doors are for."

My payback is coming. At the moment, I can hit the override button when my girls launch into one of their wild decorating schemes. However, when I look at their rooms, decorated with co-ordinating Pierre Deux fabrics, hand-painted wallpaper, and dolls carefully coiffed on a shelf, I wonder when they'll want their rooms to be more a reflection of them and less of me. How will I handle it when they hit their teens and want to paint their rooms black or hang body-pierced, tattooed, barely clad rock idols on the wall?

Will I say: "When you're paying the mortgage, you can decorate the way you like"? Will I be like Mom and bend like a green reed? Or will I compromise and let them bring me their proposals and exercise judicious veto privilege? In my heart, I believe home should be a place where kids can express their own emerging styles—which human nature dictates must contrast with the style of their parents.

Not long after I spoke with the experts about kids' rooms, I put their philosophies to the test. The day came that my older daughter was becoming a teenager and had moved past the flowered bedspread and dolls. . . .

Teen Decorating: A Language All Its Own

My thirteen-year-old daughter had been badgering me to redecorate her room for months. I was stalling for good reason. Last time

It's healthy for children to express themselves. However, letting kids actually do as they please with their bedroom décor takes a level of parental tolerance I'm not sure I have. So I called in some experts, and here's the consensus:

- **Choose your battles.** The family therapists agree that it's not worth fighting about little stuff—as in room décor. Save your hard stands for the day your daughter wants to ride on the back of a Harley with a Hell's Angel and no helmet.
- **Create controlled areas for "expression."** "I put bulletin board material on their walls and let them put up what they like," said Carol Lindquist, a therapist friend of mine who has two teenage sons. "They'll be gone so soon. Then I can decorate however I want."
- **Compromise.** "At some point you need to relinquish the room to them," said James Charles. "Do the fundamentals: furniture, bedding, drapery, paint, and carpet, and let them 'accessorize.' No designer can envision what a teen wants."
- **Close the door.** Good design has to take a back seat to good relationships (just, please, don't tell my husband). If letting kids create their own space makes home a place they feel accepted, that's probably worth a little visual discomfort.

we did her room, when she was six, I could get what I liked while making her think it was her idea. Now that she's older and on to me, she has opinions. Loud, clashing, ugly opinions. She also has her own language. To understand our decorating discussions, you need a glossary:

Burns—a searingly painful experience. When I kiss her good-bye in front of her friends, "It burns."

Deep—good. Her horse is deep.

Dorm—her bedroom.

Rude—any minor criticism, as in: "Honey, you need to wash your hair." "How rude."

Sick and Wrong—any minor allusion to reproduction, as in "The Johnsons' golden retriever had puppies." "That's just sick and wrong."

Snaps—really works. A good party snaps.

Undeep—not good. Her history teacher is undeep.

So she wants a "dorm that snaps" because "the dolls, the pink, and the flowers are totally undeep." True, her room no longer reflects her. She's grown into a non-frilly young woman who can't walk in heels, couldn't care less about make-up, and likes horses, horses, and horses, in that order. I, however, was not ready to give up the pink and the dolls.

"So what do you want?" I ask.

"Horse stuff."

"Like a bale of hay?"

"How rude."

"Why no pink?"

"It burns."

"Pink is feminine. Don't you want to be feminine?"

"That's just sick and wrong."

I establish ground rules. We have to work with the ballet-pink bathroom tiles. And we aren't going to paint; her walls are already a nice sage green. We'll limit the redecorating to fabric treatments: new bedding, a chair slipcover, and curtains for the window and shower. And we'll replace the dolls on the shelf with horse stuff.

"Snaps for me," she says.

"What colors were you thinking of?" I ask.

"Black."

"Black?" My eyebrows shoot up, where they will stay until my children are out of their teens.

"Black is deep."

"What else?"

"Brown. Maybe green."

"Sounds like an army jeep."

We head to the fabric store. "We need a lead fabric," I tell her, "a main fabric we can build around."

She pulls a red bandana print embossed into faux leather.

I light on a soft gray and green harlequin pattern.

She finds a lime leopard print.

I offer a large-scale charcoal, cream, and raspberry plaid.

She grabs a black and brown snakeskin.

And so it goes.

I practice the breathing exercises I learned in childbirth classes, which still come in handy at times like this.

"What are you doing?" she asks.

"Lamaze breaths," I pant.

"That's just sick and wrong."

At our fourth and final fabric store, I stumble across a charcoal and cream toile by Ralph Lauren with horse scenes all over it. It's lovely but can't be my idea. I set it out so my daughter can't miss it. When she discovers it, her eyes widen. "Score!" she yelps.

"YESS!" I think silently, but play down the victory and say, with a tinge of doubt, "We can probably work with that." We agree to make her bedspread out of the horse toile, then to add a green-

---

Amazingly, my daughter's ultimate choices followed the experts' rules for mixing patterns—and she didn't even know it. Here's a pattern primer:

- **Dare to mix.** It takes nerve, but a variety of well-mixed patterns not only energizes a room, but also makes the difference between a room that's boring and predictable and one that's creatively custom.
- **Know the five main pattern categories.** They are (1) textured, such as stamped velvet, damask, and sheer; (2) geometric, non-organic shapes, including herringbones, medallions, and chevrons; (3) stripes, checks, and plaids; (4) florals; and (5) large-scale motifs.
- **Choose a color palette.** The easiest is a two-tone palette. Pick varied patterns in only these two colors, say blue and cream, and you'll be safe. But if you opt for more colors, try to stick to three colors plus one or two neutrals, such as black, white, cream, or gray.
- **Choose the mood.** Brocade, damask, and velvet say luxurious. Cotton and corduroy say casual.
- **Choose a lead fabric.** Start with a main fabric that will be prominent in the room, say on the bedspread. This pattern often has a larger motif or floral design. Next pull in a geometric, plaid, or check; a stripe; and a textured solid to complement it.
- **Get samples.** Don't bypass this stage. The larger the samples, the better. Be sure to view them together in the room where you will be using them.
- **Anchor with solids.** When blending patterns, throw in a solid for grounding.
- **Pay attention to detail.** Reprise patterns and colors in trims, fringes, and fabric-covered edging.
- **Be tactful (or sneaky, if necessary).** When doing this for your child's room, make sure the child believes the choices are all his or her own.

striped ticking, a small black check, a raspberry solid linen (which I call light red—not pink) to tie in the bath tiles, and, against all reason, a soft green fabric she loves, which has cream polka dots the size of marbles. The combination looks as weird as it sounds, but it also all works, because it's her. Back in my daughter's dorm, we roll out the fabrics.

"Do you like them?" I ask.

"Pretty deep," she says. "But it would really snap if we added a zebra fur pillow."

"That burns."

27

Home Theaters for Household Drama

The makings of a home theater widow

IN THE STILL OF THE NIGHT I hear him moan: "Marantz, Paradigm, Triad."

Mixed in his business papers is more sound evidence: glossy pictures of speakers, woofers, DVD players, and receivers. Sometimes he says he's going to run errands and doesn't come home for hours.

And I know.

"Visiting sound rooms again, are you?" I say, arching one eyebrow accusingly.

"All right," Dan confesses. "I really want a home theater."

"But our home *is* a theater."

"I want a good system with a great set of speakers to make music and movies sound better, even sports." I don't point out that the only way sports could sound better is with a mute button. "I want surround sound."

"What, the kids, dogs, vacuum cleaner, and dishwasher all running at once aren't enough for you?"

"You don't understand."

"All right," I relent. I know how fragile and vulnerable men can feel at certain stages of their lives, the way women feel their entire lives. "If it makes you happy and you promise to never wear gold neck chains or dye your hair."

See, I could have easily lived in the days of Jane Austen, when family rooms were called drawing rooms, because they actually drew people together to converse, read, do stitchery, draw, and play chess or piano. But, alas, drawing rooms have devolved into family rooms, frequently outfitted with big screens and sound systems. And, for the truly obsessive, home theaters, which, Dan explains, include not two but *six* speakers, a big screen, a DVD player, a VCR, a CD player, and a receiver, which plays quarterback for all the above.

"So," I say, struggling to put this in some relevant context, "home theaters are to televisions and stereos what Isabella Fiore is to handbags?"

"Right, I think," Dan says, warily.

Over the next few months, he spends hours poring over manuals and Web sites. His eyes become bloodshot and his forehead perpetually wrinkled. "Why's this so hard?" I ask.

"You go to these sound rooms. Every system sounds great. Everyone tells you his system is best. You can't compare any side by side, or know how any will sound in your room. And there are no deals."

He finds out that higher-end manufacturers only work with authorized dealers, who don't discount the products. This is heartbreaking for a man who gets an A+ in bargain hunting (which, averaged with my grade, brings the household GPA to about a C+). Like a good therapist, I let him talk.

"You wonder whether you'd really notice the difference between a $1,200 receiver and a $3,000 receiver. One guy insists you need

To help others in their quest for a home theater, I combined tips from Mark Cleveland, home theater consultant with Listen Up in Denver, with Dan's novice efforts:

- **Don't go strictly by demos,** because how a system sounds in a demo room isn't what counts; how it sounds in your home is what counts. Many dealers will demo speakers in your home. Ask what recourse you have if they sound lousy after they're installed.

- **Expect to be totally confused** by the process, but don't fall prey to sales hype. Trust your own eyes and ears.

- **Do your homework** by visiting lots of demo rooms and friends' home theaters. When you know what you're after, decide on a budget. Systems can range from $400 to $300,000. "Realism gets better with money," said Cleveland, adding that owners of homes in the $300,000 to $500,000 range tend to spend $10,000 to $15,000 on a system. Find a home-theater expert you trust who'll take you through the process.

- **Splurge on speakers.** When determining where to spend the most money, remember: Your speakers, more than anything else, will determine how your system will sound. Don't overspend on the components or cables.

- **Don't be tempted** by the price cutting on the gray market. You can get some items for less over the Internet, but you won't have the warranty or the technical support and guarantee that a local company can provide.

- **If you wind up with more remotes** than you have arms and legs, get one remote that integrates all others. "Remotes are by far the biggest problem," said Cleveland. "They seem like an afterthought, but they're the most important piece of equipment." He likes the versions that have a small TV monitor in them and operate like Windows software. Get your home theater guru to program it. With practice, even a Luddite like me can use one of these.

- **If you don't share your partner's home theater passion,** go back to the drawing room.

$2,000 silver strand cable; another says his $200 cable system would be fine. Who do you believe? I don't want to buy more than I can appreciate."

And so he goes, ferreting his innocent way through the caveat emptor of cost, labels, real quality, and braggadocio.

Six months later, he's made his decisions, the system is in, and love is in the air. Dan rubs his hands over the components, inhales their newness, and sighs. As for me, the home theater widow, I'm out of the picture. I don't even know how to turn the TV on anymore.

A few weeks after the system is in, I have to call Dan while he's out of town on business. "Help!" I cry, interrupting his business dinner. "The girls want to watch a DVD!" He starts giving me instructions so complicated I have my youngest take over. The process involves three of our six remotes. But before he hangs up, he asks to speak to me again.

"Yes?" I say, hoping for sweet nothings.

"I miss my home theater," he says. And I know I'll need to make room for this new love.

Home Theater Static: You Want to Put That Where?

"How big?" I say, incredulously. The installer for our home theater system is standing in our family room discussing speaker size and placement, and already there's static. "I'm not sure I heard you," I continue. "You want to put the rear speakers on 3-foot stands, so they're at ear level?"

"Ideally," he says, "the assembly stands about this high." He puts his hand at the level of my mouth and I'm tempted to bite him. "But you can get the wood veneer in any color you like," he adds, as if color solves the problem.

Having two faceless totem poles at the rear of my family room isn't in my decorating plan. I say this as politely as I can, which makes my husband cringe. Dan hates looking like an idiot, even by proxy. Me, I don't mind. Turns out this home theater system, which Dan has spent months obsessing over, has six speakers and a stack of components almost as tall as I am. I would like to make them heard and not seen.

"What's plan B?" I ask. We agree to mount the rear speakers in the ceiling and place the subwoofer behind the sofa—not acoustically ideal, but aesthetically acceptable. The three front speakers, the installer says, we can mount "unobtrusively" (love that) inside the shelves of our built-in. "Can we push them way back on the shelf and put books or plants in front of them?"

He looks at Dan sympathetically. "Ma'am, you're looking to maximize vertical and horizontal sound dispersion."

"No, I'm looking to make sure my family room doesn't look as if it's a set-up for a Who concert."

"Who?"

"Oh never mind." It's okay if sound system professionals make me feel like an idiot, but I hate when they make me feel old.

"It's the same in every house," says the installer, trying to be diplomatic because he wants the business. "The lady wants something discreet that blends. The husband wants big and functional."

Left to Dan and the installer, the family room décor would consist of a large bean-bag chair and a cooler for a six-pack, encircled by giant speakers and one huge screen television. Which is why the world has wives.

Actually, long ago Dan and I made a deal. We agreed that if one partner wanted something in the home design arena that the other partner didn't, then the reluctant party had to cave in, so long as what the gung-ho party wanted was not immoral or illegal. This was an essential pact for maintaining my sanity, since, just for example, I'm married to a man who believes box springs aren't necessary and that headboards are a total waste.

If you're on the verge of installing a home theater system, here's more advice from Listen Up's Mark Cleveland:

- **The good news.** Speakers don't have to be eyesores. Ceiling or wall-mounted speakers can always replace big ugly box speakers. Speaker screens come in many colors, and their borders can be painted, stained, or wallpapered to disappear into the background.
- **The bad news.** You can't hide speakers behind the drapes or a bookcase. And mounting speakers in the wall or ceiling will compromise sound quality. As Cleveland said: "A set of $14,000 inset wall speakers can sound great, but a set of $7,000 box speakers could sound even better." Most homeowners (who want to continue living happily with their mates) sacrifice a little sound quality for aesthetics. Mature men have learned: What flies in a frat house won't in most family rooms.
- **Pad the cell.** The quality of the sound will be better if the room has rugs, drapes, and furniture. So, men, get your priorities straight.
- **Get the right installer.** If you buy components from a source that does not provide the installation, you will have to pick an installer, which can be as hard as picking components. Interview several installers, but be aware that most come with a product line and an agenda. Using one company for everything has advantages.
- **Get the installation quote.** Be sure to ask for a cap on labor costs. Our installer bid ten hours and billed for seventeen. We paid for fourteen but ended in an argument. According to Cleveland, fixed bids work best.
- **Consider it an investment.** Done well, a home theater system is a feature home buyers appreciate—and even expect to see in higher-end homes.
- **Intruder alert. If you hear odd noises,** or think someone may be bombing the house, check the home theater before dialing 911.

Two weeks after the system is in, Dan is sitting in the metrically perfect place on the sofa calibrated to receive maximum listening and viewing pleasure, and grinning like Alfred E. Neuman. He's watching *Pearl Harbor* on DVD, not so much because he likes the movie, but because he wants to experience the bombing scene. This is the fundamental difference between men and women. The scene with the dive bombers begins. "Listen to that!" he shouts like I'm deaf and starts whooping in a way I haven't heard since the Rams beat the Patriots. "The planes sound like they're right over us!"

If you'd like to keep up with the times and fashionably hide your big screen, here are some options:

- **Store it in an armoire.** This is a lovely option if you have the space. If the armoire is old, be sure the interior shelves will support the television. You may need to add reinforcement. Be prepared to cut a hole in the back for cords.

- **Build in custom cabinets.** If you can sink the television into the wall or cabinet, you've won half the aesthetic battle—hiding the sides (not an issue for plasmas). When designing a built-in, consider putting the television on a shelf that can pull out and swivel. Add doors to cover the screen when it's tucked away. Build it with access in mind for the day the repairman needs to come.

- **Have a trunk show.** A clever carpenter can build the television into a trunk, so it rises out with the touch of a remote. Great for the foot of the bed.

- **Install shutters.** Covering the face of the television with shutters only works if the unit sits flush on an exterior wall. (On an interior wall, this seems hokey.) When the television is on, fold open the shutters as if on a window.

- **Make it a mirror.** Some sets, including one made by Philips, turn into framed mirrors when off. Check that the reflective glass doesn't impair TV quality.

"I can get the same effect driving by the airport on the freeway!" I yell back, still not getting why we had to spend all this money on better noise.

"It's so real!" he shouts.

Indeed. The other night, right after I'd put the girls to bed, I heard thumping. "Stop kicking the wall!" I yelled up the stairs.

"Honey," Dan said, "that's not the kids, it's the woofer." He pointed behind the couch. I got that idiot feeling again, followed by feelings of vertigo and the need to sit down.

("If you'd like to keep up with..." continued)

- **Hang a tapestry.** You can install a tapestry on a rod in front of the set if the screen is flush with the wall. Have the rod swivel open, or add a cord to pull the tapestry up like a roman shade.
- **Use a decorative folding screen.** If the TV sits in a corner, you can install the screen in front of it, or use a pair of screens on hinges attached to the wall. For viewing, fold these open.
- **Disguise it as a masterpiece.** Several companies offer framed artwork to cover your screen. VisionArt paintings allow the canvas to roll up inside the top of the frame. When the canvas is up, you watch television through the frame. (Costs range from $3,500 to $18,000.) TV CoverUp systems lift the painting on hinges so it projects 90-degrees from the wall. (Costs range from $300 for a manual lift to $2,600 for an automatic lift.) You can select art from the company's collection or provide your own. Tip: Don't pick a painting everyone knows.
- **Paint your own cover-up.** Ultimately, my artistic friend created her own cover up. On a large stretched canvas, she painted an abstract picture using colors in her room. To keep it lightweight, she didn't add a frame. When not watching the television, she props the canvas on the mantel over the television. Cost: $100, including paint and canvas. "I like that it's low-tech," she said. "It's one less thing that can break."

"Maybe," I said, "I'd feel better if you could just surround me with a little soft music."

Masking the speaker is one issue, but what about the big screen? If, like me, you dislike the look of anything TV or hi-fi related, you'll appreciate the lengths some people go to screen their big screens. And who can blame them? Here's to the effort! . . .

The Great TV Cover-Up

Something's wrong with this picture: In the 1960s, a television was the coolest thing a living room could have, better than an original Warhol. In the 1970s, color television was hotter than denim. By the 1980s—the decade quantity trumped substance—having several prominently displayed televisions equaled status. TV sets invaded kitchens, bedrooms, bathrooms, and car headrests. The 1990s were all about size; televisions grew large enough to cover a wall. After 2000, screens shrank to Calista Flockhart thin, and now they have so much definition you can see the nose hairs on a ladybug.

But no matter how televisions changed over the decades, this didn't: People shamelessly flaunted them.

Now *that's* changing. Recently, an entire industry has emerged to make televisions vanish, appearing only when needed, like a well-trained butler. This conspiracy to cover up has ushered in a new way to spend money to hide money you've spent. I'm no sociologist, but a trajectory of buy, buy better, buy bigger, now hide it can only mean one thing: As a culture, we're embarrassed and should be.

Frankly, I'm thankful we're over our need to show off our big screens. Televisions are ugly and not just when Barney or Camilla Bowles is on. Off, they look like scary slabs of one-way glass. As a child, I believed that if I could see the people inside the television, they could see me, even when the set was off. I'm still not sure that isn't the case, though now I don't think it's the actors who can see me but the FBI and my mother.

Though the trend is toward screening the screen, not everyone agrees on the best way. A friend told me about the afternoon she found a strange man in her bedroom showing her husband this screen-masking contraption, a framed painting you hang over your plasma.

"You push this button here," the salesman demonstrated, "and the screen comes down over the television. Et voilà! Van Gogh!"

Her gadget-loving husband was ecstatic. My art snob friend was horrified. While she looked for a motion-sickness bag, her husband looked for the checkbook. They needed to talk.

28

Home Office Is an Oxymoron

A warning to all those who say they want to work from home

I CAN STILL SEE HER AT THE KITCHEN TABLE. My youngest daughter, only three years old, all set up with her crayons, coloring. As I started moving a few crayons to set the table for dinner, she stretched her arms over her precious work space and screamed: "Don't! This is my office!"

"Hmm," I said, casting a casual glance at Dan. "Wonder where she learned that?"

Okay, so I'm a little territorial when it comes to my home office, where I try to patch together a livelihood as a freelance journalist and syndicated columnist. But you try carving out a domain in a home where your family thinks you only work to fill the dull moments between the times they need you. (What constitutes a "need," of course, is debatable.)

After a dozen or more years of trying to make working at home work, I've discovered that "home office" is an oxymoron. The term is an inherent conflict, like "necessary evil" and "blessed curse."

While working from home has definite advantages—no commute, flexible hours, more time with kids, lower dry-cleaning bills, and easy refrigerator access—it also has drawbacks. For one, I get no good watercooler scoop. Dan is no help there. Every day, it's the same: "Any good gossip from work?" I ask.

"Nope."

But the real problem is boundaries. In a real office, people know your role and let you do it. At home, you have a dozen roles, all blurred: I'm wife, mother, psychologist, plumber, nurse, cook, dog handler, chauffeur, forgotten violin or soccer uniform fetcher, and scribe on deadline.

After years of conditioning, my kids know that if I'm typing on the keyboard, they best not interrupt. Instead, they hover. They stand behind my back and breathe audibly. This is worse than if they'd just blurt out whatever they so desperately need, which is usually along the lines of, "Can I have an Oreo?"

Just as I'm finally getting my thoughts around the most profound passage I'm likely to write that day and start tapping it into the computer, a small arm reaches past me. BZZZT! The arm, attached to one daughter, sets off the electric pencil sharpener two feet from my ear, launching me out of my chair.

Dan generally tempers his approach, starting with something like, "Sorry, but . . ." and ending unpleasantly, as in "weren't the videos due back yesterday?" Or "Since you're home all day" (read "doing nothing while I'm traveling for a real job") "would you mind . . . having the garage door fixed . . . reseeding the lawn . . . and so on."

I can't imagine these scenes occurring in the Bonafide Workplace, which I often fantasize about. I picture myself dressed in nice, tailored clothes, riding an elevator with a bunch of soberly dressed people wearing contemplative expressions. We're discussing things like the stock market or North Korea, while holding steaming cups of black coffee. Ahh, civilization.

Then other days my family brings me back to earth. Like the day my kids snuck into my office to give me pictures they had each drawn of the plum tree outside. The tree had just let out its first pink blossoms, and they remembered how much I like the coming of spring. As they taped the pictures quietly above my desk, I stopped writing, hugged them both, and thought, for the hundredth time, how bittersweet it is, this home office.

Family Office! Whose Idea Was This?

So, knowing what I'd been through, you can imagine my shock when I came across an article in the *Wall Street Journal* reporting on a new design trend: the family home office. Now usually I don't recognize a bad home design idea until I've invested in it. But I knew instantly that at my home a family office would be as welcome as flu.

Proponents argue that having one room with dedicated workstations for every family member promotes family bonding. But how do you bond when Dad's on his blackberry, Mom's on the phone, and Johnny's playing a computer game?

I don't need more family rooms, I need fewer! At my house every square foot—including my so-called private office—is a family room. Take my vanity area, a 3-foot-long counter where I try to transform myself from Frankenstein's bride into someone you might want to have breakfast with. I've always envisioned my vanity as a place where I would sit in solitary reflection brushing my hair like the pensive subjects in a Mary Cassatt painting. Hardly! On a typical morning both my daughters are closer to me than clowns in a phone booth while they scavenge my drawers for make-up, jewelry, and hair products. Meanwhile, Dan inserts himself like a comma to swipe a hairbrush because one of the girls— exactly who remains the subject of debate—took his brush to school. Then they all follow me downstairs like a gaggle of geese wondering what's for breakfast.

And now we're supposed to share an office? Trying to be productive with the kids around is like trying to play chess in an amusement park. When we bought our last home, I was seduced by the home office in the model. It featured a built-in partner's desk, which we copied. I figured I'd have my work space, and Dan, when he needed to work at home, would have his—on the other side. Among the many reasons the partner desk arrangement failed was because Dan doesn't clean up anything until it supports plant life. Without going into any more gory details, just know this was a failed marital experiment. Spare yourself.

After we sold that house, we wedged ourselves into a small condo for several months while the home we're now in was being built. By small I mean you could vacuum the whole condo without moving the plug from the outlet. The dining area doubled as a group workspace. You want to feel stupid, sit with middle schoolers while they ask you to help them find the slope of a line, recall the continent that contains Swaziland, or give a scientific explanation of how waves are formed. This only confirms what kids already suspect: Parents don't know anything.

Humiliation aside, productivity loss is the real reason not to create a family office. Even Virginia Woolf recognized that to get anything done, a woman must have a room of her own. She addressed women, because men secure their own private spaces automatically by their tendency to have belly gas and to treat everyone around them as a secretary.

Seriously, to build healthy family relationships, reduce the rate of domestic assaults, and get some work done, every family member needs both a place in the home to bond with other family members, and a place to retreat so they can create voodoo dolls of other family members. Whether your family shares a home office or not, every student or working adult should have a work space to call his own.

Although they're an eyesore everywhere, cords and cables are at their worst in the home office. If cord management has you tied in knots, let's commiserate. . . .

If you are contemplating giving up a real office to work at home, or putting in an office where you live that isn't just for looks, heed this:

- **Lay ground rules.** Establish office hours, or a closed-door policy. Mine is: If the door's closed, don't come in unless you're dripping blood. Which, of course, happens. If you really want to get some work done, know your best times are between midnight and 4 A.M.
- **Don't share your office with another room.** Forget setting your office up as part of the kitchen, or family room, or even the master. Set up your office in a separate, dedicated room with doors and no other purpose.
- **Don't share your office with another person.**

Space permitting, an ideal workstation should have the following:

- **An adjustable chair.** This not only allows adults to set up ergonomic workstations but also means you won't have to buy a new chair as your child grows.
- **Dedicated storage.** If more than one person shares a work area, set aside storage space for each person. Have a common area for shared materials, such as scissors, staplers, and paper.
- **Light control.** If the area has a window, be sure you can pull blinds or curtains to prevent glare on computer screens.
- **Task lighting.** The area should have ambient light, from the ceiling, and task lighting over the desk or reading areas.
- **Open-door policy.** Have kids use computers in the open. This way parents can make screen checks to be sure Susie really is writing her Civil War paper and not just updating her MySpace page.

In Knots over Cord Management

A few times a year, I treat myself to a much-needed and—in my humble opinion—much-deserved massage. Lorrie, my masseuse, cracks my kinks and kneads through the knots I manufacture while sitting with bad posture at my desk and enduring the stress of family life, home remodeling, and deadlines. While she pummels my lumps, I vent my latest home improvement saga.

"I keep telling you," she says. "Live like me: Live in a rental and use your body for a living." She's got a point. Have you ever known a stressed massage therapist? She's not lying on this table in knots. "What is it this time?" she asks.

"Cords," I say.

"These in your neck?" She presses into a set that feels like tight ropes.

"Oww, no," I say. "The ones in my office. They're out of control. They look like a Medusa's head. Cords from the printer, the computer, the fax, the modem, three from the phone alone, all tumble off the desk like serpents. I think they're breeding. They slither onto the floor, and work their way under my skin. Now they're in my neck."

"Uh-hmm." She presses her thumbs into a knot the size of a hamster.

"Ouch," I say.

"Relax."

I breathe deeply and look at the wall clock. I'm ten minutes into a fifty-minute massage and I'd better get busy if I'm going to unwind. Then, through the dimmed lights, I notice the wall clock's dark cord trailing down the light-colored wall to the outlet five feet below. To the left, I see her electric massage-oil warmer sitting on a skirted table beside assorted aromatic oils. The warmer's brown cord travels several horizontal feet, dipping slightly before plugging into an outlet.

"Don't these cords bug you?"

"What cords?"

"The ones crawling all over your walls."

"Nope."

"There are experts for this kind of thing."

"And medications."

"Seriously. I just called a cord-management consultant."

"A what?"

"He's going to squirrel away all my cables and cords."

"Good, because your problems are way beyond what I can do for you."

"You're saying I shouldn't worry about the cords in my life."

Of course, I grilled the cord-management expert and discovered these trade secrets:

- **For cord jungles** under a desk or around a home theater, experts recommend wrapping or bundling cords with wire wraps or flexible tubes. These can then be buried in cabinets and channeled to power strips.
- **For cords on walls** or ceilings (say from a swag lamp), surface runways will cover the cord and stick to the wall and ceiling. These runways come in different colors, and some you can paint. You can find an assortment of these, plus more cord-management accessories, at www.cableorganizer.com. (Love this site.)
- **For cords crossing the floor,** cord covers are tougher than surface runways and will withstand foot traffic. Low-profile ones look best and work on hard or carpeted floors. Some are thin enough to run under a carpet, if the carpet is plush. More ideal—and more costly—is to have an electrician put an outlet in the floor where you need it. Your kids might complain, as this eliminates cord jump rope.
- **For a last resort,** have an electrician add outlets. This generally involves drywall repair and paint, but it is a clean solution.
- **For the cheapest solution,** rearrange furniture to hide cords or use an artfully placed plant.

"I'm saying, I think you're nuts."

As I leave, I hand Lorrie her tip along with the name of the cord expert: "Call him."

"Is he single?"

It's no use. Soon after I leave, I'm stressed again. Everywhere I go—restaurants, friends' houses, offices—I see cords. I become obsessed with ways to conquer this spaghetti jungle. I mentally add outlets, bury cords in walls, and rearrange furniture. I fantasize about a wireless future.

Does anyone else notice? Does anyone care? My husband and kids don't.

"Honey," I say to my daughter, "if we moved your bookcase to that wall, you wouldn't have to look at that lamp cord."

"Mom, it's a lamp. It has a cord. It's fine."

The next week my cord-management expert arrives. I tell him about my cord issues. He sympathizes.

"People think I'm crazy because cords bother me so much," I say.

"People are different," he says. "Some, for example, can live with messy drawers and others can't."

I want to ask about his drawers, but something tells me that's too personal. He cuts a circular hole in my desktop, runs the cords underneath the cabinetry, wraps them in tidy bundles, channels them to a power strip or concealed phone jack, then covers the desktop hole with a round grommet. I love this man.

Next time I see Lorrie, I bring her a bushy artificial tree I bought at a used furniture store. It looks pretty fake in the daylight, but will pass for real in the dim light of her massage room.

"What's that for?" she asks.

"To camouflage your clock cord."

"You didn't have to do that."

"Yes, I did. Now I can relax."

29

Company's Coming and the Guest Room Needs Gutting

They're he-ere

*No guest is so welcome in a friend's house that he will not become a nuisance
after three days.*
> —TITUS MACCIUS PLAUTUS, ROMAN PLAYWRIGHT, C. 200 BCE,

COMPANY'S COMING. No two words strike panic in my soul quite
like these. When you consider that 48 percent of Americans who
travel for leisure stay with friends or relatives, according to the
Travel Industry Association of America, you have to figure that
the other half of us are frantically making our homes guest-ready.
This calls for a support group.

Now, I love my family and friends. Well, most of them. But having houseguests always sends me into a fit of domestic frenzy.

I worry that the guests will find those two never-uncovered
Easter eggs stuffed between the sofa cushions. I worry that my kids

will put a whoopee cushion on the guest-bath commode during the night. And I worry that, despite all my lectures, the dogs will still lick their private parts in front of the company.

Then there's the matter of the guest room.

It's my fault for bragging to everyone I know that my new house would be bigger and have—and here I drew my breath in dramatically—a guest room. That meant my kids would no longer have to play musical beds when company came, and that no one would sleep on the floor, in the old crib, or in that sofa bed that has caused more than one spinal injury. Since boasting, I got what I deserved: company.

The phone rang. "Guess what? We can come!" Feelings of delight and dread collided in me as I calibrated my voice to match the caller's enthusiastic pitch. Phrases like "no trouble," "stay the week!" and "the guest room's all ready" tumbled out of my lying mouth. I hung up and faced the truth: Having a room that you plan to turn into a guest room and having a guest room are not remotely the same thing. I had two weeks to work a miracle.

The door to the so-called guest room had been closed since the last time someone walked in and got a concussion. With the door closed, I could delude myself into believing that inside lay a pristine room that smelled of spring flowers and fresh soap and that had the ambience of a Laura Ashley B&B in Vermont.

I peer in. The blinds are mercifully closed. My eyes adjust. I gradually make out a treadmill covered in spider webs, a desk piled with tax returns dating back to 1987, a broken television, and a colony of fire ants. The smell is a combination of dust mites and gym socks. This isn't a guest room; it's a catchall. I shut the door and wonder if *Fear Factor* is nearby filming.

A week before they arrive, I clear the room. Moving the treadmill almost gives me a hernia, but it's the most exercise I've gotten out of that contraption yet. I paint. Then I selectively move in the essentials: a bed with a good mattress (also good if ever I'm not speaking to my husband), a bedside table with a reading lamp, and a small empty dresser.

Right on time, my guests arrive. I've just hung the last picture and put in a vase of fresh daisies. Still sweaty with exertion, I answer the door and welcome them.

I looked into what a nice guest room needs and picked up these expert clues:

- **Let yourself go crazy.** Since you don't have to live in the guest room, you can go a little wild with the décor. Import an African, tropical, or rustic mountain theme. If guests tire of the look, they've stayed too long.
- **Use the finest cottons.** When outfitting the room, go for sheets with high thread count, towels of Egyptian cotton, window treatments that offer light control and privacy, and blankets of different weights, so guests can adjust as they please.
- **Move out.** This is a guest room, not a dumping station. Have empty hangers in the closet and empty drawer space. Scented drawer liners add a nice touch. If you put anything in the closet, make it a clean robe, fresh slippers, and maybe a jacket guests can wear.
- **Detail the bathroom like a nice hotel.** Put in travel-size containers of shampoo, conditioner, bath gel, and lotion. (The mini bottles are cute and remind guests they're not staying forever.) Include a nightlight, blow dryer, new toothbrushes, razors, deodorant, and cologne. This may be your only chance to drop a hygiene hint.
- **Add creature comforts.** Place some magazines and books in the room, along with a basket of granola bars and fresh fruit and some literature on local attractions, bus schedules, and restaurants.
- **Splash on fragrance.** Even if you changed the sheets after the last visitor, refresh the linens by throwing a few sachets under the covers or spritzing the sheets with lavender or rosewater. Then add a welcome bouquet of fresh flowers or a flowering plant.

"Oh!" the wife gasps, when I show her the room. "This is lovely. I hope you didn't go to any trouble."

"Trouble? This was no trouble at all," I wink at the dog. "All we did was fluff a few pillows."

30

Utility Rooms and Garages

Note to men: Say it with tools

AFTER MANY YEARS OF LIVING with the same person, I've learned there are only a few times a woman has real leverage. Childbirth is one of those times. "Honey, remember that 3-carat diamond at Tiffany's? . . . Aaaaargh!! Is the head out yet?"

Or that gap of time between when a man proposes and a woman says yes. During that crucial interval, I negotiated to keep my maiden name, have the final say in the number and timing of children, and always have a dog. After that negotiations pretty much came to a standstill.

Another time a domestic partner has leverage is when he or she gets a call from the local jail to pick up her mate after a drunken brawl. Fortunately, I don't have firsthand knowledge of that experience but seems like it would warrant a favor or two.

My point is, when these leveraging moments occur, women must seize them like a lifetime supply of Retin A cream, and men like a forever supply of antibalding lotion.

On the eve of a recent Mother's Day, I encountered such a moment. The day before the Hallmark-induced day of matriarchal genuflection, I could pretty much bet my wedding ring that neither Dan nor the kids had thought of a card, let alone a gift. I worried about what they might pull off last minute. I don't enjoy gratuitous brunches where you stuff yourself with food covered in hollandaise sauce, and drink champagne so cheap the waiters keep the label covered. I always leave feeling as if a bicycle has run over my head and landed in my stomach. I didn't want another scarf or bottle of perfume. So I waited for the right moment, and, while holding an overflowing laundry basket as a prop, said, "Honey, I know work has been really stressful for you, and you need something to take your mind off it."

Take Home for Guys: Next time you owe your lady a favor, don't say it with flowers. Say it with tools. Now go read the sports section, while I share these tips for gals.

Hints for Gals: When trying to get the man of the house to hit the honey-do list, try these leveraging tactics, gleaned and tested over years of marriage:

- **#1 Timing is everything.** Pick the right moment—say, when you've just posted bail for him—and milk it.
- **#2 Make it all about how good this is for him.** Example: The more equity you put into the house, the sooner you can retire.
- **#3 Spill what you want fast.** Say it in fewer than ten words to keep his brain from flooding.
- **#4 Close the deal.** When your man is processing the request, come in for the close with your final argument: Did I ever mention how sexy a man using power tools is?
- **#5 Leave immediately.** Don't stand around for his response. Retreat and let him come to you.

If you make over your mudroom, factor in these Mudroom Musts, developed after four years of dreaming about it:

TIPS

- **Design for your family,** not someone else's. Don't just stick up hooks and shelves. Figure out the best way to configure your space for your household's needs. For instance, a home with a hockey player could use a tall cubby space for sticks and knee pads and a sturdy hook to hang skates.
- **Sketch it out,** then measure the space and buy supplies to build shelves, a bench, and a coat rack. Or buy these items ready-made to fit your space. (Be sure they'll fit through the door before you buy them. A friend of mine had to saw her cabinets in half to get them in.)
- **Cut visual clutter** by covering it. Have cabinets as opposed to open shelving, closets with doors, and boxed-in rather than plank benches.

Must Haves

- **Coat hooks.** Plan on two hooks for every member of the household, and one for the dog's leash. Make a hook rack by screwing heavy-duty hooks into a 1" x 4" piece of painted or stained wood.
- **Key tray.** Depending on how your home functions, this may be a place to put a series of smaller hooks for keys, or a key bowl, and a basket for mail.
- **Easy-to-clean surfaces.** Install easy-to-wipe counters of ceramic tile or laminate; walls or wainscoting painted in semi-gloss or varnished; hard floors of wood, stone, or non-skid tile; and a durable area rug that you can shake out in a color that blends with grime.
- **Functional closet.** If the room has a closet, consider two poles, the lower one at a good height for kids. Or add a shelf tower for hats, scarves, umbrellas, and gloves.
- **A bench.** Offer a place to sit down to remove shoes. Even better, have a bench that doubles as a storage bin.
- **Message board and mirror.** A small chalkboard for messages and a mirror to check your hair before you dash may aid frequent comings and goings.
- **Art.** Hang something pretty here, something that says, "Aren't you glad to be home?"

That got his attention. He actually looked up from the sports page. I continued: "So why don't you build out the mudroom? Put in a storage bench for shoes and rotting lunch pails, add coat hooks and a hat shelf?"

He uttered a syllable of indeterminate meaning. When I knew he hadn't yet set himself against the idea, I quickly lobbed two closing arguments: "Using power tools always makes you feel better. Plus, a great mudroom will improve our home's value." Then, I hauled my laundry basket into the mudroom and did my best to look overworked and deserving.

As in many homes, our mudroom, which doubles as a laundry room, is the most overused and underdecorated room in the house. The neglected dumping station for dirt-bronzed shoes, Roquefort-smelly gym bags, lethal sports equipment, and laundry so filthy it walks is also the room we enter and leave the house from 98 percent of the time. To put this in perspective, we share the entrance with the dogs' door.

I've never understood why so many people, including me, spend so much more time and energy fluffing up the main entry of their homes, installing nice furniture and art, while leaving the room they really use to come and go—the transition room off the garage—looking like a cross between a toolshed and a Laundromat. Who's more important, the guests we have once every couple of months who use the nice entry, or we who pay the mortgage?

Nothing about our mudroom said, "Welcome home." Instead it said, "Turn around! Get out while you still can!"

I've lobbied for a mudroom makeover before, but nobody in the family saw the point when so many other projects needed doing. The campaign really lost traction after I got an estimate to build it out like I wanted for $2,700. That put the nail in the bench seat right there.

A few minutes later Dan came into the laundry room and said, "Draw up what you have in mind." Faster than you could say, "You owe me," I penciled out a scaled drawing on 1/4-inch graph paper, easy since I'd done this in my head a hundred times. I wanted 4-foot-high wainscoting all around topped with a chair rail. I wanted a built-in storage bench with sections inside for each person's boots and stolen property. Above that, I wanted more bead board with half a dozen coat hooks and a hat shelf. Soon after, Dan was off to the home improvement store. And I was doing the victory dance.

The next day, Mother's Day, I awoke not to a predictable breakfast in bed of rubber eggs and cold coffee, but to the scree of a power saw. Dan was at work in the garage. My heart turned a happy somersault. After four years in this home, I was finally getting my mudroom makeover.

Don't tell my husband, but postponing home improvements has an upside: When you put off a home improvement—and delay is the norm at my house—your house tells you what it needs. For instance, if I'd built the mudroom out day one, I wouldn't have foreseen that this space would need to accommodate a horseback rider, a soccer player, a trail runner, and a golfer. I wouldn't have known that people who weigh less than 70 pounds could consume so much real estate. And I couldn't have imagined throwing myself across the threshold between this room and the rest of the house and saying, "Don't take another step inside until you have a funeral for those gym shoes, which smell like stale starfish."

So my mood soared with the music of Dan's hammering and sawing. When it was done, my made-over mudroom offered more than a comfortable place to take off shoes and hang coats. Now, whether we're coming in from work, shopping, the yard, the barn, the jogging trail, the soccer field, the golf course, or from burying a bone, this room says, "Welcome home."

What Would Norm Do?

"That's mine," Dan claimed.

"No, it came addressed to me." My husband and I were fighting over the Norm Abram calendar that came in the mail.

"But I'm the Norm Abram fan," he argued. True, Dan devours every episode of *The New Yankee Workshop* on the PBS and DIY networks. The show stars Abram, the friendly woodworker who can turn a stack of Popsicle sticks into fine furniture.

"But I'm the home design columnist, so Norm sent it to me."

"Norm didn't send it. His PR people did."

"You don't know."

"You don't even watch Norm."

"Apparently he wants me to."

"Give me that."

"No way."

"Life is not fair."

I understood. If George Clooney had sent Dan a calendar, I'd be crushed, too. But I clung to my calendar mainly because being a home design columnist brings almost no perks. Dan gets free computers and plane trips through his work. I get weird stuff in the mail. For instance, in one sixty-day period I received a water-saving faucet that doubles as a drinking fountain, a mosquito net, a string of plastic light-up garage tools, and a book on punk and Goth knitting projects. (If you'd like to knit a beanie that looks like a Mohawk, I can help.) So when I get anything remotely desirable—like a Norm Abram calendar—I get possessive.

A year after the calendar tussle, I was still feeling guilty. And now Dan was headlong into another Norm-type project—installing the bead-board wainscoting in the mud/laundry room (the Mother's Day weekend project was now into its sixth week). As Dan juggled saws and figured his way out of tight corners, he muttered, "What would Norm do?"

Out of earshot, I muttered, "Norm would have done the project in an episode." But I put up with the disruption (no washer all this time) because you know how I've wanted wainscoting in this room.

Though it was too late to reconsider my wainscoting decision, I decided to call a real expert to find out the general rules for where and how to install wainscoting and wood paneling. I caught up with Norm himself in his New Yankee Workshop.

"A utility room is a perfect place for wainscoting," Abram said, to my great relief. "Wainscoting has been common in utility rooms and kitchens since the early colonial and farmhouse days because it's more durable than plaster walls. In old farmhouses, people used to hammer planks horizontally on the bottom half of walls, forming a crude but functional kind of wainscoting."

Today, he added, wainscoting and wood paneling can kick any room up a notch. The crafted wall treatment is at home in informal rooms, like laundry rooms, as well as in formal rooms, like dining or living rooms.

A few days later, as Dan was applying the last coat of white semi-gloss to the wainscoting, I handed him a box. "For you," I said. He pulled out a New Yankee Workshop mug bearing Norm's likeness.

"How'd you get that?" he asked, happily surprised.

"He was out of calendars."

"Norm Abram sent you this?"

"Being a home columnist has its perks."

Here's what else Norm Abram had to say about installing wainscoting:

- **Wainscoting goes best** in traditional, Old World, and seaside interiors. It's trickier to apply in contemporary homes. Stained wood panels can look great in home offices and commercial spaces like banks or law firms.
- **You can find interlocking assembly systems** at most home improvement stores. Choose pre-primed paint grade or stain grade.
- **Height is subjective.** Most wainscoting comes up between 32 and 36 inches from the floor. We came up higher in our laundry room, to 48 inches, because our ceiling is 10 feet and we wanted the wainscoting higher than the washer and dryer. Don't divide the wall exactly in half, but you can come up higher than midway to cover, say, two-thirds of the wall, which we did to form a coat rack over a bench seat.
- **To install, use a level** and draw a line around the room at the finished height (wainscoting plus chair-rail cap). Most walls aren't square, and most floors aren't even. Let the level be your guide.
- **The biggest mistake amateurs make,** said Abram, is not first laying materials out around the room. Before you cut, pencil in where each piece will go. If you foresee an awkward transition, change the layout so the weird connection goes in the least visible corner.
- **Remove baseboards** and switchplate covers. Using a stud finder, mark studs with an X. Measure and cut wainscoting. Cut holes for outlets, and wrap window frames. Attach material to the wall using finish nails. Hammer nails into studs at the top and bottom of the wainscoting so that baseboards and cap rails will cover the nail holes. Apply liquid nails to the back of the wainscoting for added wall adhesive.
- **Add the cap rail and baseboards.** Use a coping saw or a miter saw scribe inside corners, and miter the outside ones. Practice on scrap.
- **Hide seams and nail heads** with spackle or wood putty. Sand, prime, and paint or stain.
- **Be fussy,** said Abram. "The place where people get stuck and say 'That's good enough,' is the place other people notice."

Now All That's Missing from My Laundry Room Is Someone to Do the Wash!

Let me air my dirty laundry: Just because I now have a tricked-out laundry room, blessed by Norm, doesn't mean I suddenly enjoy doing the laundry. When I'm in the laundry room, my intuitive family has figured out that they'd better be any place but. Anyone who walks in while I'm doing this dirty job is likely to hear a rant about how I didn't go to college and learn about Shakespeare and the Krebs cycle so I could stand in a room muggier than Kansas in August, fold other people's underwear, and match socks. I don't do this graciously, or well. Just ask Dan, who had to wear pink athletic socks for three weeks until the bleach kicked in. But I do the laundry because I'm the most qualified person in my household to do it, which isn't saying much.

Unlike those far more together wives and mothers who do a load a day, and stay on top of this household chore, I wait till it's an emergency. I don't just wait until everyone is out of undies, and the towels have gangrene. I wait until every wearable garment is in the hamper and Dan and the kids have taken to wrapping themselves in bed sheets toga style, a fashion trend inspired by enlightened Greek women who got sick and tired of washing clothes in the river among the reeds. I totally get that.

When I finally do take the laundry seriously, I stand at the bottom of the stairs and yell like a fishwife: "If you want clean clothes git your laundry down here in the next three minutes!" Dan and the girls hustle their overflowing baskets down the stairs, followed by the dogs who think it's Christmas for all the excitement. The ensuing stampede sounds like a cross between a football drill and charging rhinos. Dan, who most appreciates the value of clean briefs, leads the charge. Then I sort clothes into a small mountain range: peaks of whites, lights, darks, and delicates and start the

IQ-lowering process of wash, dry, fold, and sort again into baskets by owner. I don't do this with June Cleaver cheeriness. And I'll never be one of those women who smile as they pour Tide into the washer and rave over its stain-lifting properties.

But I realize that this task won't go away until I'm in a nursing home and someone is doing my sheets. Thankfully, now that Dan has made over the utility room, if I'm going to be miserable, I'll be miserable in a nice place.

Cross over the threshold of most utility rooms and you often find yourself in a major male domain—the garage. More than a place to park the car, today's garages are buffed out. Here men change more than oil. I learned most of what I know about garages from a top authority, my dad. . . .

Before Dan remodeled the laundry room, I did some research to be sure I'd wind up with the best laundry room I could. I called a real housework pro, Cynthia Townley Ewer, author of *House Works*, and CEO of Organizedhome.com, for her down and dirty tips. Here's the plan:

- **Ample shelving** for detergent and laundry products. If space is a premium, consider storage units designed to slip between washers and dryers.
- **Lots of clean counter space** for folding and sorting clothes.
- **A large sink** for hand-washing unmentionables, fishing gear, or the dog.
- **A hanging rack** for freshly pressed items and a drying rack.
- **Room for an ironing board** near an outlet, and a handy place to store it when not in use. For a tight space, some ironing boards can be wall mounted to fold away.
- **Excellent lighting.**
- **A person** to do the work for you.

Shop Talk

My dad's a garage kind of guy. As a girl, I remember him there more than anywhere. He'd spend hours in his workshop tinkering, working on the cars, and giving advice. I'd sidle up to him, because here, in his masculine domain, he talked.

To hear a complete sentence from Dad was about as rare as hearing the mating call of an endangered bird in the outback. For every ten words my parents spoke, Mom said nine. (Which, come to think of it, resembles the ratio between Dan and me today.) But in the garage, I could hear firsthand where Dad stood on matters large and small. And I tuned in. Sometimes he was even interesting. If it weren't for our garage conversations, I may never have heard some of the best life advice I ever got. Usually, the advice was car related, but we both knew it had broader applications:

- Turn off your radio once in a while and listen.
- Always keep your eye on your pressures and your treads.
- Watch the car two cars ahead.
- Drive in the center lane so you have two ways out.
- Steer clear of cars with dents and out-of-state plates.
- Don't run the air when you can put the windows down.
- Axle grease is like sex. It's great in the right place, say on a differential or in a marriage, but in the wrong place, it's just dirt and smut.

Axle grease. Sex. Got it.

The garage of my girlhood was a two-car affair, prominently featured at the front of a single-story ranch house. The place smelled like a musty combination of wet rope and sawdust, kind of like Dad. Cement floors, raw wood rafters, and a wood plank set the color scheme of dirt brown and gunmetal gray. Cat litter coated the oil spots, and old coffee cans and jars, filled with assorted nails, screws, and rolls of Tums, lined the workbench. And because, like most California homes, our house had neither a basement nor an attic, the garage had junk sprouting from the walls and rafters: my old sawed-off leg cast, Aunt Ruth's awful oil painting, a stringless tennis racquet, the old slide projector with the Grand Canyon slides still in, a papier-mâché bust of John Lennon, and an errant strand of Christmas lights.

"Hurry!" I can still hear Mom yell. "Shut the garage door before the company comes!"

True, the place was unsightly, and the door—much to Mom's embarrassment—was usually open. Any kid who needed a bike repair knew they could pull up to our garage for a fix. Grown-up neighbors, too, would come in, ostensibly to borrow a tool, but

---

Many companies can tell you how to transform your garage into a place that looks as tidy as a Montessori School. I look forward to the day ours is a priority and we get to that. My vision for our garage borrows from the garage culture of yesterday and the garage aesthetics of today. Here's what I imagine:

- **A place** for the man of the house to pursue his hobbies, whether cars, model planes, or moonshine.
- **A place** his wife can send him when he gets on her nerves, and where he can go when she gets on his.
- **A place** with an open-door attitude that says come on in.
- **A place** where kids and dads can have meaningful conversations or just be quiet for hours, while someone fixes the lawn mower.
- **A place** that looks good with the door open.
- **A place** where men can be men, only neater.
- **And, most important, a place** where they can build things like carburetors and children.

really to talk about stuff like liver tumors. It was that kind of neighborhood. That kind of garage. That kind of dad. For him, the room between his house and the world was a buffer zone, a place he worked out the stresses from his engineering job, or an argument with Mom, though I never heard one. In short, it was a port for everyone when the heat in the house got too hot and the world outside seemed too cold.

In the years since, garage design has come a long way. Today's garages are buff. The nicer ones have outdoor carpeting or floors painted with industrial paint. Peg-Board lines the walls, displaying tools the men own but never use. These garages have sound systems, televisions, and sleek laminate cabinets that hide designer sports equipment. They are immaculate, all right, but do they have soul? Many are just fancy car barns, places men beautify but only use to come and go.

My husband is not a garage kind of guy. He prefers his big screen, golf, and the newspaper. He doesn't weld or change spark plugs. I don't know many men this side of sixty who do, which is sad. (But then I don't darn socks or make pie crust from scratch either.) Though our garage isn't "done" yet, when it is, I hope it doesn't become just a storage bin and a place to park.

PART VI

Taking It
Outside

Tackling the yard:
From design to maintenance,
decks to patio furnishings

"Fabulous Yard Potential," blared the real estate ad, trying to lure buyers to the lot Dan and I ultimately bought outside Denver. The home site was really nothing more than a scrubby acre with a home in the framing stage and a dream. Calling that pile of sticks a home was a stretch, but calling that barren, wind-whipped knoll a yard was like calling a jungle gym a theme park.

I'm no gardener, nor is Dan. But we wanted a great yard. We believed the "potential" part of the ad and really thought that given the Rocky Mountain views, and the size of the property, the yard could rock. All we needed was a good landscape plan and some decent contractors.

Okay, I can tell you're laughing already.

Who knew that realizing that dream—and we finally did—would involve burning through three incompetent landscapers and fighting with the city and the homeowner's association? It would also cost two and a half times our initial estimate. The project literally became a full-time job, and both Dan and I had full-time jobs. Over the three years we battled the project, we did, however, learn a lot of lessons, which I'll share with you. I hope they will spare you similar trauma, keep your cursing to a minimum, and keep your bank account to a maximum. I'm going to need a lot of antacid tablets and maybe a bottle of vodka if I'm going to recount all of this for you, but here goes. . . .

31

The Not-So-Great Outdoors

Taking on weeds, sinkholes, Mother Nature, the HOA, and bad landscapers

DEAR MR. WINKELMAN, I KNOW *we have a few weeds, but isn't saying "infested" (a word I'd save for cockroaches or crime) a little harsh? . . .* I'm drafting this letter in my head to the chairman of the landscape committee in response to his letter to me, which stated:

It has come to the attention of the Homes Association that installation of the landscaping on the property listed above has not been completed. There are dead and/or dying trees and it is weed infested.

The letter went on to cite a couple of picky bylaws and said we had ten days to clear the weeds or be fined.

So hang a scarlet letter on us.

As in many new communities, our homeowners association—or HOA, which stands for Heckle Ostracize Admonish—requires new residents to landscape their front yard within six months of moving in. We actually did hire a landscaper, who put in landscaping that died. Then the patio caved in. Then the weeds took over, and the landscaper skipped town. The yard had become our albatross.

After owning five residences, Dan and I have experienced almost every domestic drag: foundation failures, earthquake damage, roof leaks, nudist neighbors, rats, mold. But a weed epidemic? Never. Now that we've stepped up in the world—(hah!) bought the bigger house on the bigger lot—we're in over our heads. To think an acre once sounded romantic.

Dear Mr. Winkelman, I know our yard must look to you like a foreclosed property formerly run by slumlords, but that's not for lack of effort or, heaven knows, spending. . . .

It's no use. Surely Mr. Winkelman, being a bylaws kind of guy, won't care that our luck with landscapers rivals a celebrity starlet's luck with men. We've plowed through three. Landscaper One put in a paver patio (which soon collapsed, the subject of the next section) and a rock wall, got most of his money but didn't finish the job, and blew town. We bought the trees he'd specified from Home Depot ourselves, and hired a few guys to plant them. The trees all died.

Landscaper Two planted a second round of trees, added boulders, and put in a water feature that jutted 15 feet over our property line, causing a boundary feud reminiscent of Hatfield and McCoy. (You'll read all about that, too.) In planting the trees, however, Landscaper Two trashed the irrigation system that Landscaper One had installed, actually rather well. Now more trees were dead of thirst. While we were at a standoff with Landscaper Two over the water feature and the trees, we hired Landscaper Three. He's bitter because he didn't get the work first and has attitude about cleaning up his competitors' messes. Now that he's fixed the irrigation system, the weeds are in overdrive, but it's too late for the trees.

So now, despite the small fortune we've spent on landscaping, we have to start over with a clean plot of ground and a replenished bank account, neither of which we have. So Dan and I are tackling the weeds ourselves, though I briefly considered calling the local jail hoping to haul in one of those inmate crews that clear weeds on freeways. Dan comes back from Home Depot and hands me a weed digger and some gardening gloves.

"Thanks," I grunt. We're already grumpy.

"Get the roots," he says.

"I *know* you're supposed to get the roots," I say. But my haughtiness dissolves moments later when I have to ask Dan the difference between the weeds and the few surviving plants that Landscaper One put in.

As usual, Dan and I disagree on how to approach the problem, so we split the yard. My way involves digging each weed out by hand and putting it in a trash bag. He hacks weed tops off with a scythe, then mows them to a nub, then sprays what's left with a herbicide that kills roots. After two days, he'll rake up the mess. I tell him to keep his toxic chemicals on his side.

We try to get the girls to help. "It will be fun!" We lie. We try bribes. Dan buys each a pair of flowered gardening gloves. They see through us.

"What's wrong with the weeds?" our oldest asks. "At least they're green, unlike our trees. Besides, it was nice of them to volunteer." With that, she finds her Razor and scoots off.

The youngest starts to help, then gasps: "They have flowers!"

"Some weeds do," I say.

She looks at me as if I'm the executioner at the dog pound. "You can't pull flowers!" she says, then goes inside.

"Where are the girls?" Dan asks when he sees me weeding alone.

"Conscientiously objecting."

Dear Mr. Winkelman, My daughter is very sensitive. She doesn't feel we should pull out anything that has flowers. I'm inclined to agree. Remember the words of Ralph Waldo Emerson: "What is a weed? A plant whose virtues have not yet been discovered." Which leads me to ask, what does your committee have against native vegetation?

I weed alone. I'm so bored, my brain sprouts corny analogies like, well, weeds: Weeds are like gray hairs; no matter how many you pull, they come back, only worse. I find the Zen of weeding. I dig deep. I chase down roots so long I swear I'm pulling up cable. Any minute, I expect the girls to holler: "Mom! The phone's dead!"

After two weekends of toil, the weeds are better, but my hands look like a farmer's. Dirt's so imbedded in my nails that I fear it's tattooed. So I treat myself to a manicure. At the nail salon, I overhear two customers, apparently old friends, talking. One is a real

---

Overwhelmed, I called Bob Dolibois, executive vice president of the American Nursery and Landscape Association. He defined a weed as simply the wrong plant in the wrong place and offered these steps for control:

- **Know your options.** You can eradicate weeds three ways.
  - Pull them, roots and all.
  - Smother them. All plants need light to live. If you deprive them, they'll die. Cover large areas with black plastic or thick paper weed barrier until the weeds die. This takes time but will work faster in Florida than Minnesota.
  - Nuke them. If you're in a hurry, like us, use chemical warfare. Round-Up is the most popular herbicide. It kills the weeds but allows you to replant soon. However, many organic weedkillers are also on the market. Ask at your garden center for the most effective ones for your soil type.

- **Turn the soil.** After you've cleared the ground of weeds, turn it. Weeds spread by roots, stolon (runners), and seeds. You have to get rid of them all. Turning helps snuff them out.
- **Start a prevention plan.** To keep weeds from coming back, prepare soil properly. Use a weed block. (This really worked.) This is protective paperlike fabric that you lay over the ground then cover with mulch or gravel. Weeds can't come up from below and aren't likely to take root in the mulch, but water can get through. Punch holes where you want to stick plants. Planting the right plants in the right places will ward off weeds.

estate agent; the other just sold her home. Both seem older than I am and wiser.

"Why did you sell?" the real estate agent asks.

"We got a place with less land," the other says. "An acre is just too much work."

"Try telling younger buyers that. They all want big yards."

"Well, they're all nuts."

Landscapers divide their work into two broad categories: softscape and hardscape. Softscape is the stuff in dirt: lawns, trees, shrubs, flowering plants. Hardscape involves wood and cement: patios, decks, and pools. Usually you want to put the hardscape in first so the earthmovers and Bobcats don't trash the softscape. But getting our patio and deck in right proved harder than hard. . . .

The Day the Earth Moved:
Patio Pitfalls

This story begins with a simple, American backyard dream: a finished patio and built-in barbecue. The landscaper's proposal said it would take six weeks. It took three years. A sinkhole, a near-death experience, and a contractor who disappeared off to the Virgin Islands slowed progress.

Right after we moved into our Colorado home, Landscaper One installed a patio out of interlocking pavers. The patio sat off the kitchen door at the bottom of a few steps. The workers also ran a gas line under the pavers to the spot where we wanted a built-in barbecue.

So far so good.

Until the patio caved. I don't mean dipped like a cat saucer. I mean plummeted three feet, kerplunk, taking the stairs off the kitchen with it. One day I hear the dogs barking at the back door but don't see them. I look out, then down, and see that another household project has reached an all-time low. I hop out the door, sink to my waist, and hoist the dogs in.

I hear the kids. The younger one sees me first. "What happened?" she asks.

"A bubble underground burst," I say, using my best geology.

The preteen comes in: "Why are you down there?"

"The ground burped," says the younger.

Dan walks in, "What's everyone looking at?" He peers over the ledge.

"Our patio has gas," says the preteen, then looks disgusted and adds, "I bet this doesn't happen in other families."

And we lived like this, crawling in and out of our house on hands and knees, which humbles you. Some days, I'd forget, step out the kitchen door into midair, and do the bicycle like a cartoon character before falling straight down off the ledge. On the upside, if someone complained about my cooking, I'd just push him off the cliff.

Next, a lively finger-pointing game of chain blame started: The patio contractor blamed the homebuilder, saying the ground wasn't right. The builder blamed the soil-compacting company, which was supposed to compress the soil around the house so it would support things like patios. The compacting company blamed the builder because the basement window wells, which are at ground level, made compacting the soil correctly impossible. I blamed Dan because he's my husband; he blamed the dogs who blamed the gophers.

With the patio war under way, Dan and I focused on the barbecue project. We hired a stone mason, Ed, to build a stone structure to house an outdoor grill. We picked a granite slab for the countertop, which Ed had custom cut to fit around the barbecue. Before Ed could install the granite, however, we had to install the barbecue and hook it to gas.

Here comes the near-death part.

We noticed an odd smell. We thought the water feature needed servicing. We have one of those manmade waterfall streams out back, and you know how some can smell like warm fish guts. My youngest thought the smell was from the patio's intestinal trouble. The night Dan inaugurated the grill, he came in with no eyebrows and soot in his further receded hair. We then figured out the smell was from a gas leak. The patio had crushed the gas line.

We're 0 for 2. No patio, no barbecue. I revise my dream: I just want to walk outside and not feel as if I'm in an elevator shaft filled with explosives. Meanwhile, because I can't install nice patio fencing until I know the new patio's elevation, and I need to keep my dogs home, though they probably want to run away as badly as I do, I've put up a cheesy foldable dog fence, purchased from the pet store. Altogether, the fallen steps, the collapsed patio, and the cheesy fence create a landscape you might expect to see in the poorer sections of Arkansas. We get another letter from Mr. Winkelman saying, and I'll paraphrase, that our home is an eyesore. As if we didn't know!

Although this experience may illustrate that I know less than you do about hardscape, I humbly offer these tips from the trenches.

- **Whenever something sinks** in your yard—like a pool, a driveway, or a retaining wall—assume the worst, then multiply that by five.
- **Start with a level paving field.** As with a good paint job, preparing the surface on which a patio or deck will sit is key. When setting pavers, level and compact the soil well. Put in a layer of sand and tamp hard again. Be sure the surface slopes slightly away from the house.
- **When you hire a landscaper**—even if your project is small—get all the guy's numbers: cell, home, office, wife, ex-wife, travel agent, and parole officer.
- **If something smells fishy,** assume that it could explode.

Finally, after fifteen months and three restraining orders, the builder and ground pounder agreed that if the ground pounder would remove the pavers and repound the ground at his cost, the builder would pay to repair the gas line, replace the pavers, and put in new stairs to the kitchen. Afterward, we called Ed to tell him he could finally set that granite top. After weeks of having our messages go unanswered, we called his friend to learn that Ed was living on a boat off the Virgin Islands. The friend said something about an inheritance, but I'd stopped listening.

After the dust settled, we had a level patio flanked by tacky dog fences, and a working barbecue set in a big open stone-wrapped hole with no countertop. (I'm expecting another letter from Mr. Winkelman.) We're still waiting on the fence builder and a new granite guy. They've given me their promises, which I cling to, because I have this dream.

Men, Cooking, and the Great Outdoors

Dan is outside talking to our neighbor Brian about size. This can only mean one of two things: big screens or barbecues.

"Mine's 36 inches."

"Mine's 36 plus 12, with the attachment."

"Oh, I got the attachment."

"But did you get the warming shelf?"

Definitely barbecues. To men of a certain age—that is, men who aren't what they once were on the basketball court—certain home improvements become a competitive sport. Too bad this competitiveness doesn't kick in when buying furniture or window treatments. It only applies to guy domains: home theaters, wine cellars, outdoor appliances.

After several minutes of playing mine's bigger, and trying in various ways to out-grill each other, Dan and Brian realize they've ordered the exact same barbecue. Well, high-fives all around. I'm relieved because I watched Dan while he researched. He practically knit his eyebrows into tiny sweaters as he compared: Gas vs. charcoal? Side burner vs. more grill space? Do we want a rotisserie or smoker? He spent more time choosing his barbecue than he did his internist. Ultimately—to put this into a truly relevant perspective— the grill he picked is to outdoor barbecues what Lulu Guinness is to high heels. Too bad his grilling skills aren't in the same league. "Is that a shrimp, honey, or a Pink Pearl eraser?"

Now that Brian's getting the same grill, Dan is all grins. Not only has his barbecue choice been affirmed, but the neighbor didn't one-up him. It's male bonding at its best, and it gets better when they decide that, since they're ordering the same barbecue from the same company, they'll save on shipping and have the company send two barbecues in one shipment to the same address. Hey, what are neighbors for?

As Dan shares this bonanza with me, I think this would be a good time to bring up the drapes, but he hijacks the conversation to talk about the high points of our soon-to-be outdoor kitchen. "Once the barbecue is in, we'll get that granite counter installed and make it big enough for people to sit at and have a drink while I cook." I cough to send a subliminal message that the last place I want to sit is downwind from a barbecue. "We'll get a new patio set that seats more people, and heating lamps for cool nights," he carries on. I don't dare interrupt because I've learned to never stand between a man and something burning.

Besides, the more cooking Dan does, the better. Then again, he may be doing this out of self-preservation. He recently shared a quote he'd heard: "My wife dresses to kill, which is also how she cooks." Hah, hah, hah! So, Mr. Comedian, you can just take your long tongs outside and do something about that.

Two weeks later, Brian calls to say the barbecues are in. Dan hustles over, so the two of them can figure out how to best get the box, which looks as if it contains a Chevrolet, over to our back-yard. He comes home long-faced.

"What's the matter?" I ask.

"Brian's outdoor kitchen has a sink and a refrigerator," he says. Brian also beat him at golf last week, so I can imagine what this must be doing to his testosterone. I try to think of what a guy would say at a time like this, but before I can muster the right se-

---

According to the Hearth, Patio and Barbecue Association (HPBA), barbecue buyers should consider these factors when choosing:

- **Fuel:** The most popular types are gas and charcoal. (Electric grills are less popular, but they don't smoke.) Charcoal barbecues cost less and are often portable, but they're messier. We chose gas, because it's cleaner and we knew we wanted a built-in.
- **Price:** Charcoal barbecues range from $50 to $400. Gas grills can range from $130 on the low end, to $1,000 in the mid-range, and up to $10,000 for super deluxe, but 80 percent of gas grills sell for under $300.
- **Location:** Grills smoke and flare up, so don't park them under the eaves or beneath the old sycamore.
- **Features:** According to an HPBA survey, 72 percent of gas grill buyers wanted a large cooking surface. (It's that size thing.) Fifty-three percent wanted side shelves; 36 percent wanted a warming shelf; and 20 percent wanted a side burner. Other popular features include smokers, grill lights, and rotisseries.
- **Flavor:** For a true smoky flavor, you need to add real wood (hard-wood pellets or mesquite) or woody herbs such as rosemary. Or get a smoker. We opted for a grill with a smoker drawer, which you fill with wood chips. Smokers live up to their name, so alert the fire department and stay upwind.
- **Competition:** Before making a move, find out what the neighbors are getting.

ries of caveman grunts, I notice Dan is smiling. It's a creepy smile that reminds me a little of Nixon's.

"What's so funny?"

His eyes twinkle devilishly: "But my big screen is bigger."

I shake my head and just wish I could channel some of that male drive into new drapes.

As you know, the barbecue installation didn't go swimmingly, and the yard hassles didn't end there. Actually, they grew worse. . . .

Home of the Botanically Challenged

The next humiliating incident occurred at the local country club. The club was hosting a cocktail party for new residents, trying to drum up members. But at the party, guests weren't talking about membership. They were talking about—what else?—new house woes.

"Which home is yours?" We ask one another, entering the ritual of new neighbor bonding. The answer usually fetches a compliment, as in: "Great view," or, "We've admired your pavers." Though we all pretend otherwise, everyone in that room knows every house in the area that's recently been for sale. They know asking and sales prices, and have been in your bedroom, but won't admit it. While they say: "Love your driveway," they're thinking: "I can't believe someone bought that house with the vomit-yellow bathroom."

"The tall brown house," I answer, when two couples ask Dan and me which house is ours. They look blank. "At the end of the road by the park," I add. Still no recollection.

Then Dan chimes: "With the dead trees out front."

"Oh!" all four say in unison. "The one with the dead trees!"

We smile, nodding, grateful for the posthumous recognition. It is, however, humbling. We might as well have a banner out front: "Home of the Botanically Challenged!"

"It's your fault," I say, shoving my elbow into Dan's side as we leave the party.

"What? I never set out to make us the poster couple for the Sierra Club. I was just trying to save money."

"Yeah, well now our dead trees are not only an eyesore, they're a landmark!"

"Thank goodness for Home Depot," he says, referring to the store's policy to guarantee any plant purchased from its nursery if it dies within one year (and if you can find the receipt).

As in many covenant-controlled communities, our HOA (remember Heckle, Oversee, and Aggravate) required that part of our front yard plan include seventeen pine trees between 10 and 14 feet tall. Have you priced trees lately?

They wanted this done within ninety days of closing escrow on the home, and they didn't care that during the first ninety days after closing on a new home families like ours not only have a limited landscape budget, they don't even have a food budget. But cross the HOA and Mr. Winkelman and you'll find a dead fish in your bed.

We had started honorably. We paid Landscaper One to draw up a plan before we moved into the house. The plan included a diagram of where the patio and deck would go, a water feature, and all flowers, shrubs, and trees, labeled by specific name, size, and location. It was our roadmap. It came with a staggering price tag to put it all in. To prune the landscape budget, we chose to buy the plants and trees ourselves from Home Depot and hire our own workers to plant them (saving 50 percent over what the landscape company wanted to charge).

Here's where the landscaper's experience might have saved us. Wonderful as Home Depot is, the store's trees were a problem. Being a nationwide supplier, Home Depot can purchase plants from all over the country. But trees that thrive in one state often die in another—particularly when the two states are as climatically diverse as Oregon, where our trees came from, and Colorado, where we live.

Meanwhile, Brian next-door was foresting his property with towering lush pines, piñons, and firs. As these beauties went in, Dan and I stared enviously out our window. This overt display of prodigious pinery triggered the genetically wired male combat response: Do Better! The comment at the country-club cocktail party sealed it. Dan uncovered the neighbor's secret weapon: A Tree Man. Dan cornered him to ask where we'd gone wrong.

As the Tree Man (whose name I'm withholding because we had future problems with him you'll hear about) set to work, I found myself learning what I wish I'd known sooner about trees:

- **Picking:** Only put in trees that are indigenous to your area and raised in your area or in a comparable climate zone.
- **Planting:** Don't over-amend the soil. Plants, like people, get hooked on drugs, then suffer when they run out. Put them in the same type of soil they came out of. Try to keep a ball of their original soil around the roots. Don't plant trees too deep. Trees should be planted on mounds, not in wells. Keep the tree's soil line exactly where it was before transplanting.
- **Placement:** Clump trees in groups of odd numbers. Think triangles. Don't space them evenly unless you're planting an orchard.
- **Watering:** Better to give a lot of water, slowly and less often, than a little water every day. Ideal: 10 gallons of water per inch of tree width twice a week in summer and once a month in winter. Put them on a drip system.
- **Console yourself:** Though expensive, healthy mature trees add tremendous character to a home and can quickly make a too-new-looking home look established. Too bad you can't eat them.

"Oregon, right?" the Tree Man (ultimately Landscaper Two) guessed.

Dan nodded.

"This is what you'd expect." He took a clump of dry pine needles between his fingers and snapped them like toothpicks. When trees used to sea level and 55 annual inches of rain hit our dry, cold climate at 6,600 feet, well, it isn't long before you can find more plant life on Mars, he explained. Then he pointed to the 10-inch length of tree trunk between the layered rows of branches. "These trees have been plugged with growth hormones," he said. "That's why they shoot up so much each year. They'll never look full."

We called Home Depot, which was very good about all the death. The garden center manager refunded our money for the dead trees. We handed the refund to the Tree Man, who charged us three times the price. Ouch. But we'd learned that cheap is expensive. He pulled out the dead transplants and replaced them with old, homegrown pines and firs. They looked tall and thick, and they began thriving. When it snowed, their branches looked like Belgian lace. We loved them, even as we admired them from our kitchen table, where we sat clipping coupons, still wondering what happened to our food budget.

Women, War, and the Land

With the weeds gone, the patio resurrected, the trees and rocks in, and the water feature running, we thought our landscape troubles were over. Nope. The Tree Man, it turned out, was better at landscaping than he was at business. And his people skills were along the lines of Yasser Arafat's. Getting him to cooperate when the next wave of yard problems started used up a year's supply of charm. To win this ground war, I used every weapon in my personal arsenal: threats, feminine wiles, beer, tears, persistence, flattery, even bribes. Who says a woman can't be president?

"No wonder I couldn't get them to do anything," Dan said as he stood back and watched the drama unfold. "I just tried to be direct."

"Direct only works when you're going to the airport." Which is why every home project needs a woman. The male approach got us into this mess. Like most men, Dan and the Tree Man dealt in round numbers, big ideas, and handshakes. Me, I'm a detail person. I like clipboards, checklists, agreements in writing.

After we hired the Tree Man to replace our first round of dead trees, the failed Oregon transplants, he planted more than sixty new trees, with a one-year guarantee. He also put in the rock water feature and pond. But just as his crew was finishing, we got a letter from the local water district telling us that our water feature—Whoops!—intruded 15 feet onto the district's property. It had to move. The Tree Man, who had our lot map, had miscalculated our lot line. He told us not to worry. He'd get the water company to come around.

Come around? We were on their land! We worried.

The water company said no deal. We told the Tree Man no money for the water feature until this territorial dispute got resolved. We did pay him for the trees and the rest of the landscaping. As the finger pointing continued, twenty of the sixtysome trees died of ips beetle, which infests and kills trees under stress. (If it attacked people, I'd be a goner.) The Tree Man wouldn't replace the trees he guaranteed until we paid for the water feature. Dan said we'd pay when the water feature was on our property. This went on for months until Dan and the Tree Man realized they had to stop speaking to one another or someone would get hurt.

That's when I stepped in with my clipboard. I drafted a contract listing the problems I wanted fixed and a financial schedule. Then I lay in wait. Several days later I saw the Tree Man in the neighborhood. He was in his SUV talking on his cell phone. Clipboard in hand, I climbed into his passenger seat. He looked startled and hung up. I said I wasn't getting out until we resolved our problems. Given his size versus mine (six-foot-four to my five-foot-three), I prayed that he was raised not to hit girls. I also brought the strongest weapon of all: a big fat check for 25 percent of the outstanding balance made out to him. It was his only if we came to terms.

We debated and argued. I cried and ranted. He handed me a Kleenex. I asked if he cared about his reputation. I threatened to

---

To avoid run-ins with your landscaper, consider these conflict-avoidance and resolution measures:

- **Get the deal in writing.** Your landscaper should work from an approved landscape plan that specifies every tree, shrub, and flower by type and size. He should itemize costs for all plants, hardscape and irrigation materials, soil enhancers, and labor.
- **Get a written guarantee.** The Tree Man said he would guarantee any tree that died in a year, but we never got that in writing. Later, he showed me his guarantee, which said it didn't cover trees that died from ips.
- **Get a mediator.** To resolve disputes, bring in someone objective. I hired an arborist from the Colorado State Forest Service. He charged $35 to visit my house, render the verdict on the health of our trees, and approve replacements. Of our sixty-three trees, twenty were dead or dying from ips. Another fifteen had been hit by the less lethal red turpentine beetle; these would likely pull through.
- **Know your property lines.** Have them staked out before you begin any landscaping work. Also be aware of any setbacks or easements before your landscaper gets started.
- **Be nice.** It may make a big difference in the outcome of the job. Be polite and friendly toward every person on the job, from the boss to the bricklayer. Learn their names, their kids' names, and their favorite libations. In the end, as with so many things worth pursuing in life, success boils down to people skills, bribes, and beer.

call his wife. He turned red. I told him to breathe. I periodically waved the check. Two hours later, we signed the agreement, which said I'd pay 25 percent now, 25 percent when the water feature was out and the diseased trees were replaced, and 50 percent when the new water feature was in and the other landscape problems were fixed. I got out of his SUV feeling like Reagan after his talks with Gorbachev, weary but victorious.

Over the next two weeks, the Tree Man's crew was all over my yard like fudge on a sundae. They moved the water feature, rebuilt it more beautifully, removed and replaced twenty trees, fixed drainage issues, and covered the yard with rich brown mulch. To keep his crew motivated, I went outside often to marvel at how strong they were and to talk to them about their kids and future landscape careers. When the Tree Man gave them heat for spending too much time (and mulch) on my job, I bought them a case of dark ale. I offered to sponsor a soccer team that one of their kids played on. Soon there was nothing they wouldn't do for me.

Three weeks later—not counting the eight-month stand off— our side won.

"From now on, I'm putting you in charge of all projects that involve men," Dan marveled.

Little does he know, my most challenging project is him.

32

All Decked Out

Building and finishing outdoor living spaces

"**Norm!**" I holler to Dan, whom I've taken to calling Norm, after his idol Norm Abram.

BZZRRRT.

Norm can't hear me over his power saw. He's out back building a 1,500-square-foot deck. I'm worried. I can't blame him for tackling this himself, given our luck with landscapers. But what really tripped all this was a five-figure bid that sent Dan, who had not yet become Norm, straight to the home improvement store for a book on deck building. Every night for two weeks, he pored over the book, scribbling in the margins. When we went out to dinner, he'd grab matchbooks from the bar, fold the covers into right angles, tear matches out and line them up on the folded covers like planks. He muttered calculations: "X pounds per square inch, equals the load of a stone fire pit, minus the square root of pi." It was troublesome.

"Sure you want to do this?" I said, trying to sound concerned for his well-being, when really I didn't want something that looked as if beavers built it attached to the back of our house. I hate when something doesn't look professional and—*because of certain egos*—you have to pretend it does.

"I can build it for a third the price."

"Grass is easier."

"You don't have to mow a deck."

"Keep in mind, just because Norm Abram makes woodworking look as simple as Legos, doesn't mean it's for everyone. Remember when I tried to copy Emeril in the kitchen?" A sick look crossed Dan's face as he recalled the time I made Emeril's crispy crabmeat ravioli with sweet corn maque choux. In my hands the recipe became Cajun chewing gum.

"Oh, I get it. You're afraid it will look like an amateur did it."

"Never!" I said, acting appalled.

"You watch!" The gauntlet was down.

He drew up plans and headed to the building department. With permit in hand, he set to work.

BBZZRRTT! "Norm!" I yelled again, when the saw paused.

He looked up from behind a cloud of sawdust. "Yeah?"

"Would losing your fingers be worth the money we're saving?"

He looked at his grit-worn hands: "I think so," he said and smiled recklessly, like a boy who has just discovered the thrill of acceleration. He's sporting three or four days of beard growth, and I worry that this is so he can save on sandpaper, too. But, truth is, he's happy. Every minute he can spare, and some he can't, he's working on the deck. He works in snow, rain, and once in a wind so strong it blew a cat off the neighbor's wall. If the weather's nice he comes home too early from work. Like any addiction, this one, I worry, could hurt his career. Sometimes he tries to hide from me the fact that he's playing hooky. He parks quietly in the garage and goes straight out back, not bothering to come through the house, where I might look at my watch and raise an eyebrow. He thinks I won't notice, but then the compressor revs up, which starts the nail gun firing. For a panicked second, I think I'm in Fallujah.

Twelve weeks later, the deck is done. I have to admit, it looks great, professional even. Because we don't yet have deck furniture, I pull two kitchen chairs onto the new terrace and bring out a couple glasses of wine to enjoy while the sun sets.

"Surprised?" Norm says, when he catches me admiring his handiwork.

Here are some deck-building tips straight from my Norm and Doug Meidling, owner of Big Sky Deck and Fence, in Aurora, Colorado:

- **Before starting,** check with your building department. Some decks require a building permit, some don't. Plus, the folks there can give structural advice.
- **When setting deck posts** into cement footings, use metal post brackets and set them straight. If they're off, they trigger a chain reaction of crookedness: Posts will tilt, beams won't lie true, and ultimately, the deck will look as if it needs to be exorcised.
- **Get a palm nailer.** The device costs about $80, runs off a compressor (which you can buy, rent, or borrow), works like a nail gun, and beats driving in hundreds of nails with a hammer. You'll also need several saws, including a circular saw, a chop saw, and a jigsaw.
- **Pick materials with care.** Your biggest—and most expensive—decision is your deck material. Real wood looks great and usually costs less than composite decking—a blend of hardwood and plastic. But wood needs maintenance or it can rot, warp, and weather until it's decrepit. Composite decking outlasts wood. To maintain it, you just hose it down. We chose composite, selecting a variety that had a low fade rate, showed no screws, and could withstand a lot of weight. (We've heard horror stories of decks caving in under hot tubs. Mom? That you down there?)

"Who, me?" I raise my glass for a toast.

With the deck finally done, our next task was to furnish it. Having done this wrong twice, I did my outdoor furniture homework this time. . . .

Outdoor Furniture:
How to Buy It Right the First Time

I'm going through the patio furniture store like a body builder, picking up chairs and coffee tables in a dead lift. If I can hoist them with ease, I move on.

"Lift that," I say to Dan, pointing to a metal table.

"Why?"

"Because if it gives you a hernia, we're on the right track."

Weight, not appearance, was my number one priority in picking outdoor furniture for the deck. This marked the third time in fifteen years I would make what I thought was a one-time purchase. This time I wanted to get it right.

My first set of patio furniture, purchased fifteen years ago, was a charming white wrought-iron table and chairs. Because I've never been together enough to put plastic vinyl covers over my patio furniture, it rusted. Every summer I could count on going through five spray cans of white Rustoleum to freshen the set. The paint made the furniture look younger all right, but the process whitened my hair and eyebrows, too, aging me twenty years. Eventually, all the iron rusted and returned to its native earth, until only bonded layers of oxidized paint held the set together.

So I decided my second set, purchased seven years later, would be rustproof. I went for teakwood. I lived in Southern California at the time. Forget how it looks during the Rose Parade; Southern California weather is way overrated. Those Santa Ana winds could lift a house off its foundation and hurl it to Kansas. That's the kind of wind we were having when I looked out my window and saw all my teak patio furniture—table, umbrella, four chairs, two lounges—had vanished. Poof! I went outside to look around and saw it all lying on the bottom of the swimming pool, like a shipwreck. Now before you give me one of your our-weather-is-worse-than-yours stories, you try to single-handedly haul a waterlogged picnic table out of the deep end.

To help you avoid the mistakes I've made when buying outdoor furniture, here are some lessons learned. If you get this right, maybe you—unlike me—really can make this investment only once.

- **Create a layout.** Before you buy outdoor furniture, look at your space. Ask what pieces would nicely fill it and meet your needs. Decide whether you want lots of seating, an ample dining area, or a place for private, quiet relaxation. Try taping out where pieces will go to get the scale and flow right.
- **Select frame material.** Pick your frame based on three criteria: the look you want, your climate, and your commitment to outdoor furniture care—and be honest.
  - *Resin-molded* furniture, made of PVC type tubing, is lightweight, relatively inexpensive, easy to clean, and practical.
  - *Wicker* is romantic, but it doesn't weather well. Newer *all-weather wickers* fare better over the long haul, but they are a better choice for enclosed patios and porches.
  - *Wood,* such as teak, is timeless and traditional. If you don't mind that it grays as it weathers, this may be a good choice. It's also low maintenance. However, if you want to preserve the rich brown color, you will have to oil it.
  - *Wrought iron* has a Victorian charm and won't blow away, but it will rust if you don't keep it dry and covered. Plan to repaint it every year or two.

So this third time I wanted heavy *and* rust-proof. In the Rocky Mountain foothills, the intense sun and freezing temps strip even the most stubborn finishes. If you want to peel a banana, just hold it outside two minutes. The wind can really get blowing, too, and I didn't want to go chasing down my furniture at the local cowboy bar and find the cushions had run off to the county fair, fun as that might sound. So I opted for solid cast aluminum outdoor furniture with heavy-duty, all-weather cushions I could tie on tight. I can only hope it lasts.

Fast-forward one year. My new patio furniture has weathered a year of the elements, with no help from me. But now it needs CPR. . . .

("To help you avoid the mistakes I've made..." continued)

- *Cast aluminum* is pricey, but it is heavy and rustproof, and it comes in lots of finishes and styles.
- **Choose Cushions.** You can buy inexpensive seasonal cushions and replace them every year. Or you can invest in more durable all-weather cushions, which can sit out all year. Cushions made from Sunbrella all-weather fabric are durable and popular. The solution-dyed acrylic fabric won't fade or deteriorate if left outside year round. Threads holding the cushion together may, but the fabric itself won't.
- **Shop around.** Look for bargains by shopping online and comparing prices. Factor in shipping costs and timing. You may pay less online for the product itself, but you may wait half the summer for your furniture to arrive and pay a lot in shipping. Be sure items are in stock when you order, and that you can cancel at no charge if the order doesn't arrive by a guaranteed date.

TIP: The trend today is toward fewer chaises and more chairs, because people are sunbathing less. Also, if you buy any piece that has wheels, such as a cart, be sure the wheels lock.

Outdoor Furniture Care:
Relief for Furniture Abuse

If there were laws against furniture abuse, I'd be in jail. All winter every winter, I leave my patio furniture outside, uncovered, to endure freezing temps, hammering rain, hide-peeling sun, and berry-eating bird assaults. Meanwhile, I stay warm, dry, and sun-protected inside. Then, come late spring, I expect my outdoor furniture and I to pick up where we left off.

Turns out I have some making up to do.

The cast aluminum furniture I bought new the year before didn't blow away and still looked good. No need to paint or oil. However,

---

Here are Jennifer Litwin's guidelines for bringing your outdoor furniture out of a season of neglect:

- **To clean patio furniture,** use a hose. If you need a deeper clean, try a mild solution of dishwashing soap and warm water. Brighten cast iron and aluminum furniture with car wax. Avoid harsh cleaning solutions. Don't clean patio furniture in the swimming pool. The chlorinated water will degrade the finish.
- **To clean the straps** on vinyl sling or strap furniture, which can get stained with suntan oil, pool chlorine, unfiltered irrigation water, and tree droppings, try the same soapy solution. If stains persist, add a couple tablespoons of bleach to a half gallon of the soapy solution. Apply and rinse well. If that doesn't work, increase the strength of the bleach solution. If a 50/50 mix of bleach and soapy water doesn't work, replace the straps.
- **When vinyl straps stop bouncing back,** don't toss the chair. For just a few dollars you can replace straps in an updated color. When choosing strap colors, note that dark colors get hotter and fade faster than light colors. Light colors wear better. Don't put off replacing old straps. Worn straps break easily, which is just embarrassing no matter how much you weigh.

the cushions had taken a beating. The main reason my cushions languish outside all year is that the time is never right to bring them in. When it's nice out, I don't want to bring them in because it's nice out. I might want to sit outside. When it's crummy out, I don't want to bring them in because it's crummy out. I don't want to be outside. When the sky clears, the cushions are wet or covered with snow, and I don't want to bring them in until they dry. So I wait till it's nice again. The cycle continues until, before I know it, we're back to warm weather.

So when I heard that outdoor-furniture makers had started making furniture and fabrics that could withstand this abuse, I got even more excited than I did when Starbucks got drive-through. I felt vindicated.

("Here are Jennifer Litwin's guidelines ..." continued)

- **To clean cushions,** beat them to get the dust out, then vacuum them, and wipe them with a damp sponge or rag, says Spooky Apple, spokesperson for Glen Raven, makers of Sunbrella all-weather fabric. To treat spots, mist the spot using a spray bottle filled with a mild laundry detergent solution. Rub the spot with a soft towel or sponge (not a brush). Then mist again with clear water to rinse. For a really bad stain, try a little diluted bleach, after first spot testing.
- **If you can remove cushion covers** from their fillers, machine wash them in cold water using a mild detergent, like Woolite. Air dry. Don't put cushion covers in the dryer.
- **If your cushions get soaked** in a spring shower, turn them on their edges, so water runs out the sides, rather than collecting. Often cushions that feel dry on the surface have water lurking inside. You don't discover this soggy surprise until ten minutes after you've sat down.
- **If you have a pool,** encourage people to use towels. Sparing the furniture from a barrage of suntan oil and chlorine could double its life.

"Gone are the days of slip-covering outdoor furniture at the end of the season," said Jennifer Litwin, a furniture expert and author of *Best Furniture Buying Tips Ever*, who was singing my song. "Today's outdoor furniture is durable and can withstand cold temperatures, wind, rain, and snow. It's heartier, sturdier, and has less chance of rust and deterioration."

In other words, outdoor-furniture makers finally acknowledged that furniture abuse was a way of life. They addressed the pleas of time-pressed patio owners who demanded outdoor furniture that could stand the heat, and cold, and bird doo.

For furniture abusers like me, that meant that the price of neglect had gotten cheaper. If you buy frames and cushions that can weather the elements well, you won't pay the price of replacement nearly as often. You will, however, have to give the furniture a good cleaning when the weather gets nice, or lose all friends who wear white pants. Next, I'm hoping someone comes up with self-cleaning furniture, which would be even better than a Starbucks drive-through.

33

Color Me Floral

An idiot's guide to flowerpots

"DID YOU GET A KITTEN?" asks the friendly cashier at the gas and go.

"No, why?"

"That's how my arms looked when I got my kitten."

I look down at my bare arms, which are covered in a web of fresh scratches and scabs. "I've been gardening."

"Cactus?" she asks.

"Annuals," I say, realizing how pathetic that seems. I mean, who plants flowers and comes out looking as if they've had a run-in with a mountain lion?

Forget the Zen of gardening. For me, gardening is like combat: I go in fully armed—trowel, gloves, mosquito repellent—and invariably come out wounded and defeated. The defeat comes later when everything dies.

Now that the major yard headaches are resolved—the trees are actually thriving; the patio is holding up; the barbecue is cooking, not killing, with gas; and the deck is finished, furnished, and ready to entertain, which only took three years from the day we moved in—I want to roll up my sleeves and plant some color. Determined, I bought some flowers and pots to embellish our home's front steps, deck, and patio. No way am I hiring a landscaper for this. I'm sick of them and broke.

"What a gorgeous day!" I say sprightly, trying to infect the family with my plan. "Who wants to go get some flowers to plant?"

"I have to study for geography," my oldest daughter says.

"School's out," I say.

"For next year."

"C'mon."

"How much will you pay me?"

"I pay you all the time in chauffeur services. Besides, this isn't work. It's fun!" Just then out of the corner of my eye I see the side door open a crack, then close. My youngest has vanished. While my attention is diverted, the oldest steals out the other door. "How about you?" I say to the only human left in the room, my husband.

"Maybe after the golf tournament?" Dan says. "How much will you pay me?" I thump him hard on the arm and huff off to the garden center.

I load up with plant containers, flowers, and planting mix. One bag of mix sprouts a hole and leaves the inside of my car smelling like a recycled waste facility. Two of the new containers are sawed-in-half whiskey barrels, knee high, almost 3 feet wide, heavy, and awkward. Once home, I wrestle each one to the backyard, which is like waltzing with a whale wearing wool. Hence the arm damage.

Besides scratched arms, my overall jean shorts are covered in brown muck. I've stuffed my hair under a baseball cap and have potting soil in my ears. Times like this I tend to run into ex-boyfriends.

Later, as I'm watering, I overhear Dan talking with our neighbor Brian, who's saying how nice the planters look. "It's sunk money," Dan says. "They'll be dead in a week."

My eyes turn into little slits in my face as I train my glare on him. "Will not!" I yell. Now I'm doubly determined to make sure the flowers survive. I'm counting on botanical science. According to a Harris poll conducted for the National Gardening Association, the number of households planting container gardens has increased 50 percent in the past six years. The trend is up—I'm theorizing—because suppliers have decided that brown thumbs like me are a big market, and so they've worked to make flowerpot gardening idiot-proof.

After I'd planted my planters, I called a real gardener—my dad. I told him I'd spent the day planting.

"Bet it was quiet," he said.

"How did you know?"

"When you and your brother were kids, if I ever wanted a quiet moment, I'd just go out and work in the garden."

"You really didn't want our help?"

"Worked every time."

"I'll remember that."

Maybe I've found the Zen to gardening after all.

As it happened, the flower containers didn't do so well. Dan was right about the sunk money, and I hate when that happens. When I was done planting, the pots looked great—for about three weeks. By mid-July, they looked as burned out as a beach fire pit the morning after the weenie roast. A neighbor kid confirmed my failure when he asked why we had so many ashtrays around the yard. Before Dan could say something snide, I bought a bunch of fake tulips and stuck them in the pots. From a distance, provided your sunglasses were dirty, they almost looked convincing. Sunk money was right.

The next summer, I called in a pro, Kat Stewart, a real plant person, for help. Stewart used to work in a nursery and now has a plant service. She walked around my yard and peered into the fried planters.

"Where'd I go wrong?" I asked, as we looked at the crispy dead foliage inside a half-whiskey-barrel planter. Among the remains lay little plant markers, like tombstones in a forgotten graveyard.

If you're like me and don't have the naturalist's knack for plants, but you want summer color, here, with Kat Stewart's help, is an Idiot's Guide to Flowerpots.

- **Selection:** Don't just pick plants you like and put them wherever you think they'll look good, as I did the first time I attempted to have beautiful flowerpots. You could get lucky, but most likely you'll wind up with lovely plants that can't tolerate sun in the sunny spots, and sun-loving flowers in the shady spots. Instead, note what kind of sun the plant likes. Read their tags, or ask someone knowledgeable at your garden center. Choose annuals (Idiot's tip—these you pull up at the end of the season) over perennials (which can last years, particularly if you replant them in the ground after their flowerpot experience is over). Perennials cost more, and their bigger root systems hog available space and water, which will dry the soil in the pots out faster.
- **Drainage:** When preparing a pot, Stewart puts the plastic containers the plants come in upside down in the bottom half of the pot, then pours potting soil over that to fill the top half. This helps with drainage and makes the filled pots lighter. A clever garden store clerk gave me this tip: Since I had shallow-rooting plants, I could fill part of my whiskey barrels with Styrofoam peanuts. They're cheaper than potting soil, aid drainage, and won't make the planters so heavy. Sold! Bonus: Putting in this drainage layer will force more blooms; because the roots will have less soil to grow down into, plants will grow upward.
- **Soil:** Get a nutrient-rich soil that feeds plants after they're in. Mix 50 percent Miracle Grow Potting Soil with 50 percent less expensive potting soil.
- **Placement:** Ignore instructions that say to plant the flowers 4 to 6 inches apart. When filling pots, cram plants in to avoid skimpy-looking pots.
- **Water:** Check pots daily. If they're getting dry, water. If they are dry, soak. In humid climates, don't overwater or the roots will rot. To avoid sun-scorched leaves, water around the foliage in the early morning or at dusk. Because containers dry out faster than

"Once their little lives held so much promise," I said in my grave-side voice.

"Part of the problem is placement." She pulled the markers out: viola, lobelia, pansy, and foxglove. "These like shade. Here you have full sun."

"There's shade at night," I said.

"If the tag says 'sun to part shade,' in the heat of summer that really means no sun."

("If you're like me and don't have ..." continued)

flowerbeds, garden suppliers now offer soil additives that help the soil retain water longer. There are also water-retaining mats that line containers and release water as urns dry.

- **Fertilizer:** New potting-soil mixes are fortified to feed plants for up to thirty days. After that, you'll need to add more. You can also stick timed-release fertilizer pellets into the soil, which will dispense fertilizer for months. If only feeding my kids were as easy. Once a month, sprinkle a handful of slow-release all-purpose plant food directly onto the soil.

- **New, improved containers:** New planters look good and, unlike older styles, won't break your toes when you drop them. Not long ago, only a few types of planters were available: terra cotta, cheapo plastic, or ceramic, cement, or iron. With the exception of the plastic ones, these types weigh as much as a train car when filled. Now, garden centers sell vessels that look like weathered stone but are actually very light. They're made of molded resin. I bought two faux stone urns at Home Depot for $40 each. Dan drilled a hole in the bottom for drainage. Weight also worried me when I was deciding whether to buy those two half whiskey barrels. I love the look of these classic wood planters, which retain moisture (like me) and look better as they weather (unlike me). Plus, I loved the price: $17 each.

"Why don't they say so?"

Stewart pointed out that the front and back of my house get full sun squared. "How often did you water?" she asked.

"Every day. Almost. Except on days I didn't. Okay, maybe twice a week."

"Flowers need daily attention."

"So do my kids, my husband, the dogs, the fish, and the horse. The flowers will need to get in line. I can barely get out the door in the mornings with my hair combed and shoes matched let alone the plants watered."

"Plants aren't for everyone."

"Sorry, I didn't mean to turn this into a confessional."

She offered her watering service, which I declined. Paying someone to plant your flowerpots seems pathetic enough.

Two days later, she brought a bushel of sun-tolerant plants: geraniums, petunias, zinnias, and African daisies. In two hours my pots were brimming with life. She charged $125 for her time plus the cost of the plants she had bought for me. And I didn't have to ruin my manicure, get my knees dirty, or commit plantocide.

"How long will they last?" I asked.

"Until the first frost, if you keep them watered."

"Oh, I will," I promised, giving her the sign of the Girl Scout pledge. But just in case, I hung on to those fake tulips.

A few days after Stewart left, I went to water my planters. Inside one of the half whiskey barrels, someone had placed a small cardboard marker: "Rest in Peace," it said. My husband. Am I going to show him.

If you lack the time or talent to maintain your yard—and I lack both—a weekly gardening service can keep your yard from looking like a haven for drug traffickers. But good luck finding a decent one. . . .

34

Yard Maintenance

Managing the lazy mow-blow-and-go lawn service, first frosts, and the amazing matters of mulch

THERE'S A KNOCK AT THE DOOR. It's a strange man in dirty clothes with a three-day-old beard.

"I just want to tell you today is my last day," the man says.

"Of what?"

"Of being your gardener."

"We have a gardener?"

"Until spring. I'll be back in April to turn your sprinklers on again. I'm shutting them off today, and blowing out your pipes because the freeze is coming."

"Who is it, honey?" Dan calls from the family room.

"Our gardener."

"We have a gardener?"

"You sure you have the right house?" I say to the man. "I mean, we've been paying a monthly gardener, and I occasionally see someone blow by with a lawn mower, but . . . have we ever met?"

"I left that card in your mailbox and you called," he reminds me.

"Right."

"We try not to be too intrusive."

"You're doing your job there."

"But you would have known you didn't have a gardener when your pipes exploded like a herd of burrito-eating buffalo—if we didn't blow them out, that is."

"I see." (*Wait till you read the next section.*)

Apart from the fact that the yard's not exploding, you can't tell we have a gardener. Sure, once in a while the grass is shorter, but a hungry goat could do that. Still we pay every month because that's what you do if you're yard-work impaired and your own kids overcharge for their services.

Now I'm not singling out this guy. Every gardener we've ever hired started with big promises of lawn care, weeding, fertilizing, pruning, and planter tending. Then their service quickly degenerated into mow, blow, and go. I occasionally see their rake-filled truck. (The rakes are props.) A couple workers hop out, make sounds with their blowers that separate skin from skeleton, and put a bill in your mailbox.

If you're fast enough, you can sometimes catch them. The other day, for instance, I was fed up with the maple tree that had grown over our driveway. It reminded me of the Whomping Willow from the Harry Potter series. I knew it was about to snatch up my car and hurl it into oblivion. So that week, I lay in wait. I saw the rake-filled truck, then noticed a couple guys eating lunch in my yard. "Hey," I said, "could you prune that tree blocking my driveway?"

Silence. You'd think I'd asked them to hand over their beer supply and walk on hot coals. Then one finally said, "Our boss told us not to prune in case the customers don't like it."

"What I don't like is the car-eating tree in my driveway."

More silence. You could have heard the grass grow.

Before they left, one guy, holding what looked like an electric swordfish, buzzed the tree, which now looks like a big P, shaved up one side, puffy on the other.

Although dissatisfaction with gardening services is widespread, it says right there in the *National Enquirer,* people are amazingly loyal. My parents, for instance, have used the same gardening

Next time I hire a gardener, I'm taking the advice of Joanne Kostecky, president of the American Nursery and Landscape Association and a landscape designer in Allentown, Pennsylvania. Below are ways she said people like me could get a better shake from their gardeners. As usual, I learned that most of the problem was my fault:

- **There are three tiers of garden professionals.** Landscapers design and create outdoor spaces. Gardeners maintain planter beds and keep the yard looking cared for. Lawn-maintenance folks do lawns. I need a lawn-care service and a gardener. Though lawn-care companies will say they do it all, few really do. Bluntly put, lawn-care companies aren't good in beds.
- **When interviewing gardeners,** ask how they prune. If they use electric sheers, move on. Find someone who uses non-powered hand clippers.
- **Don't wait for spring** to hire. Interview in winter, when business is slow for the landscape companies and their prices are negotiable. Make your needs clear and outline them in a written agreement.
- **Pay by the hour.** Monthly lawn services make money by getting as many clients as they can, then moving through their yards fast. Kostecky suggested that I ask my lawn guy what he would charge by the hour to just maintain the lawn—aerate, mow, fertilize (lawn only), and manage the sprinklers. Then use the remaining money saved to pay an hourly gardener to maintain the rest. Depending on where you live, a good gardener may cost between $25 and $40 an hour. Lawn service should be less. When I divided my monthly payment ($170) by the hours the crew was here (four a month max), I saw I was spending more than $40 an hour. No wonder this makes me cranky.

service for thirty-five years. At first, Vince did an okay job, though my parents complained about him. Then he died. His son took over, and the yard went from looking benignly neglected to abandoned. But my parents won't change services because they don't want to offend Vince. People are strange that way.

Of course, our invisible gardener was nowhere to be found the day the pipes blew. . . .

Frost Fight

"I'm from California," I say, hoping that explains to my plumber how, now that I live in Colorado, I could let my waterlines freeze.

"Um-hmm," the plumber nods while examining the broken pipe.

It's November. Three of us—the plumber, Dan, and I—have gathered outside in the freezing cold around the cracked plumbing part. I'm shivering in my jacket and wool scarf. The plumber wears short sleeves and doesn't even have goose bumps. This is another difference between Californians and Coloradans. The regulator to our sprinkler system has burst. The part, which looks like a giant's knuckle in brass, has a San-Andreas-Fault-like crack down its side.

I wish I hadn't said I was from California. The statement hangs like regret in the frosty air. I've learned that the *I'm from California* line cuts many ways—not all good. For instance, to non-Californians it explains why you speak decent broken Spanish; have skin cancer at age fourteen; can sleep, cook dinner, shave, and hold a business meeting while driving your car; feel okay about having an actor in the governor's mansion; don't own a pair of socks; think a million-dollar house is the norm; expect to see green floral plant life 365 days a year; and know exactly where to find traffic and surf reports on your AM dial. But you need to be careful where you leak this information.

Folks in Colorado rank second in the nation—after Oregonians—in their collective dislike for Californians, particularly Southern Californians. They enjoy seeing California transplants suffer. Their faces break into gratified smirks when a car with California license plates slides off the road in the snow. These veterans of real winters know how to drive on snow and ice. They also know how to winterize their plumbing. Thanks to my big mouth, this plumber will probably give me a California surcharge.

I try to defend myself. "Our lawn-service company was supposed to have cleared our lines."

The plumber looks at me as if to say that if I don't know better than to check up on my lawn-service people then I must have the IQ of plankton, then says, "Some things you just need to do for yourself."

"Perhaps," I say, "I shouldn't have mentioned California. But I'm not like you think. I mean I've changed. We've changed." I wag a finger between Dan and me.

"Honey," Dan says, "that's too much information."

"Um-hmm," the plumber says.

"We didn't have to move here," I continue. "It wasn't a job change or anything. We wanted to live here. I mean we knew about the winter here and everything."

"Um-hmm," the plumber says.

Dan looks at me and runs his fingers across his lips as if pulling a zipper.

"This is only our second winter here. And we obviously still have a lot to learn before we're *seasoned*. Get it?"

"For Heaven's sake," Dan interrupts, "he's a plumber not a therapist."

"I'm just trying to show him that not all Californians are idiots."

Dan rolls his eyes.

Finally the plumber speaks: "$75 for the part and $100 for labor."

"That's the price of not listening to Mother Nature?" I ask.

He looks at me as if I'm as dumb as a corncob. "No. It's the price of a new regulator."

"Right. I knew that." We pay the man, grateful the pipe broke outside not in, and vow to do better next year, and not leave this matter to the gardener, whoever he is.

The following year, we got a jump on Jack Frost and Mother Nature. I called Tom Quilon, a local plumber with thirty-one years of practice, and asked him to give this California girl a primer on winterizing water pipes.

- **If you spend the winter** in a freezing climate, winterize your plumbing between September 15 and October 30. Listen to the news for rumblings of the first hard freeze.
- **First turn off the main shutoff valve** to your outdoor irrigation system. This is tied into your home's main plumbing system but should have a separate shutoff.
- **Bleed and blow.** Near the shutoff valve is a round screw. Grab a bucket, remove the screw, and water from the lines should run out—or bleed.
- **Next go to where each section of sprinklers is headquartered.** This is the "solenoid manifold," a fancy phrase for sprinkler line convention. Look for an opening at the core of this gathering. Then use an air compressor, air tank, or even a bicycle pump to force air into the sprinkler lines and clear them. That's the blow part. If you suffer from fall allergies, try this on your sinuses.
- **Ask whoever installed your sprinklers** where the vacuum breaker is. Either blow the water out of it, or remove it and let it hibernate in your garage next to the beach umbrella. If water freezes in this vacuum, it will break, and cost $300 to $700 to replace.
- **Go to each outside faucet.** Remove the garden hose. Dump all water out, coil it, and store it with the beach umbrella. Shake each outdoor hose bib (the part that attaches to the hose) dry. You can also buy frost-free outdoor faucets that self-drain and won't freeze.

Come spring, we realized we had to do more to get our yard spiffed up than turn on the sprinklers. For one, we wondered, what happened to our mulch?

Mulling the Matter of Mulch

Oyster shells? Shredded tires? My husband and I are in the family room discussing mulch options.

Note to anyone under thirty-something who still has a chance of not letting middle-aged home ownership consume his or her life: Get out while you still can! This is where the dream of marriage and a house with a yard will lead.

Our landscaper had put wood mulch all over the yard two years before this. I naively thought that once you put mulch down, it stayed down, like a driveway. It doesn't. See, at night mulch sprouts little wings and flies off. The pieces of mulch that stay behind then degenerate until the ground looks as dull and thin as an old man's hair. One day, you have a rich, deep layer of mulch that is doing its job—murdering weeds and smothering the ground below—and the next, poof! Your yard is bald. And you're sitting in your family room having an inane yet somehow serious discussion about your mulch options.

Ground corncobs? Carpet scraps?

Coming up with new mulch varieties has preoccupied the deepest, darkest recesses of human imagination for years. Inventive people think about what garbage they can grind up and throw all over their gardens. The super industrious ones then sell it.

Before that, nature herself had the monopoly on mulch: Leaves fell from trees, creating a crunchy, protective carpet to snuff out competitors. Or prairie grass died and collapsed to protect new shoots until the young'uns got tough enough to push through.

Now companies all over the globe manufacture mulch out of burlap, coconut hulls, newspaper, poultry litter, seaweed, rice, fiberglass, cow manure, oyster shells, recycled tires, and peanut hulls, which makes bark chips seem dull.

Some have even used the remains of human corpses. And I thought manure was disgusting. Now people can sit in their garden and commune with their late Uncle Arthur, or someone else's uncle.

When mulching your yard shows up on your to-do list, consider these expert tips:

- **Type:** No one mulch works for every yard and garden. Your choice depends on your climate, application, needs, and, possibly, your quirks—poultry litter, anyone? A xeriscape or Japanese garden will do well with gravel mulch, but a bed of ferns won't. Organic mulches will add nutrients to the soil as they decompose and will encourage worm activity, which is good for the soil but also explains why you never mulch your computer. The non-organic stuff, like the recycled tires, lasts ten times longer and doesn't have little mulch wings, so it won't fly away or decompose. Ask your local garden shop for recommendations.
- **Benefits:** Mulch does more than make a yard look well tended. It protects the ground from erosion and evaporation, controls weeds, buffers extreme soil temperatures (keeps soil warm longer in winter and cooler in summer), and can enrich the soil. Because it holds water and prevents run-off, you need to water less.
- **Timing:** The best time to mulch is late spring after the ground has warmed. If you apply mulch too early, you might keep the ground from warming enough. The timing depends on where you live. Many gardeners like to refresh their mulch in the fall.
- **Depth:** Most experts recommend a mulch depth of 3–6 inches. However, don't make mulch so thick that plants can't take root in the soil below. And take care not to pile it too heavily around the base of young plants. Mulch is like parenting—the best protects without smothering.

The human corpse idea, apparently, came out of Sweden, a society I've always pegged as being unusually liberal with their bodies.

After mulling our mulch options—and we had to think this through, as we needed 20 cubic yards delivered, or two large trucks full—Dan and I again decided on cedar mulch—a boring but reassuring choice.

As Dan and the helpers spread it over the yard, they won't be burying any skeletons—that I know of.

Let's Take It Outside—
Contractor Conflicts

For some baffling reason, my daughter's eighth-grade girlfriends elected me as the mom they would most like to back them up in a bar fight. Unlikely as that scenario is (besides, they have no business being in a bar—ever!), I take this as perhaps the best compliment I've ever received.

Oh, but that their tough-mom perceptions were true. I could use a shot of confidence just now as I head into conflict with a landscaper. I'd like a "Bar Fighter Mom" T-shirt and a matching attitude, because, in truth, in the face of conflict I crumble like coffee cake.

The fight started in the backyard, with the infamous water feature that you're already acquainted with. That water feature—rather, that problem-ridden rock pile that squirts water—is more temperamental than Mike Tyson.

Every year we need to get the feature serviced. This time, instead of asking my mysterious lawn-maintenance guy—whose skill-set shrinks each year—to help, I asked the local pond supply store to refer me to someone. The scheduler for this Water Feature Specialist, whom we'll call WFS, explained that WFS would charge $20 to show up, and $20 for every fifteen minutes, which told me two things: I'm in the wrong line of work, and he'd better make it snappy.

Afterward, I wondered how I might better handle future contractor conflicts. I called Matt Maury, president of Home Owners Club, a Seattle company that helps home-owners solve home upkeep issues. The company also runs www.homeownersclub.org, which offers subscribers information on home maintenance, finding specialists, and fraud protection. Here's what Maury advised:

- **Stop that check.** If you've paid the contractor, and the situation sours right away, stop payment on the check or call your credit card company and ask for a pay freeze. This buys you time to solve the problem.
- **Finish with the person you started with.** Unless you really don't want this contractor back to your home, give him the chance to make things right.
- **Use leverage.** Invoking the name of the person or company that referred you is often enough to make the contractor want to save his reputation—and his referral source.
- **Assume the best.** Save the accusations. Start gently, with the assumption that most contractors care about their reputations and want to do the right thing.
- **Focus on the problem.** Whether dealing with the worker or the supervisor, you'll get better results if you focus on what still isn't right than if you focus on the worker's incompetence. (My mistake: Complaining to the boss about his employee made the boss defensive.)
- **Contact your Better Business Bureau.** The BBB has a dispute resolution service that can help. Since the BBB can put a ding on a company's record, business owners usually take it seriously.
- **Accept the olive branch.** If an owner makes good, and points out extra work you need done, he's trying to regain your confidence. "That's a good sign," said Maury. Or maybe he's heard what I'd be like in a bar fight.

WFS spent thirty minutes fixing the two pumps and fifteen minutes oiling and adjusting the auto refill feature. Technically, he was done, but apparently WFS has learned to bill from lawyers, because he spent the next thirty minutes explaining and

Here's more advice on hiring contractors from Stephen Brobeck, executive director of the Consumer Federation of America. He agreed that lots of great contractors exist; the trick is finding them:

- **The best protection is prevention.** Select with great care. Use only well-established companies that have done satisfactory work for people you know.
- **Use licensed contractors.** Ask for their license, then check with the licensing board to be sure it's current and that it's for the type of work you want done. If you're hiring an electrician, he could be licensed—as a plumber.
- **Get a written contract.** The contract should define the work, the price, and the payment schedule. As changes occur, write those in, too.
- **Pay as you go.** Beware of the contractor who wants a big deposit. Brobeck likes to pay 50 percent when half the job is complete, the balance at the end. Hold back at least 30 percent until the project is finished. How a contractor responds to those terms tells you a lot about him.
- **Don't pay cash.** Get a receipt for each payment.
- **Consider a completion clause.** I've stated that I'll pay 10 percent more if the worker finishes two weeks early. I'll pay the amount we've agreed to if he finishes on time, and subtract 10 percent if he completes the job two weeks late.
- **Take action.** If a contractor leaves you in the lurch, you have two options:
  - Ask your local Consumer Protection Agency, a branch of the attorney general's office, to help resolve the matter.
  - Take the contractor to small claims court. However, if you win, collecting may be tough.

re-explaining what he had done, thirty minutes talking me into buying chemicals to treat an algae problem we didn't have, and fifteen minutes writing a receipt, while smoking, time he also charged me for. The bill for his time, his supplies, and the ridiculously expensive chemicals ($120!) came to $320. After he left, I sat on my front steps fanning my fury with my greatly diminished checkbook.

Fifteen minutes later, half the water feature stopped working. I felt that bar fighter in me rise up. I thought about calling WFS but was afraid he'd start the clock again. I called WFS's boss, the company owner. Our phone conversation quickly turned uncivil and included these lines:

Owner: "I'm trying to understand how we're to blame here."

Me: "If you would let me finish before interrupting."

It degenerated from there.

Eventually, he said he and WFS would be over, making clear that if this was a new problem, I'd be charged. I braced myself for one of those auto-shop confrontations, where the guy says he can't help that your transmission fell out the minute you left the shop; that had nothing to do with the new brakes he put in. I ate a handful of Tums, answered the door with my jaw set, and pretended I was wearing my "Bar Fighter Mom" T-shirt.

In the end—and I don't know whether the owner thought WFS had botched the job, or just didn't want me to complain to the referring pond shop about him—they got my water feature running right and didn't charge more. The owner did, however, recommend about $400 more work to improve my feature. I asked for a written bid. I'm still waiting.

PART VII

Homes for the Holidays

Create festive tables, deck the halls, and get ready to party

Why, a visitor to earth might ask, do people in civilized countries go to so much expense and trouble to beautify their homes? Why do so many put themselves through the agony of endless design decisions and projects that seem to make them miserable?

Why? I'll tell you why. To create beautiful memories. When we look back on the movie that is our life, the scenes of Christmas morning, the birthday celebrations, the dinner parties, the friends who dropped by and stayed, that's what we'll recall. And the backdrop for all that should be worthy of the moments. Thoughtfully decorated homes honor not only those who live in them but also every guest who comes through the door. So now that you've brought your home this far, don't stop here. Make your home ready for holidays and special occasions—without going nuts.

35

Thoughts on the Table

Tasteful table settings
for festive feasts

DOES ANYONE ELSE WONDER where you put the food? Ahh, the food. Walk into any home store between Halloween and Christmas, and you can't miss them. Dining tables bedecked with so many layers of linen, china, silver, crystal, and ornamentation that it would take an archaeologist six weeks to unearth the table beneath.

The food, my friends, is secondary. What's primary is that these stores sell you more linen, china, silver, crystal, and ornamentation than you'll ever need so they can pay for their own merry Christmas. To do so they need to first set up an unrealistic expectation of how your holiday table should look. Make no mistake. These tables have one purpose: to make you feel inferior so you buy more stuff to clog your cupboards and line their coffers.

Enough already.

That doesn't mean your holiday table should look like the school cafeteria's. Just that chances are, you already have what you need to make it perfect. Also, just because some chi-chi magazine says sprinkling fresh cranberries on your table runner is a great idea doesn't make it true. I tried that. My kids took up a game of cranberry marble shooting, which landed the berries on the carpet, where they left a stain and made the dogs sick. I'm not sure who's to blame, the magazine for suggesting such a dimwitted idea, or me for falling for it. Though I have my own thoughts on holiday tables, I researched what current opinion leaders say about dressing the holiday table. Big surprise: They don't agree.

One expert from a culinary arts school says tablecloths and plates should always be white with no pattern, so they don't compete with the food. The food should be the color. Glasses should

---

Here are a few more thoughts to put on the table:

- **Don't make centerpieces too big.** Too tall and guests must forge a jungle to talk across the table. Too wide and the centerpiece takes up so much real estate that you can't put platters down. If you've ever removed a centerpiece to make room for food, you know.
- **Keep festive touches simple.** Use a remnant of fabric that has a holiday motif and bunch it under a candelabra, hurricane lamp, or bowl of flowers. A crystal bowl of shiny ball ornaments also makes an easy, low-maintenance holiday centerpiece.
- **Use something old and something new.** Heirlooms enhance tradition. I like to fill my great aunt's crystal bowl with fresh flowers.
- **Light candles.** Whether long tapers or small votives, they help make Aunt May's Jell-O salad look appetizing and they soften facial wrinkles. But make them unscented. You want to cast a spell, not a smell.
- **Don't overachieve.** When you get that urge to create a table like a store display, remember that this isn't a competition. The store's job is to sell you tableware. Your job is to create a backdrop for a warm, memorable holiday.
- **Use common sense.** Don't let anyone tell you cranberries make a good table accent. Cheers.

always be clear so one can appreciate the wine's hue. I say, leave the pure white table settings to the five-star restaurants with laundry service. Putting austere white plates on white cloths puts a lot of pressure on parents of messy kids—messy kids being, of course, redundant—and on the cook. If I can distract folks from the fact that I've oversteamed the asparagus, I've succeeded.

On the other extreme, a prominent designer said, "both formal and informal tables welcome a multicolored palette in glassware and tabletop accessories." Another encouraged people to combine casual and formal dishes with colored crystal or glassware "for a sense of style and sophistication." I've dined at tables so overdone with "style and sophistication" that I was afraid to pick up my glass for fear there wouldn't be a spot to set it back down.

"Hey, wait! That was my spot."

"Sorry. You moved your glass."

Passing platters involved negotiating an obstacle course.

"Would you mind holding these candlesticks while I pass the stuffing?"

"Not if you'll cover for me while I dodge the stemware for that gravy boat."

So who's right? The purists, or those with more creative bravura? Both. To me, the prettiest tables have color but are restrained enough to let the table serve its purpose: *to be the backdrop for the meal and the conversation.* But don't get in a rut. The most memorable tables have an element of surprise.

Years ago I interviewed Barbara Barry, a top Los Angeles designer. She had just finished designing the dinner party for the opening of the Getty Center Museum. It's an illustrious place, with grand halls of white marble, as you'd expect. But Barry didn't do what you'd expect. Instead of dressing tables in white linens with white china and white roses, she used burlap tablecloths, wooden plates, and centerpieces of eucalyptus and succulents. It took guts.

"The place impresses you enough," she said. "The dinner settings had to be humble." Her story taught me this: The unexpected is fun. Important occasions don't have to be fancy. And don't take any of this too seriously. It's better to be a little whimsical than too safe.

As soon as the Thanksgiving leftovers have turned into soup, the competition begins. . . .

36

Christmas Tree Olympics

And other holiday décor sports

LADIES: START YOUR ENGINES. Forget football. Our country's real national pastime engages more players, entails more movement in more directions at once, and requires maneuvering not one but hundreds of balls at Indy speed.

The sport: Christmas tree decorating. And the race is on.

As men sit by the tube and watch overweight jocks in spandex knock each other over and hurl obscenities, we women are dashing to hobby stores, pushing each other out of the way for the last box of burgundy ornaments, and grabbing the last of the mini white twinkle lights. When we yell, "Score!" it's because we've found a collectible Radko ornament on sale. All to bring home and hang on a dying old sap.

"Who are you calling an old sap?"

"Go back to your game, honey."

Then we slow dance with a tree that feels like a porcupine with rigor mortis, set it up in a prominent location—such as the front window—for all to see, and dress it funny. I'm no psychologist, but I believe the reason spouses and kids don't listen when women tell them what to wear is that they've seen what we do to Christmas trees.

Motivating us to pursue this extreme sport are the neighbors. Just when we think our tree looks pretty good, we go to, say, the Swansons' house. Their tree is wrapped in gold lamé, is dripping with Swarovski crystals, has lights that flicker like real candle flames, twirls in place, and sings "Oh, Christmas Tree." The Hoffmans' tree has an electric train running through its branches around a village made of hand-carved Dickens characters. We vow to do better.

Up until a couple of years ago—when my domestic competitive streak kicked in—my Christmas tree always looked the same. A humble hodgepodge of good intentions and eclectic excess. Like my mother—and I assumed most other people—I just hung every ornament that anyone had ever given me (including the ones my kids made in preschool) on my poor pine until it looked as if it had torpedoed through Michael's craft store with a magnet.

Candy canes made of twisted pipe cleaners hung beside the red and green Santa face that said "Our First Christmas" (like anyone cared), which hung alongside the Mrs. Claus made of an old nylon stocking stuffed with dryer lint (a gift from a crafty neighbor). If my tree had had a theme—which I later learned it should—it would have been "Ghosts of Christmases Past."

My problem wasn't bad taste, I realized; it was sentiment, hollow ornamental sentiment at that. But could I part with all that sentiment for the sake of beauty? You bet. That pivotal year, my holiday motto became *"Trees need tough love, too."*

To help me let go, I talked to some top tree designers. I went to Christmas tree shows. I studied and deconstructed the trees I saw and liked. I fretted. I obsessed. I drove my family crazy. Then I put the methods I had gathered into practice. Now I could have hired a professional designer to do this. One offered to for $100—per foot! Times 8 feet, and uhh, there goes the gift budget.

So I did it solo. Then, when I opened my home for a small holiday party, the first woman who arrived gushed: "How did you do your tree? It looks like a department store's!" Ahh, flattery, my favorite song.

"Oh, it was simple," I said, lying. Why spoil the magic?

Ever since then, however, the once peaceful family ritual of tree trimming at my house has turned monomaniacal. We start out well. We make hot cider and play holiday music. At halftime my husband does his part—the lights. Soon, he's redder than a Santa hat and holding up progress because the lights are tangled and the game's back on. My children then hear all the words he's learned from football, and I don't mean "Touchdown!" After we've consumed so much hot cider that the whites of our eyes are amber, the girls and I start with the base layer of ornaments, about 200 matching glass balls that I insist get hung in pairs.

"Clumps of two!" I say, moving an ornament someone has spaced too far from its neighbor. The older daughter twirls a circle around her ear—intimating that I'm crazy—and says, "OCD," to the younger. I'm used to this. Just because I'm picky, my family says I have an obsessive-compulsive disorder, like those people with annoying repetitive behaviors like hand washing or door locking, which I do not have, do not have, do not have. Then—*Keesh!* We all turn at the sound of glass ornament meeting stone floor. Everyone's quiet while we wait to see who's going to get it. And we're not even to the fun ornaments yet. Soon, I'm decorating by myself. The girls are hanging stockings by the fire and role-playing with the nutcrackers. "I bet your mother wasn't this picky about her tree," one nutcracker says to the other.

"Picky!" the other answers. "Geez, last time I helped decorate, she turned me into a wooden boy and dressed me in this stupid soldier costume."

Somewhere in the next room, my husband is yelling, "Get 'em! You loser!" over the tunes of "Deck the Hall," and *keesh!* Ahh, Christmas. Let the games begin.

Here's what I learned from top tree designers:

- **Pick a theme or a scheme.** If you want a designer tree, think unity. Pull a look together by choosing a color scheme or a theme. Keeping everything in one or two colors turns visual chaos into harmony. Any combination of jewel tones or white paired with a metallic—gold or silver—works great. Carry your theme color into other holiday decorations throughout your home. Limit content by zeroing in on a theme: teddy bears, toys, angels, and Santa and his elves are predictable routes. Or express the inner you with trees featuring just surfboards or sailboats, gardening paraphernalia, or musical instruments.

- **Lay on the lights.** You need more than you think. Picture a movie marquis. Clear lights show up best, but color to go with your theme can look great, too. Put them on first. Great Christmas trees glow from the inside. Too often people wrap lights around the tree (guilty!). Instead, wrap lights around branches, starting from the outside and moving in toward the trunk. Continue wrapping branches from the trunk to outer edge. Arrange strands so plug ends connect to the center. Affix a power strip to the main trunk to ground light strands.

- **Edit your ornaments.** This is hard, but you have to be ruthless. Some ornaments really may never see a tree branch again. That's okay. They'll find a support group somewhere. If you're afraid you'll hurt your kids' feelings, create a kids' tree! We got a second tree, a notch above Charlie Brown's, and put it upstairs. We put on a string of lights, then tied on all the homemade concoctions, er, ornaments, with matching red satin ribbons (for unity). The children were delighted, and peace reigned at home. Keep only the ornaments that go with your color scheme or theme, then buy dozens of ball ornaments, all the same color, and hang them evenly all over the tree by groups of two or three. (Don't do this while drinking hot toddies.)

- **Use fillers.** Professional designers fill gaps between branches by stuffing the spaces with color-coordinated bows, ribbons, and dried or silk flowers. I've also seen people bunch up wide swaths of festive fabric, like voile or lamé, and swirl it artistically throughout the tree.

After a pause for self-congratulation, it's time to decorate the rest of the house.

The Wrap on Banisters

Several years ago I went to a hairstylist to get my hair done for a wedding. As the stylist was creating the "up-do," she said, "My goal is to make your hair look like you did it yourself."

"Excuse me?" I thought. "Then why am I paying you?"

I understand that achieving an effortless, not-too-contrived look is an art. But there's a fine line between a natural hairstyle and a heron's nest. Which brings me to the seasonal garland on my stair banister. The first time I tried to apply this decoration all by my unprofessional self, the banister resembled a subdivision of

---

("Here's what I learned…" continued)

- **Add texture.** Mix shiny ornaments with matte ones, velvet bows with satin ones. Add silk flowers, such as showy magnolias. When decorating, put shiny ornaments in the tree's interior, and duller ones toward the surface, smaller ornaments high, larger ones low.
- **Top it off.** Take spools of wire-edged ribbon (in your color) and tie the ends together to create a large bow for the treetop. Let the ends trail over the tree to the floor. Bend waves in the ribbons so they ripple.
- **Skirt the issue.** When you're done, wrap the tree base in a festive skirt that ties into the theme. Hey, you weren't going to wear that purple bridesmaid dress again anyway, were you?
- **Brace yourself.** Last, plug the tree in, turn off the rest of the lights, put on a fire, grab that hot toddy and the one you love, and brace yourself for envy.

herons' nests. Sob! See, I bought my last house for its staircase. It swirled. Maybe I'd seen too many Hallmark commercials, but something about that curved staircase made me weak in the knees. I pictured Christmas, a gorgeous decorated garland swooning up

Here are the banister-decorating tips I learned that first year and have applied every year since:

- **Buy good greenery.** Some garland is pretty cheesy. You want bushy and real looking, not thin. Measure your banister, then buy two and a half times its length. Think lush. Skimpy screams amateur. If you want a rustic look, choose garland with pinecones or berries. Solid green looks more formal.
- **Wrap.** Twist the garland around the banister, going under and around the balusters at equal intervals so twists look even. At the base of the stair run the garland to the floor with a generous swirl at the bottom. Warning: Dogs (including mine) have mistakenly interpreted this indoor foliage as an indoor plant that needs watering.
- **Light.** Now wrap the greenery with white lights, assuming there's a convenient outlet that doesn't trip grandma.
- **Tie.** Pick a two-color scheme that ties in with your tree, home, or holiday décor. I like to see one metallic color (silver or gold) with either a jewel tone (teal, purple, red, royal blue) or white or cream. I pair burgundy and gold. Stick with two colors so your house doesn't look like a carnival. Buy a few rolls of thick-wired ribbon in these colors. Loosely wind the ribbon up the banister greenery like stripes on a barber pole.
- **Trim.** Gather silk flowers, sprigs of berries, or foliage in your color scheme and stick them into the garland. You can poke in sprigs of fake greenery, too, like ivy. Distribute accents evenly and generously.
- **Focus.** Finally, create a focal point at the base of the stair. Here you can go for it. Run the garland and decorations to the floor and let them puddle a little. Along this vertical run, attach larger floral pieces, a large bow using the same ribbon used on the banister, and beefed-up accents.

the curved stairs, my kids beautifully coiffed and posed for their holiday card photo. This never came together, of course, but we all have dreams.

In any case, I bought the house not because it was close to good schools, or because it was an easy commute to work for my husband, or because it was on a great lot. Nope, for the staircase. So, when Christmas came that first year, I attempted to make the banister look like my vision. When I was done, it looked as if the banister had lost a fight with a fake forest in Vegas. In other words, it looked like I did it myself.

The next year—and my husband still doesn't know what I paid for this indulgence—I hired a professional floral designer. For $75 an hour plus the materials (choke!), which I have used every year since, so this is amortizing nicely, she designed and decorated my banister. As she worked, I watched her like a heron. I took notes and photos. The next year, and every year since, I brazenly, and without a smidgen of guilt, copied her. In my current home, which has an even bigger curving staircase—it's an affliction—I follow the same program, which, incidentally, works on straight stairs, too. And now you can learn what my $75-an-hour designer taught me, so you, too, can do what comes unnaturally and look like a pro.

The Spirit Within

"We kept driving by not sure if this was the house," the woman said as she came through my door to our holiday party.

"Well, it is," I said brightly, taking her coat, noting the Marc Jacobs label. Hmmph.

"We were looking for lights or something," her husband added.

"All your neighbors have lights," she said, as if I didn't know that.

"Well, you would think," I laugh, feeling guilty—again—for not having more outdoor spirit. "We just didn't get around to lights this year."

"Or last year," whined my daughter, who's working as coat-check girl. I give her a glare to stop her from sharing family skeletons. But we both know the guests have kicked Mrs. Claus in her Achilles.

Although inside our house, the holiday sparkle was blinding, outside it might as well have been Labor Day. Naturally, I blame my husband. Our agreement is simple, if sexist: I decorate the inside; he decorates the outside. Just because he's unaware of this agreement doesn't mean he shouldn't abide by it.

I do my part the day after Thanksgiving, while he watches football and eats turkey sandwiches. Then I start nagging, which brings out an excuse list longer than my Christmas stocking: It's too soon. Wait till the game's over, or the weather's nicer, or the lights miraculously untangle themselves and all actually turn on. It's too late; Christmas is almost over.

Before I strangle him with garland, I do something as rare as a Santa sighting on Groundhog Day. I consider his side. Dan's not lazy. You'll recall the deck he built, and the wainscoting he installed. So what gives? Then I light (sorry) on the root of his reluctance. It's his infuriatingly practical nature. He thinks it makes perfect sense to wash dishes only once every three days. He doesn't understand why, when the elastic in his underwear makes the sound of radio static, it's time to replace them. "They're just getting broken in." He doesn't see the point of making the bed or using a hamper, and he only washes his car on high holy days. Christmas lights, therefore, don't symbolize to him the bright spirit of the season, but the height of futility—or fatality: You put them up. You take them down. Both times you risk your life.

Now I know you're thinking: If Christmas lights mean so much to me, why don't I hang them myself, or hire someone? I'm all for women's equality, but I delegate to those with more testosterone any outdoor job that requires a tall ladder and power tools. I have a friend who one year, just five days before Christmas, fell off a ladder while trying to fix her outdoor lights. She broke both her arms, and her husband still feels like a chump.

As for hiring a pro, frankly, come that time of year—well, all year—I'm cash-strapped. My family would prefer I spend that $300 on gifts.

"What?! No gifts?"

"It's the gift of light!"

To help you put light in your lives, and to spare you life, limb, electric shock, and broken marriages, I called lighting specialist Richard Beard, of Logan, Utah, who offered these outdoor holiday lighting tips:

- **Buy lights** with UL or ETL labels. They've passed minimum safety standards. Use only lights marked for outdoor use.
- **Plug into three-pronged** grounded outlets. Don't use indoor extension cords, but a sturdy, three-pronged outdoor cord. Fuses blow when people string too many strands together (usually more than three) before grounding to an outlet.
- **When reusing strings,** discard any that have frayed wires, damaged sockets, or missing bulbs. When replacing bulbs, unplug the string.
- **Use screw-in hooks** or fasteners that don't damage your house or light strings. Nails and staple guns can damage both.
- **Take down the lights** when the season's over. They're not designed to withstand prolonged weather exposure. Plus, leaving them up makes you look like a redneck.
- **Or go with a pro** and avoid all the above. Most charge between $200 and $400 to light a house. That usually covers putting the lights up, taking them down, and maintaining them. Pretty tempting. But lights or no lights, the party's still inside. The spirit is still within.

Thud. That would be the sound of falling hope. Still, I'm tempted. I've put promotional cards from house lighting services near Dan's cereal bowl. He ignores them. He resents spending money on jobs he can do himself—even if he doesn't do them. Which is another subject I need to bring up with the therapist we're surely heading for.

This year my girls and I anticipated the light wars and acted early. We chose my youngest daughter to do the bidding, because she's the hardest to refuse. My older daughter and I stood offstage and coached:

"Daddy, can we have Christmas lights this year?"

"Why your pretty smile is all the light I need."

We shake our heads violently and make motions like a referee signaling foul. Don't fall for that charm trick.

"Daddy, everybody has lights but us."

"What's the point if you only see them when you drive into the driveway at night?"

"It shows the world we have spirit."

We nod and point our thumbs up.

"We'll see," he says. And we all know what that means. Bah Humbug.

37

Party Time!

Whose idea was this?

IT STARTS INNOCENTLY. One night you're sitting by the fire with your significant other drinking eggnog that's probably too strong when one of you says, "We should have a holiday party." The warm feeling grows and pretty soon you're on the phone; the word is out, and there's no going back.

Then reality hits: You have to clean the house! I mean clean beyond what any housekeeper can do. (Housekeepers can't throw away your clutter, magazines, and mail; they just make the piles straighter.) You look around anticipating the public humiliation. You imagine your guests wrinkling their noses and whispering, "Oh, they're that kind of family." You start to notice everything you've been ignoring or stepping over: moldy socks behind the drapes, the dog's chew toy in the bread box, dead moths in the light fixture, the cooked-cabbage smell in the refrigerator, and the carpet stain where one of the dogs chewed up a watermelon-scented marker. Next thing you know, you're running around like your hair's on fire screaming, "Whose idea was this?"

Parties put the pressure on.

Yet every holiday season I have at least one. To prepare, I dart through the house like a roller derby queen armed with Pledge, Mr.

Clean, and a stun gun. My goal isn't perfection. I gave that up years ago along with the goals of six-pack abs and a caffeine-free existence. Some efforts aren't worth the agony. But I do want my home to look better than usual, usual being a cross between the epicenter of a large earthquake and a frat house.

I start with a big basket and go room to room. I fill it with the flotsam and jetsam of our lives: unpaid bills, chewed gum wads, overdue library books, dull razors, dead flowers, burned-out fireworks. When I get to my kids' rooms, I close the doors and put thick red "Biohazard" tape over them.

Beyond a good cleaning, here's what Dickey said to do to make your house party ready:

- **Clutter bust.** Put all toys in one designated playroom, ideally with the kids, a pizza, and a babysitter. Cut back your stack of books and magazines to two each, and the newspaper to that day's. Blast through the mail stack. Put what you can't throw away or file into a basket in the garage to sort after the party.
- **Strip the refrigerator.** Take off all the kids' pictures and artwork. Open it and toss anything old, smelly, or gross.
- **Edit your stuff.** If you must feature your angel collection, don't put out all fifteen; put out three of your prettiest, together. "Staging is all about selective decorating," said Dickey. "It's better to start with a clean surface and add a few carefully selected items than to figure out what to remove."
- **Get rid of the magazines.** That is, the ones in the bathroom. "No one needs to know what you're reading in there. It conjures up a weird image." Speaking of weird images, I once went into a bathroom and found a laptop. Detail this space well. Set out clean guest towels. Remove anything embarrassing from the cabinets. People look.
- **Edit your bulletin boards.** Remove appointment cards and prescriptions. No one wants to know when your next colon screening is, or that your husband's on Viagra and you're on estrogen.

I stand back and try to see my house as someone who's never seen it would. Then I get down to business. It's party time. I roll up my sleeves and start staging.

Although I have my own kamikaze way, I decided to call a staging pro. Dana Dickey is vice president of Interior Redesign Industry Specialists, a national organization based in Chicago whose members specialize in staging homes for sale and events. "It's not that people don't want to pick up," she said. "They just stop noticing what other people do." She was being kind. Most of us avoid housework like we avoid the endodontist.

But, hey, one of the best things about parties is that they make you clean up. And when you do open your doors to entertain, don't make the mistake I used to. For years, I focused not on all the

---

("Beyond a good cleaning …" continued)

- **Hide the laundry room.** However, if your guests will be in there, dump all dirty clothes in the washer and close the lid. Put a tablecloth over the washer and dryer to make back-up counter space.
- **Cut the lights.** Switch 60 watt bulbs to 40 watt for softer ambience. Light candles. They hide a lot, including dust in corners and worry lines. Pillars burn longest. Avoid scented candles, which make some people sick.
- **Do a walk-through.** Start at the front door. Plan where guests will put coats and purses, where they will head for a drink or food, and where they will go from there. Be sure the experience flows. If a place in your house usually becomes a bottleneck, rearrange furniture to open it. To get guests to gather in other parts of the house, put food there.
- **Point the way.** For large parties, place directional signs on easels that point to the coatroom, bar, or kitchen. This frees you from being traffic cop.
- **Think twice.** Make sure you want to do this before you open your big mouth and say "Party at my place!"

home improvements I had gotten done, but on what I still needed to do. I'd go through the house with guests almost apologizing: "We're still waiting on drapes here," or, "Someday we'll have art for over the fireplace." I was missing the point. Decorating a home is a process. Your whole house may never be done to your liking, or when it is, you'll probably need to start over, like those who paint the Golden Gate Bridge.

So when friends visit, or you host that soirée, don't sweat the fact that the powder room isn't finished, or the entryway still looks like it did the day you moved in. And never postpone a party because you're waiting for a new sofa. Enjoy your home and all you have done to make it yours. Live now. Always keep in mind that most basic of truths: The house is there to support you, your milestones, your traditions, your daily life. You're not there to support it. Get that, and you won't let the house win.

Now that I've started you on this truly endless journey of home improvement, I'll leave you with one more story. . . .

PART VIII

Home Economics

Make your household dollars go farther without feeling the pinch

When housing markets plummet and take the economy with them, people stress about money. We do at my house. To stretch our household income, I started to look at home economics as something other than an 8th grade class I didn't do too well in. I searched for ways to cut household spending, and, of course, I talked to experts for ways to save on everything from utility bills, to household expenses, to yard costs. See if the scenarios below sound familiar. If so, put these cost-saving tips to work.

38

Thirty Ways to Patch Money Leaks at Home

Start cutting energy, food, and yard bills now

Saving on utilities . . .

OUR HOUSE LEAKS MONEY.

We stuff money in, as if filling a turkey, and it flows out the window, up the chimney, down the drain, into the garbage, and through the door. It swirls down the vortex of our water-sucking toilets, and blows out the dryer vent. Our house leaks money faster than a sorority house leaks secrets.

That leakage, on top of collapsing home values and a snap of cold weather, puts Dan into stealth mode when it comes to saving. Thus, we are a home at war: We have water wars, light wars, and heat wars.

"Who's running half a load of laundry?" he growls.

"But our clothes are small," one daughter defends.

"Who left the lights on?"

The girls and I look at the dogs.

Every night before we sit down to dinner, Dan roams the house flicking off lights until the only one on is the one hanging over the dinner table, where the four of us sit, surrounded by darkness, looking as if we're about to be interrogated.

When Dan's not looking, the girls eke the thermostat up. When they're not looking, he shuts it off.

"It's cold," one daughter says shivering.

"Put on another sweater," he says.

"I'm already wearing three under my parka."

"Then get in bed."

Beyond shivering in the dark, here are some cost-saving home improvements and tips that Calli Schmidt, environmental communications director for the National Association of Home Builders, says can comfortably reduce money leaks at home:

- **Beef up insulation.** According to the U.S. Department of Energy, homes can lose up to 60 percent of their heating through areas where insulation or ducting is inadequate. Insulation keeps heat in when it's cold out and is cheap compared to what it saves. Consider adding an environmentally friendly insulation, such as blown-in cellulose. Cover the water heater and pipes, too

- **Patch cracks.** Use caulk, new weather stripping, or a spray foam like Great Stuff to patch cracks and openings around the house that let in cold air. Ask whether your local utility company offers free energy audits, or if they can recommend an energy professional to perform a blower test, which determines where leaks are.

- **Make the most of hot air.** When the heat is on, close ceiling vents and open floor vents. Run ceiling fans in the reverse direction to force rising warm air down and keep it circulating. Turn off heat or close heat vents and doors in unused rooms. Open window coverings on south-facing windows on sunny days.

- **Right size your HVAC.** If you're replacing or adding a heating and air conditioning unit, don't buy a bigger system than you need. Oversized units won't work better, but will cost more to operate. As with all appliances, look for the Energy-Star label.

To be fair, I, too, can be an energy miser. When the heater is running, and I notice one of the kids has her window open, my mother comes flying out of my mouth: "Just wait till you're paying the heating bills. Then you'll remember to close the windows!"

Granted, Dan's motives—save money, conserve energy—are purer than mine: Forget for a moment about the planet's limited resources, global warming, our over reliance on foreign oil, and the tough economy. To me, the real question is: Why puff money out the window when you could use it to buy a stylish pair of boots?

("Beyond shivering in the dark ..." continued)

- **Program that thermostat.** Get a thermostat that lets you set the time and temp of the heating and cooling (assuming you can get the household to agree) so you only pay for comfort when you need it. Programmable thermostats cost from $40 to $100, but save the average home 10 to 15 percent on energy bills.
- **Replace single-pane windows.** Double pane windows with glass labeled low-e (for low emissivity) reduce heat loss in winter and heat gain in summer—but only if you remember to close them. Because new windows are expensive, window insulation kits offer a cheap ($4 per window) and effective alternative. These temporary plastic sheets stick to your windows on the inside.
- **Go cold.** Turn your water heater down to 120 degrees. Wash your clothes (full loads) in cold water. Hang them dry when you can.
- **Switch to Compact Fluorescent Light bulbs.** Put them in areas that stay lit for two hours or more. Though CFLs cost more than incandescent bulbs, they save in the long run. They are four times more efficient, use 50 to 80 percent less energy, and last 10 times longer.
- **Plant trees.** Deciduous trees planted on the south and west side of your house can provide shade in warm months and cut the need for air conditioning. Plus, one tree filters 60 pounds of air pollutants each year.

Saving around the house . . .

Cutting energy bills is a good first step, but most households, including mine, leak money in other ways. As I watched the econ-

In my zeal to cut household spending, I asked kitchen coach Mary Rogers and organizing guru Cynthia Townley Ewer, author of *HouseWorks* (DK Press) and founder of organizedhome.com, for more money-saving tips:

- **Make a meal plan.** Buy fewer takeout meals. "People say they're too busy to cook, but, if you plan a week of meals, buy the ingredients for them (and only them) in one trip to the store, you'll save time, gas, and money, and will probably eat healthier," says Rogers. Make your meal plan. Write your list. Scour ads for deals. And look for store brands, which offer equivalent quality at lower prices, says Ewer.

- **Organize the pantry.** So you don't buy mustard when you have two jars in the pantry, put like with like—canned fruits and jellies in one place, condiments in another, cereals together, etc. Put small items in front, large in back, so nothing gets buried. Be sure the whole household follows the system. As you get down to your last jar of a staple, like canned tomatoes, write it on the grocery list (which you're keeping, right?). Dedicate a section to complete dinners. Stock all the ingredients for several meals, like tuna casserole. This will buffer you against emergencies.

- **Cut down on cleaning products.** "You don't need a bathroom cleaner and a kitchen cleaner," says Ewer. "A streamlined cleaning tote containing evaporating glass cleaner (like Windex), degreaser (409 or Fantastic), dishwashing liquid, and tub-and-tile cleaner handles 90 percent of household cleaning chores." Buy these in bulk from warehouse-type stores, so you pay for product not packaging. Decant them into spray bottles. To stretch them, use half what you normally use. If that works, try less, until you find the sweet spot.

omy tank, I uttered something to Dan I never thought I would: "We need to cut spending."

"Have you been taken over by aliens?" he asked.

"I've already made some cuts, deep cuts," I say, trying to convince him I've become a thrifty woman.

He raises his wary eyebrows. My fingers are in front of his face waving like two over-stimulated sea anemones. "Look, I gave up my silk nails, a $40-per-month habit."

He backs up his nose to adjust for presbyopia.

"And I've been using grocery-store hair color." I throw my head down so he can inspect the haphazard root job. "That's saving 75 salon dollars every eight weeks."

From this head-tipped vantage, I take in Dan's shoes, loafers he's worn since college, which he alternates with the tennis shoes he's

---

("In my zeal to cut household spending ..." continued)

- **Don't buy stuff to organize your stuff.** Living with clutter wastes time, which is money. But spending money on organizers just leads to organized clutter. Declutter first, then measure what you're storing, and buy organizers last, says Ewer.
- **Save on dry cleaning.** Don't fall victim to dry-clean-only labels. Some of these garments you can wash at home, by hand in cold water and mild detergent. If it's the professional pressing you like (and who doesn't), home launder certain garments and have the dry cleaner press them. You can save up to 40 percent. Look for coupons and ask your dry cleaner if he will meet the price of a competitors' coupons, or offer you a similar discount.
- **Bundle your services.** Have your Internet, phone, and cable service moved to one provider. (Find bundling offers at lowermy bills.com.) Consider whether you really need all the extras. Can you live without call waiting, premium cable, and satellite?

worn since high school. It's difficult to discuss thrift with this man, but I press on.

"And I didn't even go to the Nordstrom half-yearly sale."

"Impressive," he says, nodding above the frayed collar of his polo. He's unconvinced that a woman who has an advanced degree in consumer spending with a minor in consumer confidence can change. I also know that he's not saying what he's thinking because he's learned what it feels like to be on the business end of my elbow.

"Next," I continue, "we have to change our grocery habits."

"You don't buy groceries." This may be the only shopping area where I underachieve. Typically, about an hour before dinner, I dash to the store to buy the fewest items I need to get through one meal, which, he reminds me, is a complete waste of time, gas, and opportunity. When he grocery shops, he grabs a big cart. (I avoid the big cart like I avoid elastic waistbands and opt instead for those little hand held baskets, which, and here I must appeal to Isabella Fiori and Kate Spade, really need a redesign.) Dan whirls up every aisle shopping as if we were anticipating the Great Irish Famine. If something is on sale, he raids the shelf, which explains why we have 27 cans of albacore in water. He brings home a dozen bags, but can't answer what's for dinner.

"We're out of control!" I confess to kitchen coach Mary Collette Rogers, founder of everydaygoodeating.com, whom I appealed to for cost-saving advice.

"Neither way works," she said, but confirmed my instinct that household goods and services are areas where most of us can save a lot without feeling the pinch.

Saving around the yard . . .

I'm having lunch with Dan on the outdoor deck of a local restaurant, surrounded by a flourishing garden.

"Look how lovely the gardens are," I say, a note of wistfulness set strategically in my voice.

Dan, well trained after nineteen years of marriage, correctly translates my comment to mean, Unlike our yard, which looks like a compost pile, and responds accordingly: "Since we're saving money by not taking a crazy vacation this summer, I think we can afford to spend a little on improving our yard."

I being equally well trained don't say, It's about time! Instead, because I embrace any hope for home improvement that trickles forth in these budget-starved times, I say, "Great! I'll get some plans to fix up that dreadful patch in the front yard by the street."

"Actually," he says, "I was thinking we'd fix up the backyard around the deck."

"And we should. But first we owe it to our neighbors to make the front look better."

"I want to sit on the deck after work and enjoy my backyard."

"But they have to look at our house when they go by."

"I don't care what they see. I care what I see."

"Fixing up the front yard is a public service."

"This isn't about altruism."

"How is everything?" The waiter asks.

We screw up our faces to form unconvincing smiles.

"Fine."

"Fine."

Dan makes a pneumatic sigh, like a bus pulling up to the stop. "I can't believe we don't agree on this."

"Maybe we should take that vacation."

In the end, like most arguments, this one proved pointless. The two areas we agreed on were that we needed to economize and we needed a plan. We both know better than to landscape kamikaze style. So I called a landscaper out and asked what he would charge to draw plans for the front and back areas. The cost for plans—$500—pretty much consumed our budget. But now, at least, we'll know what to do next—if, that is, we ever agree.

Dean Hill, a landscape designer based in Indianapolis and member of the American Society of Landscape Architects, says, "Whatever money you spend on landscape, a plan is your best investment. I know it's not an instant new yard, but it's your road map for when you do have more yard money." Here are more ways Hill suggests to get the most out of your landscape dollars:

- **Plant with a plan.** "Many homeowners go to a big box garden center, see many beautiful plants in bloom, and buy one of each," says Hill. "They go home and plant them all and wind up with a hodgepodge. Nothing correlates to anything around it." A good landscape designer will know what will work in your yard, how to organize various components, and integrate them so your yard coheres. A good plan can run anywhere from $500 to $5,000, depending on the landscape designer's experience, and the size and complexity of the yard.

- **Be up front about costs.** Many landscape designers will waive the plan fee if you use them for the project. But don't be fooled. That fee is buried in the cost of the project. If you can only afford the plan at first, say so. If you do use the landscaper later to do some or all of the work, ask if he'll give you credit for the plan fee.

- **Don't feel pressured to do the whole job at once.** "It's a rare client who can pay for everything right away," says Hill. "Most do a bit at a time and do some work themselves. If a contractor gets put off by that, find another contractor."

- **Do some jobs yourself, leave others to the pros.** Hill recommends having your landscapers do anything that involves construction (patios, retaining walls, fire pits, gazebos), complex irrigation systems, and bed preparation, which involves putting the right soil amendments in different areas depending on what's going there. But homeowners can save money by buying and planting the

Saving when you sell . . .

Alas, if only life conferred with the real estate market before it dealt you a life-changing blow. But jobs change. Babies arrive. Family members move out. Dogs bark. A pedophile buys the house next door. And sometimes you must move from your dream house.

("Dean Hill, a landscape designer ..." continued)

specified trees and plants themselves, and by running basic sprinkler systems. Homeowners can also save if they buy and spread their own mulch. Landscapers charge between $50 and $100 per cubic yard of mulch installed. You can buy a cubic yard for between $25 and $35. "You'll save 50 percent or more, and all you need is a weekend and a wheelbarrow."

- **Shop end-of-season sales.** In spring and early summer it's tempting to buy up the garden center. But wait. End-of-season sales are just around the corner. Come August and September, those $20 plants will be $12 or less. Plus, fall is an ideal time to plant.
- **Grab Cuttings.** Next time you walk around your neighborhood, bring clean scissors and a bag. When you see something thriving that you like, snip a cutting. They're free and will likely thrive at your home, too. Aim for several inches of new growth and cut just below a node, where leaf joins stem. (You might ask permission first, in case the neighbor owns a shotgun.) Pluck off all but the top leaves. Back home, dip the cutting in root hormone and put it in a cup of sterile sand or non-soil planting mix. Be sure to bury two or three nodes when you plant it. For more cuttings, an aquarium works well. Keep the container in a bright warm place covered with plastic, like a mini greenhouse.
- **Use-What-You-Have Planters.** Don't spend money on fancy planters. Look around your garage and house. Old wagons, wrapper-free paint cans, wheelbarrows, baskets, old work boots, and pitchers can all make whimsical planters and give new life to objects you'd otherwise toss.

If you're thinking about putting up the for sale sign—and no I'm not moving from this house, yet—think Broadway, because you're going to be on stage. Fixing your house up for sale is different from fixing your house up for you. Knowing the inexpensive touches that attract buyers is particularly important when trying to sell in a cool real estate market.

So, if you're fixing to sell, here are ten inexpensive ways LaPorta said will help move your house faster:

- **Get the right mindset.** Once you list your home, detach yourself. It's not about you anymore. Treat the house as a commodity. Make changes that will depersonalize it and broaden its appeal.
- **Start at the curb.** Look at what people see when they pull up. Trim hedges, prune trees, mow the lawn, and plant flowers. If the mailbox is tired and address numbers are falling off, replace them. Walk around the house; get all debris off the property.
- **Paint—it's money in a can.** Outside, a coat of paint is one of the best facelifts you can give your house for a relatively low price. If you don't want to paint the whole house, paint the trim. Inside, paint walls a soft neutral like warm beige, sage, or gold. Paint says fresh start and masks odors.
- **Focus on the entry.** The front door makes a strong first impression. Make sure the door, hardware, and porch décor look fabulous.
- **Start packing.** Most homes would show much better with 50 percent less stuff. Since you're already moving, give yourself a head start by packing away clothes, books, and dishes you won't need for the next few months. Thinning out bookcases and closets lets buyers better appreciate the space and gives the illusion that the house offers more than adequate storage. If you can't get the stuff into off-site storage, stack neat, labeled boxes in the garage. While you're at it, clear surfaces. In kitchens, leave out just one appliance. On your desk leave just a phone and a lamp. Think nice hotel.

"In a hot market, the extras can fetch multiple offers. In a cool market, they can mean the difference between getting an offer or not," says Lisa LaPorta, co-host of HGTV's *Designed to Sell.*

At first, I didn't believe all those experts who said that before you put your house on the market, you should stage it. That, in part, means stripping it of your personality. Pshah, I thought. That advice is for people who have no taste, no style. They haven't seen

---

("So, if you're fixing to sell ..." continued)

- **Catch up on maintenance.** Do those minor repairs you should have done. Paying attention to details signals that you care about big stuff, too.
- **Consider new appliances.** In LaPorta's experience, sellers get back every dollar they spend on new appliances. "When people see new kitchen appliances, they often see a new kitchen. That rates high on people's radar."
- **Add house bling.** Update anything metal. People see shiny new metal, and say "Oooh." You can buy a new dining room light fixture for $200 and one for the porch for $40. Change door knobs, faucets, and curtain rods if they're worn and dull. You may only need a can of spray paint. Styles don't change, metals do. If you have dated polished brass fixtures, paint them an updated metallic that looks like oil-rubbed bronze, brushed nickel, or iron.
- **Clean house.** Clean is relative, but we often don't notice our own dirt. So look hard starting with the switch plate by front door. Wipe it down along with all light switches, doors, and baseboards. If you're not the best housekeeper, hire a service. Every surface should sparkle.
- **Banish smells.** Pet odors kill deals. When people walk in, they should smell either nothing or a really nice scent, like cinnamon or citrus. Put out potpourri or fresh flowers. Have carpets—if not re-placed—professionally cleaned and deodorized.

my home—or yours. Who wouldn't appreciate our family photos, book collections, and travel mementos?

LaPorta finally convinced me otherwise. The news felt like a body blow. "Home buyers don't want to know you better," she said. "Depersonalizing a home lets buyers imagine themselves in it."

In other words, sweetheart, unless you're Elvis and the place is Graceland, no one gives a rat's whisker about your lifestyle or the framed photos of you looking possessed with your electric guitar. Get over it. They just don't.

Here's the brutal truth: People looking to buy your home don't care who you are, what sports your kids play, how you looked on your wedding day or where you went to college. They don't care about the striped bass you caught on the Arkansas River, your painted velvet art collection, your ballroom dance trophies, your quilting project, or that photo of you standing on top of Mt. McKinley looking like a street person. If they do get intrigued by the photo of you standing with Gene Simmons or Nelson Mandela or Lance Armstrong or Queen Elizabeth, they're not focusing on your home, which is the point.

The little touches matter, said LaPorta, because today's buyers can afford to be choosy.

Now that I've started you on this truly endless journey of home improvement and more affordable home enjoyment, I'll leave you with one more bit of perspective. . . .

Final Thought

You Can Take This Home

SEVERAL YEARS AGO, my family went on a much-anticipated trip to France. As we were standing inside the Palace of Versailles, just outside Paris, gaping at the grandeur of perhaps the world's most ornate residence, I couldn't help but feel humbled to my knees as we looked around this castle that a few centuries ago had housed a succession of fancy French kings, including Louis XIV, Louis XV, and Louis XVI. Nearby, a small girl, about five years old, stood with her well-dressed parents. As the trio gazed at one of the palace's more ornate rooms, the girl slapped her hands to her cheeks and gasped:

"We are so poor!"

I could have kissed her. I knew just how she felt. Home tours, never mind palace tours, always make me feel that way. But the Palace of Versailles—think Hearst Castle on steroids—is particularly humbling, with its glacial marble walls, gilded columns, hall of mirrors, masterpiece ceilings, and tapestries the size of billboards. Being there moved me to imagine living back in the eighteenth century. I can see myself. I'd have big hair, not a franc in the bank but some great clothes, and I'd hungrily and unsuccessfully aspire to live like royalty. But, alas, my station as a commoner would keep me outside the noble court. I'd press my nose against the palace glass and ask the question that haunts me to this day, a question I posed at the beginning of this book:

"How do you get to live like this?"

A tour guide snapped me out of my reverie. She was showing us the queens' bed, where the public was invited to watch queens give birth to heirs of the throne, apparently an early effort to prevent identify theft.

"Oh, sick," said my oldest. For once we agreed. If either of us were queen, we'd get that line struck from the job description.

But back to the notion of excess, which the guide reminded me has its price. Tired of seeing the royals live so lavishly at the people's expense, the people of France ran Louis XVI and Marie Antoinette out of the palace in 1789, put them in prison, and chopped off their heads. As the guide explained this, I noticed my daughters had plugged into their iPods and were missing the point. I pulled out their earphones and restated the lesson to make sure they got it, because it's a lesson that's all too easy for all of us to forget: Although these people lived lavishly for their time, we live better than the richest kings and queens in history. They didn't have near the luxuries we take for granted. They didn't have forced-air heat or air conditioners. They relied on smoky fireplaces that led to lung problems. They didn't have hot and cold running water. They—or their servants—had to fetch water from wells and boil it for their infrequent baths. They didn't have electricity, flush toilets, or refrigeration. Instead, they had candles, bedpans, and ice houses.

"That's deep, Mom," my oldest said, before putting her earphones back in.

I can only hope this sinks in, and that someday, when they find themselves, as I often do, wishing for a piece of furniture or a home they can't afford, or maybe never will be able to, they will stop and reframe their outlook. They will look instead at all they have, not at what they don't. They will appreciate what is, not lament what isn't. They'll realize that homes are about what happens inside, the loving, the learning, the growing, the milestones, the shared traditions, and the building of memories. If all this can happen in a space designed to support us with style, grace, and beauty, even better. And if that space creates a beautiful backdrop against which all memories of home rely, that, dear readers, is a dream house.

Though I feel just as humble as that little girl when I face the excessive grandeur of palaces and even some homes, I take refuge knowing that with the many home improvements we can easily make and enjoy today, we can live better than royalty and still keep our heads. So go ahead, create your dream home. And while you do, keep your perspective and good humor. Take your time. Live well. Entertain often. And keep your home in its place.

Acknowledgments

THE PATH FROM INSPIRATION to publication is neither straight nor sure. For the fact that this book is in your hands, I am grateful to those who along the way believed in me, banked on me, and urged me on. First I'd like to thank Chris Meyer, of the *Orange County Register Home Magazine*, who had the instinct to assign me the job of writing a column that would be the antidote to the serious interior design content found in most home publications, including his, and who unwittingly started all this. I am also grateful for Eve Becker and Doug Page, who had the faith and conviction to launch the column into national syndication; for every one of the editors who have made my voice a part of their newspapers; for Bev and Bill Martin, and their divining lights; for Stephanie Abarbanel, a wonderful editor and friend, for her constant enthusiasm; and for Tracy Beckman and Eileen Roth for reading. I am especially thankful for my parents, Neal and Nancy Jameson, who showed me how a home should feel; for my agent, the amazing Faye Bender; and for the wonderful team at Perseus/Da Capo, specifically, Matthew Lore, my editor, for his perfectly calibrated guidance, and indefatigable caring.

Index

Bold page locator indicates information contained in boxes in text